A FRONTPAGE REPORTER'S VIEW OF THE GLITTER, THE FOLLY AND THE GREATNESS OF AMERICAN JOURNALISM TODAY

"Wicker's insiders stories are riveting...if you believe in the First Amendment, clap your hands – and read this book!"

— COSMOPOLITAN

"Wicker, one of the most respected journalists in the business, has been learning the pitfalls of the profession since 1949. He has written...a handbook for the average citizen who wants to know just what sort of crap he is being fed in the newspapers."

— PLAYBOY

"An eloquent personal statement...one of the most cogent and absorbing examinations of the American press ... searching...indispensible reading."

— PUBLISHERS WEEKLY

"Having been lied to by Presidents, and told truths unfit to print until it was too late, Tom Wicker insists now on his hunches, his instincts."

— THE NEW YORK TIMES

ON PRESS
TOM WICKER

A BERKLEY BOOK
published by
BERKLEY PUBLISHING CORPORATION

This Berkley book contains the complete
text of the original hardcover edition.
It has been completely reset in a type face
designed for easy reading, and was printed
from new film.

ON PRESS

A Berkley Book / published by arrangement with
The Viking Press

PRINTING HISTORY
Viking edition published 1978
Berkley edition / November 1979

ISBN: 0-425-04068-2

A BERKLEY BOOK® TM 757,375
Berkley Books are published by Berkley Publishing Corporation,
200 Madison Avenue, New York, New York 10016
PRINTED IN THE UNITED STATES OF AMERICA

Presented a copy of his family tree yesterday, President Carter said of his genealogical history: "We've uncovered some embarrassing ancestors in the not too distant past. Some horse thieves, and some people killed on Saturday nights. One of my relatives, unfortunately, was even in the newspaper business."

—*The New York Times*
June 4, 1977

Author's Note

The account on pages 27–29 of my mercifully brief experience as a sportswriter in Lumberton, North Carolina, first appeared as part of an article in *Esquire* magazine for December 1975. The appreciation of John F. Kennedy on pages 125–28 was adapted from an article in *Esquire* for June 1977. My account of covering Kennedy's assassination (pages 128–36) appeared as a chapter in *The Working Press*, edited by Ruth Adler (New York: G. P. Putnam's Sons, 1967), a collection of articles from "Times Talk," the house organ of *The New York Times*. The rescue of Arthur Krock's LBJ hat (pages 148–49) was recounted also in my introduction to his *In the Nation: 1932–1966* (New York: McGraw-Hill, 1966). The Chicago convention anecdote on pages 163–64 appeared in slightly different form in an article in *The New York Times Magazine* for August 24, 1969.

The material on newspaper mergers and chains on pages 183–85 is drawn mostly from an article by Ben Bagdikian in *Columbia Journalism Review*, March–April 1977, although he bears no responsibility for my interpretation of it. I wish also to acknowledge gratefully the important research assistance of my former colleague at the *Times*, Kathy Slobogin.

—Tom Wicker
New York, June 26, 1977

Contents

1

New Villains, New Heroes

On the morning of July 15, 1964, under a San Francisco dateline, *The New York Times* gave its readers a detailed account of a speech by General Dwight D. Eisenhower to the previous night's session of the Republican National Convention. Four paragraphs down, this passage occurred:

"'But the convention hall fairly exploded when the general told the delegates that they should not let themselves be divided by 'those outside our family, including sensation-seeking columnists and commentators. . . .' "

"Fairly exploded" was an understatement. I was in the Cow Palace that night as the *Times*'s national political correspondent. Like most other reporters, I was oppressed by the ominous air of the convention—the electric hatreds flickering between the factions, the manic joy of the delegates supporting Barry Goldwater as they anticipated his victory, the indefinable sense many of us had that these people would take us into dangerous and uncharted political seas.

But I was not prepared for Eisenhower's attack on columnists and commentators, much less for the response to it.

"There was a deafening roar of boos directed at the press stands flanking the speakers' platform and many on the convention floor jumped up and shook their fists at those in the glassed-in television booths."

I was virtually within reach of the crowd as I manned a typewriter in the press section, and I can still see those shouting, livid delegates, rising almost as one man, pointing, cursing, in some cases shaking their fists, not just at the men in the glass booths but at *me*. In the first moments after Eisenhower's words, I feared some of the delegates might actually leap over the railing separating them from the press section and attack the reporters gazing in astonishment at this sudden surge of hatred.

Eisenhower himself, never an inflammatory speaker, obviously was taken aback by the commotion he had caused; he stared in bewilderment at the yelling delegates and spectators, most of them on their feet, many braying on the ear-splitting airhorns that made that convention a particular trial. But when he could be heard again, the general plowed doggedly on—". . . because, my friends, I assure you that these are people (columnists and commentators) who couldn't care less about the good of our party . . ."—and that fired up the Cow Palace crowd again, as the delegates screamed their anger and frustration at the American press.

In retrospect, that moment in the Cow Palace seems to me to have marked the emergence of "the press" as an issue in American life and politics. Reporters and editors, long used to the self-serving complaints of offended candidates, were put on notice that the problem went far deeper than that. So, far from being "observers"—like sportswriters in the press box at an important football game—reporters, by 1964, were coming to be seen by millions of Americans as players in the game itself.

Those fists raised in anger at the men in the glassed-in booths—the "commentators" and the "anchor men"—bore this message, too: "the press" had become inextricably linked with television in the public mind.

Perhaps all that could not have been deduced, on the spot and against a deadline, from the wild response to the former president's remarks. But that response itself was palpably the real news about the Eisenhower speech.

It may seem odd, in view of the importance of that news to the *Times* and most other newspapers, that they nevertheless reported the Eisenhower speech primarily as a plea for party unity. In fact, by the time the convention opened, any good reporter knew that there was no Republican party unity and would be none that year.

Nor, by then, did anyone seriously believe that Dwight Eisenhower, for all his eminence, any longer wielded real influence in a party newly conquered by Barry Goldwater. Anyway, an ex-president preaching party unity was a political convention cliché. Yet, most of the press *did* report the Eisenhower speech at face value and *did* assign it front-page importance, as if it might actually have an effect on party unity. Here, for instance, is the *Times*'s "lead"—in which the story's most important fact was supposed to be set out with accuracy and brevity:

"SAN FRANCISCO, July 14—Former President Dwight D. Eisenhower warned Republicans tonight that they must unite behind their convention's choice of a Presidential candidate or 'drown in a whirlpool of factional strife.'"

In 1964 the most demanding editor and the most erudite professor of journalism would have had trouble finding fault with that lead, even though it entirely missed the real story—as it continued to do in the next two paragraphs, which gave such data as that Eisenhower had been interrupted forty times for applause.

Had it been my assignment, I would have written the story much as it ran in the *Times*; if I hadn't, my editors would have given me a hard time, perhaps called for a new lead or a rewrite. The chances are that the story was written in advance, from a prepared text of the speech, with the anti-press outburst only grudgingly inserted after it happened.

This was "objective journalism," which few then doubted was the only honest journalism. On politics and government, objective journalism reported mostly the contents of official documents, or statements delivered by official spokesmen. Objective journalism "analyzed" such documents or statements only in the most obvious terms—Eisenhower's speech, the *Times* told its readers owlishly, "was widely interpreted as an effort to strengthen his self-assigned role as a unifier of the warring factions during the nomination process and as a rallying point for his party during the campaign."

Objective journalism would venture no subjective suggestion that "party unity" was already lost before the general stood up, unless some official-enough spokesman could be found to say so. Objective journalism proceeded, too, from the prior assumption that a former president's remarks in such a setting were important merely because they were made by him, with no assessment of their likely futility in the actual circumstances. Objective journalism preserved, with five columns of accompanying text, the official record.

The official record conveyed, however, none of the meaning of that moment when the Cow Palace "fairly exploded." But to have based a story on such an analysis would have been considered "subjective," because there were no official spokesmen to explain the significance of the moment, and no documents to quote on its origins and consequences. For a reporter to have drawn his own conclusions would have been "editorializing in the news columns," the cardinal sin of objective journalism.

So at the moment when the hostility that the free American press aroused among its own readers first became dramatically apparent to the press itself, that press had so wrapped itself in the paper chains of "objective journalism" that it had little ability to report anything beyond the bare and undeniable fact that the Republican National Convention had "fairly exploded" at Eisenhower's words.

Numerous reporters in the Cow Palace nevertheless had a pretty good sense of what was happening. In the bitter preconvention campaign between Nelson A. Rockefeller of New York and Barry Goldwater of Arizona—left vs. right; East vs. West; old money vs. new—events had led these reporters to at least two conclusions.

One was that Goldwater's support was both wide and deep among millions of Americans who perceived him as a hero and his conservative doctrines not as "right wing" or "kooky" but as elemental Americanism. The other was that the Goldwater supporters saw the "Eastern, liberal, internationalist press" that so often seemed to criticize or belittle him, particularly television, as a powerful and concentrated force dedicated to the defeat of their champion by fair means or foul—editorial opposition, slanted news reports, distorted commentaries, even outright lies.

The passionate Goldwater conservatives, by July 1964, believed they had captured the Republican party and assured Goldwater's nomination *in spite of* the biased, corrupt, perhaps unpatriotic press. And when Eisenhower gave them the opening, their anger erupted in the Cow Palace. Those Americans shaking their fists, doubtless millions more watching at home, had been convinced by newspaper and television reaction—usually hostile or skeptical—to the Goldwater campaign that the free American press was menacing, hateful, corrupt, by their lights perhaps not American at all.

This was reasonably clear to me and many other reporters at the time, although the ferocity of the demonstration shocked me; for the first time in a fifteen-year career in journalism, I was forced to acknowledge to myself that my colleagues and I were hated and feared by millions of other Americans.

My life in the press—dating back to 1949 and a job as editor, reporter, ad salesman, Omaha folder operator, relief linotypist, mail clerk, delivery man, and general factotum for the *Sandhill Citizen* (circulation 1800 weekly) of Aberdeen, North Carolina—had not prepared me for that hatred. Nor could I foresee, that hot night in the Cow Palace, anything like the turbulent decade that lay ahead—years in which a public far more numerous than the Goldwaterites would come to perceive the press as a powerful participant, sometimes menacing, sometimes protective, in American life; years, too, in which the practice of journalism itself would be greatly altered, with even the hallowed traditions of "objectivity" beginning to yield—if slowly—to a new and less cautious ethic of disclosure.

The Goldwater nomination was almost a model for the change that lay ahead. Just as the Goldwaterites perceived the men and events of 1964 differently than those men and events seemed to be portrayed in the newspapers and on television, Americans generally began to find it more difficult in the 1960s and 1970s to reconcile "the news" they read or watched with their own perceptions, beliefs, and attitudes.

Almost immediately, for example, Goldwater—pictured by Lyndon B. Johnson and much of the press as a hawk who would precipitate a nuclear holocaust—lost the 1964 election in a landslide predicted by most reporters (and who knows to what degree the prediction may have influenced the fact?). But before the echoes of the campaign had mercifully faded, Johnson—who had pledged repeatedly that he would not send American boys to fight an Asian war—dispatched American bombers to North Vietnam.

So the same "objective journalism"—and in many cases, the same reporters and commentators—whose articles and broadcasts, derived from the "highest official sources," had assured the voters that LBJ was the peace candidate, suddenly had to explain a few months later that the same LBJ had "no choice" except to lead the nation into the war he had promised to avoid. And the same highest official sources had to be quoted in support of this contradictory proposition. (The irreverent Herblock of The Washington Post, however, pictured Johnson staring into his shaving mirror, with Goldwater looking back.)

The highest official spokesmen and sources might have been saying one thing in 1964 and another in 1965, but objective journalism required less that the contradictions be noted or explained than that the official record be kept. And if a reporter or a columnist did recall what had been said before, in contrast to what was being said later, the contradiction was seldom played as prominently as the later proclamation of official "fact."

Thus, Johnson's turnabout injured not only his own credibility but that of a press which tried dutifully to explain the President's actions as he wanted them explained. But still another element of objective journalism made it relatively easy for the new version of events in Southeast Asia to achieve prominence in the press in the early years of the Johnson administration. The ethic of objectivity required that every effort be made to get "both sides of the story." If President Johnson, for instance, said a new civil-rights bill was necessary, a reporter had to be dispatched instantly to, say, Senator Richard B. Russell of Georgia so that he could say that a new civil-rights bill was not necessary.

Probably, in the Times at least, there would be an accompanying "news analysis"—in Times jargon a "Q-header," so-called because such articles were always displayed in the same double-column fashion, topped with a headline designated as a "Q-head" in the stylebook. The Q-header would discuss the reasoning of both Johnson and Russell, and give about equal weight to the views of each, possibly with some inside dope on the legislative situation. Farther back in the paper, of course, an editorial would say that Johnson was right; there ought to be a new civil-rights bill.

But in the case of the war in Vietnam, who spoke for the "other side" of the story in 1965 and 1966? Certainly not the hawkish Republicans; certainly not the even more hawkish Goldwater conservatives; certainly not most of the liberals of either party—Senators Wayne Morse and Ernest Gruening excepted. Other liberals, even if doubtful about the war, feared to turn on Johnson because they feared him, or because they feared his liberal domestic policies might suffer, too; besides, he appeared to be carrying on a war inherited from John Kennedy and which they felt they had to be anti-Communist enough to support, lest liberalism itself be tarred with the McCarthyist brush as "soft on communism."

The only spokesmen against the war, therefore, were a few professors officially decried as insufficiently hard-nosed, a few rag-tag kids and hippies, a few professional leftists and bleeding hearts—and of course the Communists and subversives. Such opposition provided little standing or authority for the antiwar view, which critically lacked—for the purposes of objective journalism—an official spokesman or any kind of respectable institution on which to base itself.

Nor was it only the press that suffered from the need to be seen as "objective" in official eyes. At a time when only Senators Morse of Oregon and Gruening of Alaska were speaking out forcefully against the war, Senator J. W. Fulbright of Arkansas, then chairman of the Foreign Relations Committee and reported to have been the only high-ranking official to try to persuade John Kennedy to abandon the Bay of Pigs invasion, suddenly burst out in a private conversation with me:

"Hell, I'd like to be out there with Morse and Gruening. But I can't afford to have people think I'm a crackpot like that." He didn't add that he couldn't afford to have the White House think that either; he didn't need to.

At that time, moreover, after years of Cold War, the Eisenhower "father image," and the Kennedy charisma, most of the public perceived little reason to mistrust the government. Presidents were generally revered; when they donned the commander-in-chief's hat and American troops went to war, the American instinct was to rally round the White House.

So, in 1965 and 1966, the antiwar view inevitably was played, in newspaper jargon, "back among the truss ads." If it appeared on television at all, it was usually through coverage of an unmannerly demonstration by strangely clothed people more likely to repel than persuade the general public.

But problems were developing for the official version of things, not so much in Washington as in Vietnam. There, too, many reporters at first saw no alternative—or were given none by their editors—to reliance on official American spokesmen and their Vietnamese echoes. Every night in Saigon, at the so-called "Five O'Clock Follies," the spokesmen produced the "facts"—the body counts, the villages pacified, the Chieu Hoy bag (the number of Viet Cong deserting or, more euphemistically, "rallying" to the government), the endless statistics that pointed to an inevitable American and ARVN victory over the Communist invaders of democratic South Vietnam.

But no censorship was ever imposed in the "police action" that really was an undeclared war in Vietnam; censorship would have been another political burden Lyndon Johnson did not want to bear, and, ironically, the armed forces cooperated in what was to prove a large cause of the war's undoing. They gave the press almost complete access to military communications and transportation throughout Vietnam. More and more reporters, skeptical of the relentless optimism of the Follies, thus found it possible to get out in the field, not only the battlefield but among ordinary Vietnamese and low-ranking American officials in the provinces. These reporters began to engage in the most objective journalism of all—seeing for themselves, judging for themselves, backing up their judgments with their observations, often at risk of life and limb, and the government's wrath. Under this scrutiny, the claims of generals, ambassadors, spokesmen began to appear hollow and inflated. In 1966, for example, I got valuable insight into the process by which official-source journalism was being undermined—and with it the official version of the war—in Vietnam, if not yet in Washington.

I was in a small party of Washington reporters who had accompanied Vice-President Hubert H. Humphrey on a tour of Asian capitals. Humphrey's trip had been high-handedly ordered by Johnson, then at the height of his power, in an effort to enlist more Asian nations in the war. Our first stop was Vietnam itself, where Humphrey was taught his salesman's spiel in a closely guided tour of battle areas and American units and ARVN training camps and South Vietnamese government projects. The Vice-President did not see any known Viet Cong sympathizers or non-Communist Vietnamese political dissidents.

In the bar atop the Caravelle Hotel, I met an intense young ex-Marine who was working for the government as a civilian. He showed few of the grave doubts about the American effort that—as I later learned—he already had developed. This was not to be my last encounter with Daniel Ellsberg, but on that trip the most educational experience was the climactic news conference held on the terrace of Ambassador Henry Cabot Lodge's sumptuous villa.

For the occasion, Lodge and his press aides had called in from the field a number of Americans who were then serving as advisers to the Vietnamese military and civilian administrators in various areas of the country. Television cameras were in place, the Washington press visitors had notebooks in hand, and a substantial number of American correspondents regularly assigned to Saigon also attended.

Picture the scene: the Vice-President on one hand, the ambassador on the other, the field advisers in the middle, the cameras pointed at them all. Humphrey wanted to know how the war was going; so did the visiting press; the advisers said the war was going fine. The war was being won. The hearts and minds of the people were being captured. The enemy was losing his nerve and morale. Victory would not be quick but victory was certain.

Murray Fromson of CBS News, an old friend and a correspondent long assigned to Vietnam, plucked at my sleeve:

"That tall guy in the blue shirt." He indicated one of the advisers. "That was bullshit he was giving us a minute ago. You should have heard what he told me privately when I spent the night in his tent last week."

That was one of the more important moments of my professional life. I understood at once that *of course* in such circumstances the advisers had to put the best possible face on the situation. They were certainly not going to let themselves be shown on television at home telling the Vice-President and the ambassador that the war was being lost, even if they thought it.

They were bureaucrats, military men, experienced government hands. Some may even have persuaded themselves they were presenting a true picture; others may have been too inexperienced in Vietnam to see the reality beyond superficial gains.

I grasped then a singular truth of the war. The more Washington pressed for favorable results, the more Vietnam would have to provide such results—inventing them if necessary, or inflating minor accomplishments, or concealing setbacks. And the worse the situation really was, the more necessity for presenting a façade of success, and the more inevitable the lies.

A corollary was clear, too. The more reporters like Murray Fromson informed their reports to the American public with what they heard for themselves in the privacy of an adviser's tent or saw on the battlefield or learned in the ruined villages, the more those reports would be at odds with the official government pronouncements, derived from what high-level Washington was hearing through its official channels and believed by most of a trusting public. As a result, reporters like Fromson inevitably would seem "lacking in objectivity" and "too emotional"—or to be just plain liars—to those who delivered the official reports.

For the American public, moreover, the dilemma was plain. Should readers and viewers believe press accounts from Vietnam or should they accept the government's pronouncements from Washington? After the long era of the Cold War and the glorification of the presidency under Eisenhower and Kennedy, during which the press had seldom questioned the government's purposes, much less its integrity, most Americans obviously found it difficult to accept the idea that Washington was both pushing a mistaken war and lying about its progress. To them, the press was bound to be distorting and exaggerating what it saw in Vietnam. And if some might believe that, instead, a horrendous blunder was being exposed, that would only sharpen the hostility of the government toward a press that was not "on the team."

As the Humphrey news conference broke up that day in Saigon, a few quick conversations disclosed that most of the Saigon veterans agreed that a rosy picture had been painted for the Vice-President, the traveling press, above all for the cameras (and no doubt for Lodge, who was mostly isolated in Saigon). That night in Bangkok, where the Humphrey party next landed, some of us tried for hours to persuade Humphrey staff men to take the word to the Vice-President that he'd been given an overoptimistic report; but the staff men could not believe the "official" field advisers had not been giving them the "objective" truth. Men far higher in the government than they had much the same trouble, right up to the moment when the last American helicopter took off from the Saigon embassy roof in 1975. No wonder ordinary citizens found it hard to know what to believe.

Television added a powerful new dimension to the developing mistrust between press and public, press and government. By the time Vietnam became a household concern in America, the television screen had transformed the news business. "The media," thereafter, would always outweigh "the press," and for several reasons.

One was the immediacy and power of the news when *seen*; no written or spoken story could convey the shock of Jack Ruby blasting the life out of Lee Harvey Oswald, or any of thousands of other happenings. But more important was the *reach* of television. By the 1960s, the networks, the local stations, and cable systems stretched into every corner of the nation. For news and public affairs, the effect was profound—remote areas long dependent on sketchy radio news and regional or local newspapers had come to be in live and frequent contact with Washington, Yankee Stadium, an Asian war, a revolution in Greece, a civil-rights melee in Alabama, with outer space and, later, the surface of the moon.

People who once had been too isolated to know much of what was happening in the great world had become engaged with public affairs; people who had found the news an irrelevant bore saw it transformed by the power of television into fascinating visual terms. Most newspapers could only benefit from the new interest in the news generated by television.

As television spread interest in the news, it also created an interest in news-gathering and news dissemination, as well as in those who gather and disseminate it. It's hard, in fact, to imagine the rise in public concern about "the press" or "the media" without the spread of television and of interest in television-news stars like Walter Cronkite and David Brinkley. In the fall of 1977, Cronkite even became the central figure in arranging the visit to Israel of President Anwar el-Sadat of Egypt; one of the great events in modern diplomatic history was set up in separate television interviews with Sadat and Prime Minister Menachem Begin.

And in the Vietnam years, the impact, reach, and omnipresence of television produced a situation no wartime government had faced before. The war's mushroom growth in 1966 and 1967 was visible to every American with a set, and it did not always look like the war that Lyndon Johnson and Robert McNamara and Dean Rusk claimed was being won. Even the television commentators, most of whom voiced views cautiously close to the official Washington attitude, could not make the pictures more palatable.

No amount of commentary could have countered that nightly parade of battlefield images through the American living room. As much as any single factor, I believe, that parade turned most of the American public eventually against the war. The famous scene of a Marine torching a thatched-roof house with his cigarette lighter was only the most shocking of a long succession of horrors and surprises. The public revulsion that finally resulted was not just due to the intensity of these household experiences—deaths, burnings, the ghastly aftermath of a B-52 raid or a village showered with napalm, miserable refugees moving in their hopeless thousands past the unblinking cameras. It was due also to their totality, the seeming endlessness and futility of the horror, surviving one administration into another, flickering night after night, year after year in the American home, the American consciousness. Television made the war inescapable and finally sharpened to their intolerable points the essential questions: For what? To what end? No official source ever provided answers convincing enough; but until the war's essential futility finally became clear to most Americans, television's graphic and unpalatable reports were another cause for the unease and mistrust with which many viewed the press.

If reporters who saw the war at first hand and a public that saw it on television were coming to mistrust the government officials who conducted it, those officials were developing in their turn a distinct hostility to the newspapers and broadcasters they held accountable for many of their troubles.

After the 1968 "Tet offensive" had shattered official

pretensions to inevitable victory, for example, Secretary of State Rusk was asked if there had not been a failure of advance intelligence; he replied with a remarkable indictment of the press.

Rusk was talking with a group of reporters in his office. He was never satisfied, he said, that enough was known about what was happening in Vietnam. "But the point is," he said, "I don't quite see why you have to start from the dissatisfaction. There gets to be a point when the question is: Whose side are you on? Now, I'm Secretary of State of the United States and I'm on our side."

The reporters listening were not slow to take the implication that maybe *they* weren't. But Rusk continued. During World War II, he said, "there wasn't a time when you couldn't find something to bitch about. But what do you talk about? Do you talk about (how) to win this thing? Or do you throw this thing in and say everything is lost?"

It was his fifty-ninth birthday, the secretary said, and maybe he could be forgiven if he spoke his mind—because none of your papers or your broadcasting apparatuses are worth a damn unless the United States succeeds. They are trivial compared to that question. So I don't know why, to win a Pulitzer Prize, people have to go probing for the things that one can bitch about when there are two thousand stories on the same day about things that are more constructive in character."

Here was a sweeping indictment indeed—the press was irresponsible, sensation-seeking, defeatist, insufficiently interested in the success of the United States, maybe not even quite on "our side." This was worrisome enough coming from the secretary of state; but what was known about the view of the press from the White House suggested that Lyndon Johnson's animosity was even stronger.

Johnson's attitude, however, was mild compared to that of Richard Nixon, who had pledged in his 1968 campaign to "end the war and win the peace." Instead, he took over management of the war and widened it into Laos and Cambodia. Nixon and the small circle around him came into the White House with no view more passionately held than that "the liberal press" would be "out to get us." Not long after he took office, in fact, Nixon took note of published criticism that his administration was not as open as he had promised. In a memorandum for Herbert Klein and Ronald Ziegler, his press spokesmen, he told them to ignore such criticism—"If we treat the press with a little more contempt, we'll probably get better treatment."

Nixon's attitude, and the long-held suspicion of his character and veracity that was widespread in the press, made it all but inevitable that the hostility between government and press would be intensified during his administration—particularly since he continued the war that was at the root of that hostility. And these divisions were reflected in the public, part of which tended to side with the government against the press, part of which backed the press against the government—and some of which mistrusted both press and government.

In quick succession, moreover, even while the war continued, unprecedented other events in the Nixon years made the press even more controversial—to some an uncontrolled threat to national well-being, to others a beleaguered defender of democracy and the Constitution.

In the fall of 1969, for example, Vice-President Spiro T. Agnew—accurately sensing that public mistrust of the press was ripe for exploitation—launched his alliterative bolts at "nattering nabobs of negativism." On June 13, 1971, *The New York Times* began to publish the Pentagon Papers and the Nixon administration went to court to stop the presses, only to have the Supreme Court speedily rule against the desired "prior restraint" on publication.

A year later a small band of burglars was arrested in the offices of the Democratic National Committee in the Watergate office building, and *The Washington Post* assigned two unknown young reporters, Bob Woodward and Carl Bernstein, to pursue the story. They had few official sources, but the sources they did have led their stories tortuously toward the White House—ultimately to Nixon's forced resignation under threat of impeachment in August 1974.

Aside from their intrinsic importance, these events fed the ever-growing public and official concern about the press and its place in American life. How could it have been otherwise, when the Vice-President had expressed at the highest level the popular suspicion that newspapers and television were biased and conspiratorial, apostles of permissiveness and national defeatism, and in any case had too much power to shape what people thought, particularly since there was no real public or other control over that power? (Reading an Agnew text line by line,

Nixon exulted: "This really flicks the scab off, doesn't it?")

What was the public to think, in the light of Agnew's charges, when the most prestigious newspaper in the country, long an editorial opponent of the war in Vietnam, published documents that not only were classified Top Secret by those who were popularly supposed to know what ought to be secret; but documents the substance of which detailed the long-charged duplicity of the Johnson administration in the conduct of the war? Was the Nixon administration right to label the publication a grave breach of national security? Or was the *Times* right to call it a necessary disclosure of the true history of the war to a people who had been misled for years?

In 1972 and 1973 Ron Ziegler, Nixon's wind-up spokesman, could label the Woodward-Bernstein Watergate stories "shabby journalism" and "a blatant effort at character assassination" composed of "hearsay, innuendo, and guilt by assocation"—and find a ready audience of believers. And as other newspapers and television and radio took up the many threads of the Watergate investigation, and the tangled story began to be unraveled, Nixon's defenders became convinced that a savagely anti-Nixon press was out to reverse the 1972 election results.

Even many Americans who did not accept that extreme idea, but who tended to lump together "the President" and "the government" and "the nation," feared the implications of politically immobilizing or impeaching Nixon. So they questioned the propriety and responsibility of continuing press disclosures damaging to the President—rather as if "Nixon" and "the President" had become interchangeable, an idea he assiduously encouraged.

Nixon himself epitomized the hardest attitude toward the press. At a news conference on October 25, 1973, he said he had never "heard or seen such outrageous, vicious, distorted reporting in twenty-seven years of public life" as he had in the Watergate period. He was not blaming anyone, he went on characteristically, and perhaps "what we did brought it about, and therefore *the media decided that they would have to take that particular line*." (Italics mine.)

Like Rusk's complaint five years earlier, that just about said it all—"the media" were not just objectively reporting the news but had "decided" (the conspiracy theory) to take a "particular line" (the bias and get-Nixon theories). And, Nixon concluded, "when people are pounded night after night with that kind of frantic, hysterical reporting, it naturally shakes their confidence" (the unchecked-power-of-the-press theory).

But the press was damned if it did and damned if it didn't. In the Vietnam and Watergate years, vast numbers of other Americans had become persuaded not of American righteousness but that the United States government—particularly under Johnson and Nixon—was the major threat to peace in the world, freedom at home, and happiness everywhere. Dogmatically convinced that "the system" had to be changed to give "power to the people" or merely alarmed at what they saw as a drift from basic American principles, they believed the press had not done enough to end the war in Vietnam, publish its secrets and failures, scourge the military-industrial complex, and expose the repressive operations of Nixon and his Plumbers, not to mention the FBI, and CIA, and every other government police agency.

To many of these critics, the press appeared hopelessly under the control of the Establishment, the willing tool of the warlords, existing only for profit and to deceive the people into thinking their liberties were being protected. (Years earlier, with less vehemence and more reason, many blacks in the civil-rights movement had viewed the press in much the same way, as a pillar of the status quo.)

Many of a more moderate view saw the American press, after Vietnam, the Pentagon Papers, and Watergate, as a watchdog of liberty, a check on government, and a balance against power as important as any specified in the Constitution. For them, press skepticism and independence and willingness to go behind the self-serving statements of official spokesmen were vital to a functioning democracy; and perhaps Justice Potter Stewart of the Supreme Court spoke for most of them at Yale Law School in December 1974:

"The public-opinion polls I have seen indicate that some Americans firmly believe that the former Vice-President (Agnew) and the former President of the United States were hounded out of office by an arrogant and irresponsible press.

"It is my thesis that, on the contrary, the established American press in the past ten years, and particularly in the past two years, has performed precisely the function it was intended to perform by those who wrote the First Amendment of our Constitution."

An extreme version of *that* view, of course, had developed also. Some saw the men and women of the press—particularly "investigative reporters"—as the new American heroes. Woodward and Bernstein became the unchallenged idols of the campus, their books best sellers, they themselves matinee idols as played by Robert Redford and Dustin Hoffman. It was as if, suddenly, the "investigative reporter" had succeeded to the role played at various times in the American psyche by so many robust earlier heroes—Paul Revere, the watchman of liberty; the Western sheriff, as portrayed by Gary Cooper, single-handedly guaranteeing law and order; Lindbergh challenging the Atlantic in the name of progress—the fearless, fighting individual standing up for the many, daring the gods, alert on the barricades.

None of these views of the press, hostile or favorable, was entirely warranted, but it was not only the public's perception of the press that was changing; particularly owing to the pressures of Vietnam and Watergate, the practice of journalism itself had evolved slowly and grudgingly, in ways not always easy for the public to see or define, but clearly visible to old practitioners.

The enormous importance of television news had started the process of change in the printed press. In the sixties and seventies every survey showed that most Americans got the news first from television and automobile radio. The broadcast media, therefore, had taken over the front-page function of newspapers (except for "exclusive" stories they independently developed, which were not available to broadcasters). The network evening-news broadcasts were illustrated front pages, compact and convenient, tuned to by most of the nation.

Reluctantly, sometimes not admitting even to themselves what they were doing, newspapers began to move beyond the front-page function—the summary of what happened yesterday. More analysis, background, and commentary began to appear in news columns—either as separate stories or as parts of regular news stories, sometimes even on the front page itself. This was not so much by the choice of cautious editors as because of the necessary search for a role complementary to, rather than competing with, the nightly "front page" on television. Instead of "bringing the news," the printed press was evolving toward "explaining the news."

This creeping development was reasonably advanced when

the "credibility gap" of the Johnson administration and the growing doubts of many reporters and commentators about the war in Vietnam added another element. To a greater degree than would have seemed possible in the Cold War days of Truman, Eisenhower, and Kennedy, the press—television included—found itself having to scrutinize official positions, challenge official statements, turn a skeptical eye and ear toward official spokesmen. Here and there reporters and editors began to speak openly of the "adversary function" of the press.

A powerful impulse toward such press skepticism was provided by the peace movement—particularly by its student component. In the late sixties no one writing in the press or speaking on campus about the war escaped challenge, argument, confrontation—not only about the war itself but about American institutions and assumptions generally. Reluctantly, often painfully, members of the press were as profoundly affected as were many other Americans by the disillusionments and unwelcome revelations of the sixties.

Racial rioting in the central city ghettos furnished an example of what was happening. Nothing the civil-rights movement had done in ten active years had so dramatized the economic problems of the nation, the changes wrought in its cities by the huge migration of blacks out of the South since World War II and the mechanization of the farm, or the realities of persistent and pervasive racial discrimination. The years of rioting left assumptions about justice and the good life in America as shaken among reporters and editors as anyone else. Their product was bound to reflect the experience, not always to the pleasure of readers and public officials.

Watergate then made the "investigative reporter" the glamour figure of American journalism. Editors and reporters scrambled to get aboard this newest trend away from the passive, cautious "objective journalism" to which they had been so long devoted; and sensational revelations were quickly forthcoming about the CIA, the FBI, the IRS, major business corporations, Congress. To analytical, adversarial journalism was added the new ethic of disclosure; the idea that the duty of the press was to print or broadcast what it knew, rather than tailoring its content to perceived ideas of "responsibility," "the good of the community," "the national interest," and the like, was well established—if by no means universal—by the mid-seventies.

By then, too, newspapers and broadcasting had been

strongly influenced by the many young men and women of the sixties who had moved into journalism. Activist in temperament, skeptical by experience, eager—often too eager—to right the wrongs of the world, these young people were well suited to adversarial, investigative journalism. They would have pushed the press in that direction even if circumstances had not already done so.

Objective journalism, in the old sense, was by no means abandoned. Newspapers and broadcasters, all too often, continued to play "on the team." Official spokesmen not infrequently shaped stories to their liking, as before. Powerful news centers, such as the White House, had ample means to get their positions before the public advantageously. Major forces in American life—huge corporations, for the most glaring example—still were little scrutinized and mostly unchallenged in print or on the airwaves in the seventies. No "revolution" had occurred in journalism.

But the transformation of the press in the public eye—partially owing to real if limited changes in the press's outlook and practices—was virtually complete by the time of Nixon's resignation in August 1974, just ten years after that transformation first made itself known to me in the Cow Palace in 1964.

Reporters once might have been seen rather as their colleagues across the sea were derisively described by Humbert Wolfe:

> You cannot hope to bribe or twist
> Thank God! the British journalist.
> But, seeing what the man will do
> Unbribed, there's no occasion to.

But whether they worked for newspapers or television, American reporters by 1974 were no longer being viewed as raffish observers in the press box, hat brims up, phoning in to stop the presses. "The boys in the newspaper game," a condescending description of my colleagues and me which I seldom heard anymore, had become on one hand the ruthless villains of Agnew's warning vision, and on the other the stainless heroes of the Redford-Hoffman movie.

A quarter of a century in the press, from the *Sandhill Citizen* to *The New York Times*, had given me a far different view of my trade. I had seldom seen it as heroic, only occasionally as villainous, frequently as ill-advised, all too often as inaccurate, sometimes as powerfully effective.

To me, the plain meaning of the First Amendment's provision that Congress "shall make no law...abridging the freedom of...the press" was that the American press had a constitutional obligation to act as a check on and a balance against the power of government and other institutions. Even the government was not empowered to retaliate against or silence a free press; as I understood it, that freedom could only have been intended to help assure the rights of citizens, the probity of government, the rule of law.

But I thought I understood, too, what millions of Americans seemed not to grasp—that despite the freedom conferred by the Constitution, the American press operated under severe limitations, inherent in its nature and that of the country, which effectively restrained the power derived from freedom. And I *knew* what many in the press did not want to admit: that despite the advances of recent years the constitutional obligation of the American press had been more often met hesitantly, even timidly, than aggressively—and again for reasons inherent in the nature of the press and the nation itself.

I thought the press, like most American institutions, was inadequate to its responsibilities. But I saw no "reforms" that would insure improvement, primarily because most of those proposed would impair the press's freedom without recognizing what was at once its basic problem and its greatest strength—that "the press" in America was not really an institution so much as a scattered collection of human beings and organizations, going about their business with differing purposes, in differing ways, with differing consequences, all operating under the loosest of rules, which were open to differing interpretations and were seldom enforceable.

This book is about the experiences and influences on which I base those beliefs and from which I have also derived what I call the First Law of Journalism—that so human a creature as a newspaper inevitably reflects the character of its community. And I believe that the American press is neither heroic nor villainous, but that it mirrors rather well the character of the American community.

2

Personal Journalism

Monday was "court day" in Moore County, North Carolina, in 1949, and I regularly spent it at the county seat, Carthage, as correspondent for the *Sandhill Citizen*, of Aberdeen, North Carolina (population 1603). I reserved most of the afternoon for peddling ads—another of my duties—to the Carthage merchants, in keen competition with the county seat weekly, the *Moore County News*. On first arrival at the courthouse in the morning, I checked with the register of deeds, the clerk of court, the sheriff, and other officials for suits newly filed, big property transfers, scandalous foreclosures, heinous crimes, and the like; then I laboriously copied down births, deaths, and marriages of note. Later I hastened to the courtroom, where County Judge Leland McKeithen dispensed even-handed justice, or something as close to it as anything I've seen since.

That courtroom was rank with the enduring follies and foibles of mankind. It was segregated still, and in the summer months sweltering in the harsh dry heat of the North Carolina Sandhills in the days before universal air conditioning. But it provided a generous education in human nature, lawyers' tricks, oratory, and the law itself—in roughly that order. I witnessed court actions involving murders, manslaughters, crimes of property too numerous to define, vagrancies, seductions, desertions, auto offenses of every variety, bitterly disputed wills, breaches of promise and peace, recoveries of damage, alienations of affection, assaults, rapes, batteries, break-ins, reckless endangerments, ad infinitum. It seemed natural enough to me in the South of the 1940s that most defendants, and most victims, were black.

One divorce case—that of a white couple—had a particular impact on me, although I scarcely recall its details. They involved one party futilely chasing the other with an ax. The story plaintively related from the witness stand by the complainant, a worn-out woman with a ZaSu Pitts voice, haggard eyes, and hair just beginning to go gray, was the human comedy at its most ribald and perverse—Moore County transported to Chaucer's time and *The Canterbury Tales*. The spectators scattered around the courtroom, the press—another reporter and I—at its privileged table, even occasionally Judge McKeithen, rocked with laughter. The conclusion was foregone—divorce granted, with a fine crack of the gavel.

That was Monday. That afternoon, I hawked the *Citizen's* ad space, probably to no better effect than usual. The next day, armed with copious notes, I turned out a humorous account of the divorce case for my long lead over the agate type that summed up the other court cases ("Lonzo McNair, Star Route, Carthage, failure to observe stop sign, costs of court;" "A. C. Overby, Vermont Avenue, Southern Pines, aggravated assault, continued to Superior Court") and sent it back to the *Citizen's* ever-clacking Linotype machine (in a small shop in the days before offset printing, it was mandatory to keep "the machine" running, both to make the thing pay and to keep the lead pot from "freezing").

On Thursday, putting on my editor's hat, I wrote a two-column head for my court story and scheduled it for page one, above the fold—top play in the *Citizen* as in any other newspaper. We went to press routinely that night, got the mail copies to the post office in the nick of time, and went off for a few late beers.

Working late justified sleeping late; and when I dragged myself into the *Citizen* office about noon the next day, I had a visitor: a worn-out looking woman with a ZaSu Pitts voice, but whose once-haggard eyes were blazing, whose fluttering hands were clenched into fists, and whose graying hair—I suddenly saw at range closer than that of the witness stand—was that of a woman not too many years older than I, who not too long before probably had been considered a peach by the boys in her high school class.

"Mr. Wicker," she said without preamble, "why did you think you had the right to make fun out of me in your paper?"

I have never forgotten that question—and I still can't answer it. In 1949 I doubt if I even tried. I remember thinking I had not bargained for such awful moments when I had landed my first reporter's job a few months before. Accurate though my story had been, and based on a public record, it had nevertheless exploited human unhappiness for the amusement or titillation of others. I had made the woman in my office something less than what she was—a human being possessed, despite her misfortunes, of real dignity.

Seeing that, I saw too that I had not only done her an injury but missed the story I should have written. This is one of the besetting sins of journalism—sensationalism at the expense of the dignity and truth of the common human experience. I have been fortunate to have worked mostly for publishers and editors who sought to avoid that sin—not always successfully. And reading some of the more lurid journals, I've often thought that sensationalism and gossip columns tend to be techniques employed mostly by big-circulation publications for an anonymous audience. Not many editors and reporters would be callous or unseeing enough to engage in them if they had to face the victims the next morning over a battered desk in an office not much bigger than a closet.

On the other hand, in small cities and towns, where the overwhelming majority of American newspapers are published, circulating to millions more readers than *The New York Times* or *The Washington Post* ever reaches, newspaper publishers and editors have difficulty looking at their communities objectively and serving them dispassionately. Like the woman in my office, the readers are close at hand; many of them are bankers, industrialists, heavy advertisers, country club members, and golfing partners with those who own and manage the newspaper.

It's hard to be independent, much less "crusading," in such

circumstances. Commercial boosterism is more often the rule, especially since publishers usually have a heavy economic stake in their communities. They also tend to be part of, or at least cooperative with, the community power structure; and they are seldom controversial and almost never adversarial about important community institutions. This doesn't necessarily mean that respectable and useful newspapers can't be published in small cities and towns; but they are often limited in their scope and ambitions. My career in provincial journalism—from 1949 to 1960—soon impressed on me the rudiments of what became that aforementioned First Law of Journalism, that a newspaper inevitably reflects the character of its community.

The *Sandhill Citizen* was the single-handed creation of H. Clifton Blue, an unlettered but shrewd Tarheel who began publishing it as *The Captain* in 1932 on a foot-powered press that could print only two letter-sized pages at a time. Clif Blue himself supplied the foot power. His first base was the town of Vass, North Carolina (population 728), for which motorists on U.S. Highway One didn't even bother to slow down. As Blue later remembered of those Depression days:

"The bank in Vass had closed. The main store in town had closed and the next main store was in bankruptcy and I had no better sense than to think I could operate a newspaper there without a motor to run it with, which I did for about two years before getting a motor."

When a competitor folded elsewhere in Moore County, Clifton Blue took over its name—the *Sandhill Citizen*—and second-class mailing permit; *The Captain* had never had such a permit, for the good reason that its publisher had never had the $100 application fee.

In 1936 Blue moved the *Citizen* down the road to Aberdeen, which not only boasted U.S One but two railroads—what was then the Seaboard Air Line, and the Aberdeen & Rockfish, a feeder road to nearby Fort Bragg—and therefore, in the late thirties, a success story just about to happen. So, in a more modest way, was the *Sandhill Citizen.*

By the time I came along in 1949 the *Citizen* was one of three more or less prospering weeklies in Moore County, not counting the *Outlook,* which catered to rich Yankees wintering in Pinehurst. Clif Blue was by then a member of the North

Carolina General Assembly; he was later Speaker of the House and a candidate for lieutenant governor. The general assembly meets biennially in odd years, and Blue was looking for someone to manage the *Citizen* while he spent the first five or six months of 1949 politicking in Raleigh.

I was not long out of the University of North Carolina with an A.B. in journalism and an enduring piece of advice from Professor Phillips Russell: "If you're going to write a story about a bear," Professor Russell taught generations of aspiring writers, "bring on the bear," and I believed I was ready to do it. My home town was near Aberdeen, my father worked for the familiar Seaboard Air Line, and I was willing to work cheap and counted myself worth every cent Clif Blue could pay me, if not much more. For $37.50 a week, I could even call myself editor.

The *Citizen* was quartered in a one-story cinder-block building on a street connecting U.S. One with Aberdeen's downtown business section. There was a business office up front, presided over by a young woman of post-high-school age, who took subscriptions, classifieds, and "personals" over the counter or from the phone, kept the books, and sent out the bills. There was a littered editorial office I took over from Clif Blue, and the shop was out back—one Linotype, one flatbed press, two job presses, one Omaha folder, a mail-labeling device that sometimes worked, and a splendid smell of ink and hot lead. A vintage linotypist and a pressman ran this impressive plant. The pressman, Preston Blue (a distant relation of Clif's, as all Blues in that area were), doubled as photographer. We had to send his negatives to Raleigh on the bus to have engravings made, and the pictures sometimes ran a week after the stories they were supposed to illustrate.

Other than engaging in mildly lascivious repartee with the counter girl—tame stuff by today's standards—my job was mainly to sell ads to anyone who'd buy, at 40 cents per column inch, $60 the full page. I designed the typographical layout for these ads, usually wrote the copy, and laid out each page, more or less. On Thursday nights, when the *Citizen* went to press, I ran the Omaha folder—a neat trick, flipping square sheets of newsprint crackling with static electricity precisely into the thing's snapping jaws, so that four pages, printed on each side, could be mechanically folded and cut into an eight-page newspaper.

Actually, my lowest priority was to collect and "write up"

such news as there was—the discovery, for instance, of the first beaver dam in anybody's memory on a local creek. The very first news story I ever wrote to earn a living seemd to me to be right out of Ben Hecht. A quarter of a century later, my lead is graven on my memory: The long arm of the Federal Bureau of Investigation reached down into Pine Bluff last Tuesday to arrest a long-sought bank robber hiding out in a tourist court."

I also wrote editorials, but on Clif Blue's instructions they were mostly about the virtues of cornbread and pot likker, or the pleasing record of the local girls' basketball team. I did attack a pothole on a downtown street once, but after that Clif took to calling Preston Blue on Thursday night to ask, "Did Tom write anything controversial this week?" This hardly encouraged me to view the press as a watchdog of liberty and justice.

Nor was I long in perceiving that once a month, without any solicitation, a full-page ad arrived in the mail from the headquarters of Robbins Mills. This textile giant not only had a vast new plant on the outskirts of Aberdeen (beyond city taxes) but also one in a neighboring community that had been known as Hemp—until the city fathers gratefully changed its name to Robbins. The ads extolled free enterprise and the right to work, but so far as I ever saw, the *Citizen* did not have to run "puff" copy to qualify for this monthly windfall. On the other hand, I never noticed criticism of Robbins Mills creeping into our columns, either.

By the time of my encounter with the outraged divorcée, I was not a complete stranger to controversy. A local doctor, Robert F. Mobbs, had volunteered to me that the small Taylor Chemical Company plant (also just outside the town limits) was producing a fallout of dust that was dangerous to workers and families living nearby. I had no real sense, in 1949, of the volatility and importance of the environmental and industrial-safety issues, and I incautiously reported Dr. Mobbs's charges, along with the avuncular denials of the plant management. But I was too inexperienced to know how to follow up, or even that I should. Besides, I left Aberdeen for greener pastures soon after my story appeared.

Dr. Mobbs, it later developed, had hit upon one of the first indications that DDT and other insecticides might be harmful to human beings. His interest had been piqued by the death from unexplained convulsions of a three-year-old Aberdeen girl; and it occurred to him that material in the air from the Taylor plant might have been in some way involved.

On investigation, he learned that Taylor was mixing DDT, sulphur, and lindane into a crop-dusting compound; to protect workers who were bagging this mixture, the dust from it was blown by a large fan out of the plant—and allowed to go freely into the atmosphere. As early as December 1948 Dr. Mobbs had published in the *Journal of the American Medical Association* an account of how he had subjected rabbits to lindane dust and they had died—showing evidence of tissue change similar to that found in the dead child.

For the next twenty years, Robert Mobbs was one of a small band of American crusaders against insecticides like DDT; he appeared frequently before congressional and scientific committees and government agencies, mostly to no avail. In Aberdeen, as a consequence, he soon got a reputation as something of a zealot, a man who rocked the boat and who had given the town and one of its industries a bad name. Feeling "ostracized," in 1954 he moved back to his native Massachusetts, where he now practices in Wilmington—and where on June 14, 1972, he got the news that the federal government finally had banned DDT.

Dr. Mobbs's charges against Taylor Chemical was my first encounter with a so-called "whistle-blower"—one who speaks out against fraud or deception or graft or hazard that might not otherwise be detected. And his treatment in Aberdeen illustrates as well as anything the frequent necessity for whistle-blowers to hide their identities—to become "anonymous sources" protected by a reporter from the vengeance of their superiors or neighbors or competitors or peers.

Close proximity to his or her readers can sometimes impose a degree of humility on young reporters—not easy, when youth has a forum. After my apprenticeship on the *Sandhill Citizen,* for example, I moved about fifty miles east to become a general reporter, later the telegraph editor, of the afternoon daily *Robesonian* (circulation about 7000), published in Lumberton, Robeson County, North Carolina. I arrogated to myself also the title of sports editor, which reflected my real interests at the time.

That summer of 1949, I for one had little doubt that I knew as much about sports as, say, Mel Allen, whom we heard broadcasting from distant scenes of glory, or even Wilton

Garrison, the veteran sports editor of our state's largest paper, the *Charlotte Observer*. One hot night I climbed to my usual perch in the cramped press box above the wooden stands of the Lumberton baseball park, from which I regularly covered the home games of the Lumberton Auctioneers—Lumberton was a tobacco-warehouse town and the Auctioneers were a farm club of the Chicago Cubs playing in the Class D Tobacco State League. *The Robesonian* paid me not a penny more for spending my summer evenings keeping notes and score, but *The News and Observer* of Raleigh, the state capital daily, paid me three dollars a game—as I recall—for filing each night's box score by phone to its sports pages.

The '49 Auctioneers were undistinguished by anything, including success, except a locally famous first baseman named Turkey Tyson. A stoop-shouldered slap hitter with a reputation for zaniness and getting on base, Tyson derived his nickname from a gobbler-like sound of derision he made when he pulled up at first after one of the frequent singles he poked through opposing infields. The Turkey probably had played with more minor-league teams than exist today and was at the end of the line in Class D; his future was ten seasons behind him, and he was old enough to be the father of most of the post-high-school kids he played with and against.

One exception—I recall only that his first name was Mike—was a burly, blue-bearded outfielder the Auks (as I labeled them in the headlines over my stories) had obtained somewhere in midseason. He could play ball, or something resembling it, when infrequently sober, had traveled the minor leagues from coast to coast, and although younger than Tyson was also down and about to be out in Class D. (Neither got much closer to the majors than the "Game of the Day" on radio.) Mike had some difficulty handling the ball, except at the plate; he swung a bat the size of one of the telephone poles that held up the dim lights in the outfield. When he connected, he could hit the ball over those lights. More often, he took three mighty swings and hurried back to the bench for a quick swig.

I had noticed a little something about Mike and that morning in *The Robesonian* had unburdened myself of some inside dope for the avid readers I liked to imagine I had. Mike, I told them, was a first-pitch swinger, and the other Tobacco State League clubs were onto him; if he'd lay off that first pitch, I suggested, and wait for *his* pitch, his average would go up and so would the Auks.

There was a good crowd on hand that night, and in the first inning Turkey Tyson rewarded the fans with his specialty—a ground single about two inches out of reach of a flat-footed second baseman who was probably getting $80 a month and meal money and might someday make it to the Piedmont League, Class B. "Gobble-gobble" went the Turkey triumphantly from first, and Auk fans cheered. But that was nothing to the roar that went up when barrel-chested Mike, batting cleanup, strode to the plate, thumped his telephone pole twice upon it, then turned his back to the pitcher and pointed that huge bat straight up at the press box and me.

I can only imagine what it was he yelled at me, but I learned one heady thing—those fans *had* read my article in *The Robesonian*. Unfortunately, that roar also told me everyone in the park knew Mike would defy my first-pitch dictum. I prayed for the pitcher to throw him the deepest-breaking curve or the fanciest knuckle ball in the history of the game. But somehow I knew, and the crowd knew—as Mike turned back to the plate, hunched over it, waved his war club menacingly, and waggled his rump at the world—exactly what was going to happen.

It did. That pitcher came in with a fast ball that would have bounced off a window pane. I can still see that mighty swing, hear the crack of the bat connecting, watch the ball soar into outer darkness. As one of the Auks said later, "Mike just disappeared it."

I can still hear that crowd, too, roaring not just for Mike but *at* me, isolated as I was under the single light bulb in my press-box perch. In the open stands down the first- and third-base lines, they stood and pointed upward and howled with glee as Mike showboated around the bases behind Turkey Tyson and reached the plate again, jumped on it with both feet, and bowed low to the press box. Cowering above him in that naked light, I did the only thing I could do; I stood up and bowed, too, and the crowd howled some more. I thought there must be for Mike, in that moment of defiance and triumph, a certain compensation for all those long bus rides through the minor leagues, that long decline of hope and youth down to the smelly locker rooms of Class D. And I *knew* I was never going to make a sportswriter.

Like most Southern communities, Robeson County was strictly segregated; blacks and whites did not mix in the schools, churches, movie theaters, restaurants, bus and train stations. Unlike most, Robeson was segregated three ways—among blacks, whites and the Lumbee Indians, then usually thought of as an offshoot of the Cherokee, whose reservation was hundreds of miles west in the Great Smokies. These Indians were a proud people and many of them had old English names like Oxendine, Lowrie, and Locklear. For that reason, among others, they were thought to be descendants of "the lost colony"—Sir Walter Raleigh's English settlers on Roanoke Island, who had disappeared into the American wilderness between 1587 and 1591. Local legend had it that Virginia Dare, the first white child born in America, was buried somewhere in Robeson County.

Proud as the Indians were, the whites still looked down on the Lumbees enough not to mix with them. But the Indians, in their turn, looked down on the blacks, and resented any suggestion that there was black blood in their veins. All this human folly produced such ridiculous results as three separate school systems and three seating sections in the movie theaters of Lumberton—the ground floor for whites, half the balcony for blacks, and the other half for the Indians, with a chicken-wire fence separating them.

Like their pioneer ancestors, nevertheless, Robeson whites had a healthy respect for the Indians' fighting qualities. They were thought—stereotypically, of course—to be quick and proficient with knives and revolvers, especially when their honor was impugned, or their race questioned. An Indian coming out of his segregated theater entrance was not likely to be jostled around or—as would be said today—"put down" in any way.

Naturally, we had a column on the sports page of *The Robesonian* for "Negro Baseball" and another for "Indian Baseball"—that's how ludicrous segregation can be, and was. One day I routinely took a score over the phone—something like Beat Six Stars 8, Fairmont Red Sox 2. I put this, together with the line score and the batteries, into agate type under "Negro Baseball."

The next day a war party marched grimly through the *Robesonian* news room to my desk. I looked up at the hostile Indian faces surrounding me and got ready to go under the desk.

"Mister," one of my visitors growled, "the Beat Six Stars ain't niggers."

That kind of thing teaches a young reporter real respect for accuracy. Fortunately for me, the error was of the factual kind that can be put right with a correction. In the years to follow, I learned that errors of judgment, interpretation, taste, and understanding were not so easy to deal with. And sometimes even the correction of a factual error cannot undo the damage done by the error itself; by some perverse quirk of nature and journalism, corrections—usually displayed unprominently—never quite "correct" errors that have been splashed gaudily in headlines or big news stories.

But it probably was not so much my deficiencies as a sports editor that impressed the *Robesonian*'s publisher, Jack Sharpe, as it was the limitations he must have found in my work as telegraph editor. This exalted title signified that I had the responsibility of stripping the Associated Press ticker, going through the reams of copy it spewed relentlessly into the *Robesonian* news room, then editing for length and headlines the stories I had chosen for that day's issues (we had one per day, Monday through Friday afternoons).

Ordinarily, we used most of what the A.P. sent us since, like most small-town papers, *The Robesonian* had limited staff and limited ambitions, hence limited local news coverage. The latter consisted of the most obvious town and county government stories, plus sports, personals, "society," births and deaths, historical features, and an occasional oddity.

The use in local papers of extensive wire-service copy on state, national, and world stories is a widespread custom irreverently known to newspapermen as "Afghanistanism" (who can check up on or take offense at news from Afghanistan?). We were expert practitioners at *The Robesonian,* but in my tenure as telegraph editor, I at least tried to bear down heavily on North Carolina news—especially as I conceived us to be in "competition" primarily with the state capital daily, the *News and Observer.* One afternoon Jack Sharpe stalked toward my desk, holding a copy of a fresh-off-the-press *Robesonian,* as well as an early edition of that day's *Charlotte News,* an afternoon paper that reached Lumberton by truck shortly after we went to press.

Sharpe held up the *News.* Across its front page an enormous headline blared something on the order of ELEVEN DEAD IN GUN SPREE.

"Where's our story," the publisher demanded, not illogically.

I peered more closely at the *News.* "Oh, *that* story," I said. "Heh-heh. Uh . . . it's inside."

Under a polite one-column head on about page six, I had

displayed the story of how Howard Unruh, that very morning, had walked down a street in Camden, New Jersey, killing eleven people as he went. It was one of the great stories of the time and consequently Jack Sharpe was not impressed with my editorial reasoning—that New Jersey was a long way from Robeson County and I thought our front page ought to serve our particular readers. They could read about Howard Unruh in the *Charlotte News,* I said, fervently reminding him of Editor Billy Arthur's slogan for the Jacksonville *Daily News:* "The only newspaper in the world that gives a damn about Jacksonville, N.C." Sharpe rolled his eyes heavenward but kept me on the payroll.

Despite this lapse, by 1951 I was working as a copy editor and weekend telegraph editor in what I thought of as the Big Time—the *Winston-Salem* (N.C.) *Journal* (circulation about 75,000). With time out for Korean War service, I worked for the *Journal* through most of the fifties, taking a turn as sports editor, another as Sunday features editor, a year as Washington correspondent, covering city hall for a while, then writing editorials—a copious education in journalism during which I may have learned something about life.

The *Journal* at that time had a remarkable young staff headed by Executive Editor Wallace Carroll—later to be news editor of the *New York Times* Washington bureau, under James ("Scotty") Reston, still later to return to Winston-Salem as publisher of the *Journal* and the afternoon *Twin City Sentinel.* And my first year in Winston-Salem gave me a high sense of the particularity of my work and the camaraderie possible within it.

I worked at night for the morning *Journal*—going in for duty at 5:00 P.M., eating "lunch" about 11:00 P.M., getting off at 2:00 A.M. or later. Especially in a small city, this kind of off-hours routine can be exhilarating. I slept late when everyone else was struggling out of bed to punch the time clock; I saw my movies and did my reading in the afternoon; I went to work just as good householders were coming home; and when I got off in the small hours, the empty city belonged to me and my few colleagues of the late trick. With our wives, we thought nothing of beginning a bridge game at 3:00 A.M. and playing until the sun was well up; without wives, we shoveled a lot of money (for us) around the poker table.

Once, a group of us took off for Myrtle Beach in the predawn hours. We knew the all-night barbecue joints and the best places for breakfast; we regularly dropped by the hospital emergency room and the police station to chat with the few other night people. We never had any trouble finding bottled spirits, even with the legal purveyors home asleep; and we dropped much cash on the football parlay sheets to the Greek Boy, our local oddsmaker, a man who avoided the sun as a cat does water. We owned our special nighttime world, and disdained all others; and I have never again felt myself either so set apart from workaday mortals or so dominant in my own environment.

I also picked up in Winston-Salem something of the newspaper-man's tough crust, under which it's possible—sometimes, anyway—to shelter from the assaults of life around you. Violence, crime, accidents, acts of God, death, corruption, fate—all these are the stock in trade of the newsroom (no news is good news and vice versa), and I have known few newspaper people who didn't develop either calloused attitudes or a sort of protective armor. All the world's grief channels itself toward the newsroom, and no one can hope to cope without some kind of emotional shield. I threw up the first time I saw the blood flowing around a knife handle sticking out of a man's stomach, but never again.

Gowan H. ("Nutt") Caldwell, the *Journal*'s state editor, handled the obituary page; when a well-trained funeral home would call in with a death, Nutt would sing out to some reporter: "Got another deader for you!" Or a frequent variation: "Another deceasement here!" A visitor might have mistaken this irreverence for indifference; but Nutt was in fact a sentimental man (whose enduring claim to fame was that he had covered the spectacular trial of the singer Libby Holman, who in 1932 had been acquitted of the murder of Smith Reynolds, heir to the local tobacco fortune). But nobody could handle a dozen or so obituaries a night, year after year, without developing techniques. Year later, Roy Thompson, the *Journal*'s local columnist, properly wrote in Nutt Caldwell's own obituary that there was "another deceasement" to be reported.

In print, however, *Journal* obituaries were strictly controlled by the *Journal* stylebook, a document remarkable among small-city newspapers, as most of them have neither a stylebook nor a style. But the *Journal* was painstakingly edited. No one, for example, "died suddenly" in a *Journal* obituary. We held officially that death was always "sudden" and "died suddenly" always redundant, although we sometimes permitted "died unexpectedly."

Worth Bacon, the managing editor of the *Journal* and one of the best copy editors I've known, was furiously opposed to "widows"—a type slug at the top of a column which did not make up a full line of type. I've torn up whole pages to get rid of widows nobody but Worth Bacon would have noticed. He was a harassed man with a cowlick and stooped shoulders who invariably held the second high hand in poker games and gave off an air of eternal anxiety; but he taught a lot of young people something useful about words, sentences, and their proper usage.

In Worth Bacon's newspaper, John Smith never "yesterday announced" earthshaking news. Smith's and everyone's news was "announced yesterday" or not at all. No one did anything in the *Journal* at "6 o'clock at night"; he did it "at 6 P.M." and he did it, furthermore, "at 6 P.M., Tuesday" not "on Tuesday at 6 P.M.," a waste of words and space that pained Worth Bacon. We had strict rules for uniformity in capitalization and punctuation, and our headline-writers struggled under heavy constraints.

For them, there were no easy ways out, such as "Reds in New Attack." In those days, headlines contained verbs in the *Winston-Salem Journal.* Nor could a head-writer get away with "Rapes Mother, Shoots Self." Verbs had to have subjects, even in headlines. As other newspapers did in the fifties, we used "Ike" in desperation; but other abbreviations, diminutives, and slang were not for us.

Natural phrases and linkages could not be "split" from line to line; that is, head-writers could not write, say, "Cookie Sale/Raises Girl/Scout Funds" or "Girls' Cookie/Sale Raises/Scout Funds." Worth Bacon would insist on "Girl Scout/Cookie Sale/Raises Funds." No splits. Nor could our headline-writers torture the language merely to make a head fit its allotted space.

I once wrote in a single dismal night two heads, each of which used the common—I thought—headline locution "said" as a substitute for "said to be" or "reported to be" or "thought to be." Thus, I wrote something like "Police Said/Hot on Trail/Of Thieves" and again "Alderman/Said Likely/To Resign."

Through sheer bad luck, these heads appeared not far apart on the same page. The next morning, Wallace Carroll marched out of his office and pinned that page to the bulletin board. My two "said" headlines were circled with red crayon and a note was clipped to the top of the page: "These are the last headlines of this kind ever to appear in the *Winston-Salem Journal*."

Like my Indian callers in Lumberton, that kind of attention tended to teach me the trade. More than that, I learned on the *Journal* the value of high standards on apparently small matters. Details taken together become large matters, so that high standards on details almost dictate high standards on larger matters. Besides, high standards strongly sustained are the best guarantee of high morale and pride in the ranks—ask any military officer.

We were proud of the *Winston-Salem Journal* because of its standards, and we were proud of ourselves because we met those standards, night after night. When we won the N. W. Ayer Award for typographical excellence in our circulation class, the whole newsroom—including reporters who didn't know Bodoni from boldface—threw itself a monumental beer party.

One of the saddest experiences of my professional life came early—when the United Press started sending Teletype-set copy. Instead, that is, of sending in ticker copy to be set in type by our linotypists, the U.P. began sending its stories on punched tape, which could be fed directly into a device attached to our Linotype machines to set the type without the aid of a human linotypist. This wizardry eliminated substantial wage costs but the Teletype-set material was in the U.P. style—different from *Journal* style in numerous ways and far less rigidly observed by the far-away tape punchers.

Since the object was cost-saving, our management would not let us have the Teletype-set material reset where necessary to conform to our beloved *Journal* style. That was understandable but heartbreaking; for a while, we struggled along incongruously with U.P. style in some columns, and our own style in local and Associated Press copy. When the A.P. also went to the Teletypesetter, with its own style, three styles in one newspaper became too confusing.

We gave up *Journal* style, and the paper became a hodgepodge of capitalization and punctuation and usage, with only our headlines retaining anything like their former precision. I had loved that precision as a young man can love an ideal; besides, there was a profound orderliness in it that I craved in life itself, and knew I never would find. I went home one night and wept at the desecration of a thing of beauty, as someone else might have wept at the defacement of a Goya or a Rembrandt.

But those were mostly good years, full of variety and growth. For a while, as Sunday feature editor, I also was book editor, fleecing gullible New York publishers for innumerable volumes to which the *Journal* could give but cursory review. I wrote a book column for the Sunday paper and thought it raised the tone of things; but when we had a professional readership survey, my column's score was something like 1.3. "News Notes from Upper Yadkin" had more readers, and that only appeared in the mail edition.

With difficulty I persuaded those who had ordered the survey to keep the book column anyway; my argument then was as it would be now, when I have by no means overcome a life-long antipathy to readership surveys. I argued that a newspaper ought to offer something to all its readers, not just the most common denominator among them; that my 1.3 readers might be among the *Journal*'s most important and influential; and that a survey of what people *had* read ought to be no more than one guideline—never a substitute—for an editor trying to decide what readers *might* want another day.

I was then considerably more interested in books than in politics or public affairs, and I still am. But when I came back to Winston-Salem after a brief stint as Washington correspondent and was assigned the *Journal*'s best beat—city hall—in 1959, I jumped at the chance, particularly because it was a city election year. Mayor Marshall Kurfees, a colorful character who had surprised the city by winning election several terms back, then surprised it further by being a pretty good mayor, supposedly had been told by the power structure—which, in the home city of R. J. Reynolds Tobacco Company, Hanes Hosiery, the Wachovia Bank, and Goody's Headache Powder, was some structure—that he was not to run again. The mayor acquiesced tamely enough, some said owing to promises from on high. It was my job that spring to cover the power structure's search for a new mayor, suitably pliable to work with. Marshall Kurfees, rumor had it, had got a little too big for his political britches.

But no new candidate—only a lot of possibles—emerged. And for the first time in my youthful career, I suffered a shattering "beat" by a rival. Gene Whitman, the city hall man for the hated *Twin City Sentinel,* our afternoon paper, scooped me by a mile on the sensational story that Marshall Kurfees would run again after all. Biding his time like any good pro, the mayor had waited for the right moment to preempt the field—which was exactly what Whitman, an old hand at the game, had expected him to do. What's more, Whitman had had the foresight to get a pledge from Kurfees that if he *did* run, he'd break the story in the *Sentinel.* I kicked myself for weeks because if I'd thought there was even a possibility that Kurfees would run again, I could have offered him more circulation for an exclusive in the morning *Journal.* Moral: in writing about politics, the *possibilities* matter as much as the supposedly known facts, which often are not facts at all.

(Using the inspired slogan "Put the Jam on the Lower Shelf Where the Little Man Can Reach It," Kurfees won another term. But the same slogan did not help him when he tried to take a Senate seat away from Sam Ervin, Jr.; in North Carolina, it would have been more profitable to run against George Washington.)

Bill Hoyt, a wise and gentle man with a good business brain, was the publisher of the *Journal* and the *Sentinel.* I respected his character and management ability, but I assumed the professional skills of the newsroom were out of his line. One night, long before my city hall assignment, some major development took place in the Korean War; I happened to be "in the slot" as telegraph editor (no line of work has more pervasive jargon than news) and I ordered out 72-point type (an inch high) for a "banner"—a headline across the top of all eight front-page columns. I was admiring this display between editions when Bill Hoyt came in on some late errand and looked over my shoulder.

"Terrific," he said, pointing at my cherished banner. "What type will you use when the war's over?"

That not only said something to me about proportion and news values; I began to realize then that the rigid standards of the *Journal* and the high quality of our staff in those years hadn't happened by accident. We could have been putting out a paper full of boiler plate and Afghanistanism with a third of the staff and care, and the balance sheet probably would have looked better at the board meetings. But Hoyt and the owner of the papers, Gordon Gray—one of the Reynolds Tobacco Company heirs and at that time a high official in the Eisenhower administration—wanted a quality newspaper to serve Winston-

Salem well. And Hoyt had known how to go about it; he brought in good people—like Wallace Carroll, and Leon Dure before him—and gave them the leeway and support to do good work. By the time I applied for a job on the *Journal,* it was the most widely admired paper in North Carolina, at least among journalists. The basic reason was that it reflected the character of its community, even though in its limitations as well as in its strengths.

Winston-Salem was a wealthy city, strongly oriented to business, and its leading families had put down strong cultural and economic roots there—the Reynolds Building was then the tallest in the state. Community spirit was very nearly rah-rah. There was an active arts center, many lecture and music series, a good symphony orchestra (I got in a season as music critic, cribbing shamelessly from record jackets). The city's United Fund drive was annually successful; if the public didn't come through, the major businesses made up the difference. A big fund drive produced a splendid new library building with the latest audiovisual equipment; there weren't many books in it, but they came later. Local ownership like that of Gordon Gray, in such a city, was bound to result in a newspaper of high quality—which in turn got impressive support from local advertisers.

On the other hand, Winston-Salem was not a city to question itself too deeply, and the *Journal* reflected that quality, too. The names of leading citizens and companies could somehow fail to appear in disagreeable stories. Such stories themselves could be cut, rewritten, buried, or thrown away. The cigarette-cancer connection got short shrift in a newsroom from which could be smelled the tobacco odors of the Camel cigarette factory. The *Journal* did not often cut against the grain of the power structure, of which it was in fact a part, nor turn over many local rocks to see what might be underneath. It did provide solid news coverage of community affairs, brilliant feature writing and photography, sensible editorial comment, ample national and world news, and a high degree of literacy and accuracy.

When the power structure proposed a bond issue for a new hospital, the *Journal* explored the plan thoroughly, reporting its flaws as well as its advantages, but supported the proposal editorially. Just before the bond election, Worth Bacon sent me out to do a man-on-the-street poll. I came back with a story that showed my respondents fairly heavily opposed to the new hospital (the organized opposition insisted the old one could be renovated at less expense).

Looking more anxious than usual, Worth finally decided not to run my story. It would look too much like editorializing in the news columns, he told me with his usual apologetic air. With a young man's arrogance, I shouted something about "cowardice" and stalked out of the newsroom—a loser not for the last time in an encounter with objective journalism.

But Worth had a point. My survey was entirely unscientific, consisting of twenty-five or thirty people stopped at random on the street—and at that in a section of town where low-income people were most likely to be found shopping. They varied widely in their knowledge—if any—of the issue. That my story reported public sentiment, however unrepresentative and uninformed, against a new hospital might indeed have been damaging at the polls to its proponents.

But Worth himself had asked for the survey. I had conducted it honestly, if unscientifically. There was no doubt in my mind that if my respondents had *favored* the hospital, Worth would not long have worried about editorializing in the news columns. That was not his fault so much as that of the city he worked in and the tradition of journalism in which he had been trained. I did not fully realize then what I believe now—that objective journalism almost always favors Establishment positions and exists not least to avoid offense to them. If I had realized that, I would have spared a man I liked some unjustifiably harsh words.

As part of my city hall beat, I covered the city school board during some of its turbulent times following the school-desegregation decisions of the fifties and the passage of various state laws on the same subject. As such groups like to do, the school board decided that reporters or any other public representatives at their meetings were a hindrance to doing business—even though their business was taxpayers' business. Henceforth, they told me condescendingly, I could wait outside and when they'd finished conducting public affairs in secret, they'd tell me as much about what they'd done as they wanted anybody to know.

I protested loudly, but after due consideration, Reed Sarratt—who had replaced Wally Carroll as executive editor after Carroll's departure to the *Times*—said the arrangement seemed all right to him, depending on how it worked out. After the first closed meeting and my first official briefing, Sarratt told me it had worked all right, and we could live with the system. I wanted to get back to Washington anyway, and I made up my mind it was time to move on.

But if the *Journal,* faithfully reflecting a community run benevolently from the top, could be somewhat less than inquisitive and somewhat more than cooperative on some community affairs, it could and did reflect the best in the community, too. After the Supreme Court's 1954 decision in *Brown* vs. *Board of Education*, which ruled out segregated schools, Winston-Salem was one of the first cities in the South to admit a black student to one of its high schools—naturally, the R.J. Reynolds High School. That action resulted from the decision of community leaders who, whatever their racial views, did not want their cherished city torn apart, and who no doubt hoped to "contain" desegregation at the lowest level of demand from the black community. No matter—they opted for change and compliance, rather than bitterness and resistance.

The *Winston-Salem Journal* supported that decision; unlike most newspapers in the South at the time, its reporting and editorial comment provided a pillar of common sense and rationality. Meanwhile, the North Carolina legislature, only somewhat less panicked and demagogic than those of its sister states, passed something called "the Pearsall Plan." In the final analysis, it would have permitted communities to close their public schools rather than desegregate them.

Apologists for this proposal—like Governor Luther H. Hodges—explained privately that they didn't intend that any schools should actually be closed. The closing provision was necessary to get votes from red-hot segregationists for the more moderate aspects of the Pearsall Plan. It was that kind of "leadership"—actually, surrender to the loudest screamers— that led the South into the dark and futile years of what Virginians had at least the honesty to acknowledge was "massive resistance" to the law of the land.

The *Winston-Salem Journal* and the *News and Observer* of Raleigh were the only two daily newspapers in North Carolina in that sad time to oppose the Pearsall Plan. Again, the *Journal* was surely reflecting the sentiment of its community—which was, essentially, the power structure of the city—that there could be no greater folly than the closing of the public schools for any reason. I had nothing to do with the *Journal*'s editorial stand—Reed Sarratt was editor of the editorial page at the time—but I was part of the organization. And I was proud to be.

Twenty years later I know that that single editorial stand by a newspaper I loved persuaded me finally that a man might spend his life honorably and perhaps even usefully in the American press.

Representative Joseph W. Martin of Massachusetts, the House minority leader, had some news for the reporters who crowded into his Capitol Hill office on the morning of August 27, 1957, during my brief tenure as the *Journal*'s Washington correspondent. Famous for his malapropisms and collaboration with the Democratic Speaker, Sam Rayburn, Joe Martin was in effect the Eisenhower administration spokesman on what was about to become—or was it?—the Civil-Rights Act of 1957, the first such measure since the Civil War.

Martin proposed a qualification of the right to jury trial for defendants charged with criminal contempt under the bill's provisions. He suggested that judges be empowered to hear such cases without juries, but that if a judge sentenced a defendant to more than six months in jail and a $1000 fine, the offender could demand retrial by jury.

The reporters, including me, hurried across the Capitol to "the Senate side" with a sense of being the bearers of important tidings. Congress was nearing adjournment and the long battle for a civil-rights bill was at a crucial point. As the measure had been laboriously worked out by the Senate and the House from the original draft sent up by the Eisenhower administration, it empowered federal prosecutors to obtain federal injunctions against actual or threatened interference with the right to vote. This was an important matter in 1957 in the South, where blacks had routinely been threatened with anything from physical violence to loss of jobs to keep them away from registration and voting places.

As passed by the Senate earlier in the summer of 1957, the rights bill provided that persons refusing to obey such federal injunctions could be held by federal judges, sitting without a jury, to be in civil contempt of court. Such persons could be jailed until they agreed to comply; they held, in the jargon of the debate, "the key to the jail in their pocket," because they could get out at any time by their own decision.

But in cases of *criminal* contempt, where a judge sought to punish noncompliance *after* the fact rather than force compliance before the fact, Southern senators—railing powerfully against "government by injunction"—had prevailed in requiring jury trial. Without such a provision, the Southerners would have filibustered the rights bill all summer.

In the House, Southern influence was diminished by the rule against filibustering, and the usual Southern-Republican conservative coalition did not function well against a civil-rights bill. The House therefore appeared ready to reject the absolute right of jury trial in criminal contempt cases that had been written into the bill by the Senate. House civil-rights supporters rightly argued that many Southern juries would refuse to convict white defendants accused of denying blacks the right to vote The original administration bill had required no jury trial at all, for either civil or criminal contempt cases. The feeling was strong in the House that the Southern senators, with their usual ingenuity and mastery of legislative tricks, had succeeded in making jury trial for whites rather than civil rights for blacks the major issue.

What was needed, as the House prepared to vote on the Senate bill later in the day of Martin's news conference, was a compromise—enough jury trial to keep the Southern senators from filibustering against final passage, but not more jury trial than House Republicans and Democratic liberals would accept. Martin had just made the opening move.

I was by then an eight-month veteran of the Capitol press corps and believed I knew my way around "the Hill." On the day I'd reported for duty as the *Winston-Salem Journal*'s first Washington correspondent, I'd been intimidated by the fame of the politicians and newspapermen among whom I was suddenly circulating; but before that day was out, I had been in the Senate Office Building covering a caucus of Southern senators who were organizing opposition to the administration's civil-rights bill. One of "my senators"—the two North Carolinians I was supposed to be covering for the *Journal*—was Sam J. Ervin, Jr. Sixteen years before his Watergate fame, he and Richard B. Russell of Georgia were the intellectual leaders of congressional opposition to the gathering civil-rights movement. I had come to town in the right year, for a young correspondent from the South.

I quickly ran afoul, however, of the intricate customs and mores of Capitol Hill. At a party for new senators, to which the press was invited, I fell into conversation with Frank Church, then thirty-two, the newly arrived junior senator from Idaho, as green in Washington as I. When I asked how he'd been able to get elected at his age, Church joked that he'd been "in the middle between two nuts"—a reference to his opponents, Herman Welker, a conservative Republican, and Glen H. Taylor, and independent liberal who had been the running mate of Henry Wallace on the Progressive ticket in 1948.

Church and I drifted into a group that included the august Senator Russell, keeper of the Senate's rules and flame, guardian of its traditions, the acknowledged Southern leader, gernerally considered one of the ablest men in Senate history. I stole Church's thunder and told his story about being "in the middle between two nuts." No one laughed. Russell's face froze ominously; I could see Frank Church looking for a way to go through the floor. I had forgotten that both Herman Welker and Glen Taylor had been United States senators. No matter what their politics had been, they were not in Richard Russell's presence to be referred to as "nuts" by a young whippersnapper from the press . . . or a junior senator from Idaho.

There was much such trivia to be learned by any newcomer to Washington and I worked hard at learning it all in that first session of the 85th Congress. Mostly I covered Capitol Hill—the civil-rights debate and various actions having to do with tobacco and textiles, North Carolina's prime economic interests. My only office was the Senate Press Gallery—which then was the case for a surprising number of Washington reporters—but all my major stories required me also to gain some familiarity "downtown," in the maze-like corridors and rabbit-warren offices of the Agriculture, Commerce, and Justice Departments.

But the major issue throughout 1957 had been civil rights, and I knew that that struggle was coming to a climax as our group of reporters hurried from Martin's office to the "Taj Mahal," the grandiose suite of Lyndon B. Johnson, the Senate's wizard majority leader. Johnson's presidential chances for

1960—no one in 1957 was giving John Kennedy much thought—were supposed to hinge on the majority leader's ability to get a rights bill passed, thus proving himself a "national figure" without alienating his Southern base of support.

Martin's plan wouldn't do. Johnson said. It put too high a price tag on the right of jury trial. It was possible, however, that the Senate just might accept an amendment providing the right to retrial by jury if a judge, sitting without a jury, had fined an offender as much as $100 and given him thirty days or more in jail.

Obviously, Martin had at least hit on the right approach; only the numbers seemed to be at issue. The reporters trooped back across the Capitol. Johnson's plan, said Martin, was practically the same thing as unqualified jury trial. What about retrial by jury only after a fine of $750 and ninety days behind bars? Back we went to the Senate with this news—which, of course, preceded us on the wire-service tickers to which Johnson even then was addicted. All right, the majority leader said, he was a reasonable man, the Senate was a reasonable body. Make it $300 and thirty days.

On the way back to the House, I was beginning to feel foolish. Johnson and Martin obviously had better means of communicating than through a troop of reporters traipsing among the tourists from side to side of the Capitol—rather like couriers bearing messages from one satrap to another. It made a dramatic spectacle and a good story but not much sense; instead of sitting down over something tall and cool and settling their differences, the two politicians were using the press to dramatize their "negotiations."

I wrote my story that night with a sense of having been used as a spear carrier in the drama—which, not unpredictably, had ended with the right to retrial by jury priced at $300 and forty-five days in jail. Worse, like the other reporters, I had been a willing spear carrier. My Washington assignment for the *Journal* was coming to an end, but I had hopes I'd be back; and I resolved that when that time came, I would be on guard against being more than an uninvolved and disinterested reporter of the news—above all, against being used for their own purposes by politicians and government officials. I had no idea, that many years before Vietnam and Watergate, how hard it would be for any reporter to hold to such a resolution, particularly in an era in which "the media" themselves were to provide the primary arena of public affairs.

Not long before Martin and Johnson staged their charade, I had gone for the first time to one of President Eisenhower's news conferences. Because I had been following the civil-rights debate daily for more than six months, I had more detailed knowledge of it—even as a relative rookie in Washington—than did most of the less specialized reporters who crowded the Indian Treaty Room of the Old State, War, and Navy Building, where Eisenhower met the press about once a week.

Announcing my name and affiliation, as was then required, I managed with some trepidation to put a question to the affable General Eisenhower on the rights bill. He gave me a newsworthy answer that I knew would make headlines. I've long forgotten the details of question and answer, but I well remember walking on air as I went home to my P Street apartment that night.

That news conference had seemed a long way from Aberdeen, Lumberton, and the Winston-Salem school board. I had shown myself I could do the job in Washington. I knew I was where I wanted to be, and I hated the thought of going back to North Carolina. I wanted to stay in proximity to the great—as near as I could get to the heart of the matter.

It had taken me, therefore, no longer than eight months to encounter the deadliest enemy of the Washington reporter—perhaps of any reporter—the desire to be recognized, to have access where others are denied, to be on the inside, a part of things, to belong to the world of power and influence and decision, no matter how peripherally.

3

The Last War

Dwight Eisenhower was still in office but John Kennedy and Richard Nixon were readying themselves to fight for the succession. Few thought or had even heard of Vietnam. Henry Cabot Lodge was a sort of national spokesman at the United Nations, Lyndon Johnson and Sam Rayburn dominated a Southern-style Congress, Soviet Sputniks were humbling the American space effort, and the big political issues were medical care for the aged, federal aid to education, and civil rights. Those who worried about foreign affairs worried most about Berlin, the missile gap, and Fidel Castro's brand of communism, just ninety miles from Key West.

That's the way it was when I returned to Washington, after a brief stint as an editorial writer for the *Nashville Tennesseean*. I was coming back as a reporter for *The New York Times*—which, I carefully explained to the baseball fan who was my mother, was rather like playing for the Yankees. It was the election year of 1960 and I wanted to be a political reporter. But as a rookie in the *Times* Washington bureau, I had little hope of getting into campaign coverage, although my former Winston-Salem editor, Wally Carroll, was by then the bureau news editor under James Reston. I'd been hired to replace Allen Drury, a *Times* congressional reporter who had struck it rich with his novel, *Advise and Consent,* and left the bureau.

Carroll told me I would be assigned to cover "the regulatory agencies," an intimidating notion, since these agencies presided over subjects as diverse and as little known to me as television, aviation activities, and railroad freight rates. This assignment evoked snickers from old hands in the bureau, because for years almost every new *Times* Washington reporter had been told that he would cover "the regulatory agencies."

None ever did, although occasionally *Times* reporters had taken on some part of the task—say, the Federal Power Commission—in which they had a particular interest or expertise. In part, these failures had been because it was a bad idea; "the regulatory agencies" are too diverse in subject matter and procedures and personnel to make a coherent "beat" merely because they all regulate something. Beyond that, however important the regulatory agencies may be, their work is slow, mostly arcane, and only rarely productive of quick, easily understood news—let along front-page headlines. Day in and day out, there's not much news—defined in terms of headlines—in the regulatory agencies.

The *Times*'s failure really to cover the regulatory agencies reflected a major deficiency in every news organization I have known, even those not given to sex-and-crime sensation. The dull, the routine, the unexciting, is seldom seen as news, although the dull, routine, unexciting clearance of Thalidomide for the market, or the dull, routine, unexciting management of rates and routes for the railroads, truckers, and airlines may affect far more Americans in their daily lives than some relatively more glamorous presidential directive or congressional action.

Had I actually covered the regulatory agencies, or even some of them, for any length of time, I might well have become a specialist in broadcasting problems or consumer affairs or transportation; I might possibly have become an investigative reporter, since all the fields covered by the regulatory agencies offer fertile ground for digging into influence peddling, payoffs, lobbying, abuses of the public interest, and other such scandals. But, true to bureau tradition, I was quickly switched to fill Drury's shoes on Capitol Hill, where my brief tour of duty for the *Winston-Salem Journal* had given me some experience; and therefore it was to political reporting—a craft with special rules and requirements, holding perceptions and deductions about character and events more important than the so-called "facts" and "issues"—that my years in Washington were to be primarily devoted.

I was delighted with the change of assignment. The Senate was a cockpit in 1960, with Kennedy and three of his major Democratic rivals—Johnson, Humbert H. Humphrey, and W. Stuart Symington—on the floor and Vice-President Nixon frequently presiding.

Peter Braestrup—now editor of the *Wilson Quarterly*—had joined the bureau just after I did, and we both got a bad break and a good break. As rookies, we were not assigned to either party's national convention; but as rookies also, we found ourselves almost alone in the bureau in August, when most of the more senior reporters had scheduled vacations in anticipation of the long fall campaign. Unexpectedly, however, Congress reconvened that August in a "rump" session, and Braestrup and I were suddenly covering a Senate in which both presidential candidates, Nixon and Kennedy, and the Democratic vice-presidential nominee, Johnson, were heavily involved.

I was covering the minimum-wage bill, which Kennedy in his senatorial capacity was managing, and that gave me a close look at the Democratic nominee. I was less impressed with his management of the bill—which failed to get out of a deadlocked conference with the House—than I was with his ringing promise to take the matter to the people. This impression was more prophetic of his eventual administration than I knew.

I was also covering an aid-to-education bill, which eventually was tied up by a coalition of Southern Democratic and conservative Republican representatives in the recalcitrant Committee on Rules of the House. Playing a hunch—always the reporter's best weapon—I called Herb Klein, Nixon's able press secretary, and asked him if the Republican candidate was trying to pry the bill out of the committee, since it was a school-construction measure popular in the country and sponsored by Eisenhower.

He called me back shortly to say that Nixon was twisting every Republican arm on the committee; I learned by further checking that this was true, and although Nixon ultimately failed to move any of these conservatives, I had an exclusive that the *Times* played on the front page. At that time of my life, that meant more to me than a raise would have.

News stories, particularly political stories, come about in something like that fashion more often than may be apparent. A reporter knows a certain set of facts—in this case that Republicans were going to kill a Republican bill supported in the Republican platform. From that proposition, a reporter can make a logical deduction—in my story, that Nixon ought to be trying to save the bill, for his own political reasons. If such a deduction can be confirmed, the reporter has a story—and sometimes his deduction may be more of a *suggestion* that *causes* a story to happen. In any case, I formed from that experience a somewhat better impression of the Vice-President than most of my colleagues then held.

This was in spite of a disturbing personal glimpse of Nixon earlier that year, before his nomination. For some reason I had been working late in the Senate Press Gallery and was all but alone in that wing of the Capitol. The elevator was slow in coming, and I walked down the marble stairs to the Principal Floor, as it was then called. Just before I reached it, Jack Sherwood, Nixon's Secret Service guard, passed the foot of the steps. Not far behind him was Nixon himself—striding along apparently lost in thought, his hands in his pockets, his shoulders hunched over, much slighter in stature than I had thought him in glimpses from a distance; I was struck by something dark, brooding, in his face, which was shadowed as always with beard stubble, and he passed without looking to left or right, peering steadily at the floor. I had never met the Vice-President and thought he looked unpleasant, almost physically ugly. I believe now that I had glimpsed the haunted, introverted Nixon, withdrawn into some tormented inner world, that most of the public would not see until fourteen years later in the ruins of Watergate.

The August session, exciting as I found it, was only a hindrance to the real campaign and both sides got it out of the way as soon as possible and took to the road. I feared that ended my part in the 1960 election, but one red-letter day shortly thereafter, owing to some quirk of assignments in the bureau, I was told at the last minute to make a one-day trip into the South with Nixon. The enormous reception he got in Atlanta was evidence enough of the changing political temper of my home region—and a good reason, I believe, why Nixon was personally ready, eight years later, to embrace the "Southern strategy" that finally put him in the White House.

Then I was rushed out as a substitute to cover Henry Cabot Lodge, the patrician vice-presidential nominee on the Nixon ticket, who was making an early campaign swing through Florida. For the rest of the campaign, I covered Lodge and Lyndon Johnson, in rotation with other reporters, primarily Anthony Lewis. I'd be on Lodge one week, and Lewis on Johnson; the next week, vice versa.

Vice-presidential campaign planes, at least in those days, were uncrowded and informal, good vehicles for breaking into the intricacies and routines of campaign coverage. Johnson, in lurid pajamas, used to stroll through his Electra—the same one he commanded to land on the asphalt strip at the LBJ Ranch one night, leaving, as someone said, not a dry seat on the plane—keeping the bemused press up till all hours with yarns about his dealings with Joe McCarthy or how he had saved Eisenhower's neck on the Bricker Amendment. A young man named Bill D. Moyers was in charge of the Johnson entourage and practically everything else aboard the plane. Lodge was less gregarious—"even his best friends call him 'Mr. Ambassador,'" wrote Pat Furgurson in a profile for *The Baltimore Sun*—but his staff was congenial, Mrs. Lodge was everybody's favorite political wife, and the candidate paced himself cautiously enough to provide a nice change from Johnson's frenetic campaign.

Neither candidate dealt much with issues, I noted early. Each put out daily releases and had a pat little speech recited at all but the most important stops. Nobody paid much attention to either—a fact that once brought Lodge to grief. He had been saying frequently that there should be a Negro in the cabinet, without causing any excitement. Then he was asked by Nixon headquarters to deliver a "strong civil-rights speech" in New York. His speech-writer, Charles McCarry, turned out the required text and capped it off with the line: "If elected, we will fulfill these promises."

As he was about to deliver the speech in East Harlem, Lodge himself penciled in *before* that last line: "There should be a Negro in the Cabinet." It happened that a *New York Times* reporter new to the Lodge campaign was writing the story that day; he apparently didn't know Lodge had said this before, and anyway it was followed this time by the pledge to "fulfill these promises." He led his story with the cabinet remark. It drew a big headline in the *Times* and caused a sensation. Nixon—even then angling for Southern votes—repudiated the pledge almost before Lodge got across the Triborough Bridge to La Guardia Airport.

Usually, Lodge and Johnson stuck with the pat formulas they had worked out for themselves ("Henry Cabot Lodge," wrote the irrepressible Furgurson, "flew across Texas today, 16,000 feet above the issues"). Lodge regularly cautioned the voters, in reference to Kennedy's supposed youth and inexperience, that it was "no time for on-the-job training in the White House." Johnson just as regularly pointed out that a Democratic president to go with a Democratic Congress would put an end to "divided government." He also made relentless use of the phrase "Austin to Boston" and worked innumerable crowds to the point of tears by reciting the story of the wartime death of John Kennedy's brother Joe.

"Nobody asked him what his religion was when they asked him to put on the uniform," LBJ, knowing how tough was anti-Catholic sentiment in the South and Midwest, intoned with impressive solemnity from Austin to Boston. Seldom departing from his overall formula, he could nevertheless rise splendidly to the occasion, and once outdid himself on a whistle-stop tour through the South, when he leaned from the rear platform of his train as it pulled away from an early stop in Virginia, and bellowed at the receding crowd: "What did Dick Nixon ever do for Culpeper?"

Some months later the San Francisco humor columnist Art Hoppe drove from Washington to Culpeper and asked a gas-station attendant: "What did Lyndon Johnson ever do for Culpeper?"

"Who?" the attendant asked—at least according to Hoppe.

The aristocratic Lodge had the most effective, if perhaps the most meaningless, standard line. Well known in 1960 for his stern denunciations of the Russians on television from the chambers of the United Nations, Lodge billed his formula speeches in their opening sentences as "a serious talk on foreign affairs." This never failed to impress audiences in the full grip of the Cold War mentality, and Lodge then stirred them further by declaring that "I come to you tonight after eight years at the United Nations where I spoke for all the nation—North and South, East and West, regardless of party."

This lent a nonpolitical aura to what followed, invariably climaxed by this refrain:

"My friends," Lodge would say, "the Russians want to take over the United States, and the Russians want to take over the world." Ominous silence in the hall. "But let me tell you something: Nobody's going to take over the United States." Great roars of approval. "And nobody's going to take over the world!" Pandemonium.

Five presidential elections later, this remains the most effective, sure-fire, stand-up-and-yell political line I have ever heard from a total of sixteen serious presidential and vice-presidential candidates I have covered. After hearing it virtually ad infinitum, I said to "Easy Ed" Terrar, a dour Nixon aide assigned to the Lodge plane, that the line seemed a bit simplistic to me, even for a political campaign. Terrar looked at me with pity for my youth and idealism.

"You know what Nixon's best line was in 1958 when he was leading the congressional campaign?"

I confessed my ignorance

"Well, he'd say toward the end of every speech, 'My friends, let me assure you of one thing—*their* campaign is going *down* and *our* campaign is going *up*!" Never failed to bring down the house. In politics, you got to keep it clear and simple."

Nothing I have heard in any campaign in the decade and a half since then has caused me to doubt Terrar's wisdom. No matter how much candidates may pay lip service to "the issues," they are not really what most political campaigns are about.

I began to learn another important lesson about political reporting early in 1961. With a year's congressional experience behind me and the memory of the exciting 1960 campaign still fresh, I volunteered to cover Senator Barry Goldwater on a swing through Texas to campaign for an unknown Republican senatorial candidate.

He was John G. Tower, a conservative political-science teacher who was running as the only Republican candidate in a special election to fill the Senate seat that had just been given up by Vice-President Lyndon Johnson (who, Johnson-like, had run for and been elected *both* senator and vice-president the previous fall). No primaries had been held and not one but seventy Democratic candidates had been attracted by the low filing fee of $50.

These included Maury Maverick, Jr., son of the New

Deal-era congressman; Bill Blakley, formerly an owner of Braniff Airlines, who was holding the seat by appointment; Representative Jim Wright, who was to be elected House majority leader fifteen years later; Bing Crosby's father-in-law; and innumerable publicity-seekers and political opportunists.

Each, however, had some support, if only his family's, and the division of the Democratic vote among seventy candidates gave the Republican singleton, Tower, a better shot at winning a U.S. Senate seat than any member of his party from Texas had had since Reconstruction. Besides, Tower was well known already, having polled nearly a million votes against Johnson in the fall campaign.

As I had suspected, Goldwater's appearance on his behalf improved Tower's chances considerably. My story was less about the Senate election, in fact, than about what was only dimly realized in Kennedy's Washington or elsewhere in the East in 1961—that Barry Goldwater was one of the hottest political properties in the nation, that Texas and much of the West were already "Goldwater country," portending an almost certain struggle in 1964 between the then-dominant Eastern liberal Republicans and a new kind of conservative force.

Played on the front page, my story on the Texas campaign may have alerted some *Times* readers—before most other Easterners—to the rising Goldwater phenomenon; and I took home in my notebook an added dividend for later use. Political reporters should be, and most are, assiduous "string-savers." Some quote not apropos in today's story may be just right for next week's; or some note jotted down on one story may mesh with another from a second story to make still a third. "Stored" in this fasion, in the long memory any newspaperman ought to have, almost any information may become useful to a reporter.

I had been standing near Goldwater, for example, as he was saying good-by to a Texas Republican leader just before flying on to another stop in the small private plane that had been provided for his party. The Texan asked Goldwater who he thought would be the next national party chairman. With the candor that later came to be celebrated, the senator told him he didn't know, hadn't given it much thought, then added off-hand:

"I'd be for Bill Miller, I guess. He's done a good job."

Representative William E. Miller of New York was then serving as the House Republican Campaign Committee chairman, and although he was known on Capitol Hill for a waspish tongue, dapper attire, and staunchly conservative views, he had almost no national reputation. Besides, the incumbent Republican chairman, Senator Thruston B. Morton, was not talking of resignation, although that was more or less expectable, since he had presided over the losing campaign of 1960. I made a note of Goldwater's response but thought little more about it—until June, when Morton resigned the chairmanship to run for re-election to his Senate seat in a tough race with Lieutenant-Governor Wilson W. Wyatt of Kentucky.

Goldwater's casual mention of Miller came back to me immediately. In 1961, the odds-on choice for the 1964 Republican presidential nomination was Governor Nelson A. Rockefeller of New York, the unchallenged leader of Republican liberals, who was not yet divorced in order to marry a divorcée. There would be no Republican national chairman unacceptable to Rockefeller—but I thought none opposed by Goldwater conservatives, either. I sensed the possibility of a compromise—Bill Miller was a conservative but he also was from New York and presumably not immune to Rockefeller's power. Was he not a potential candidate on whom both factions might unite?

I phoned Dick Aurelio, then Senator Jacob K. Javits's press spokesman, later deputy mayor and campaign manager for Mayor John V. Lindsay of New York. Aurelio had proved himself to me as a solid source on New York and Republican politics, so I gave him my reasons for thinking Miller might be Morton's successor and asked if Aurelio could check the idea with the Rockefeller people. He could and did, and phoned me shortly to say that Bill Miller was, indeed, acceptable—at least politically—to Rockefeller.

(Why would Aurelio check out a story that had no great meaning to his employer, Senator Javits? Because he put me mildly in his debt, for one thing, which might be a help to Javits later on; but I think primarily because Aurelio, a former reporter, was an incurable political buff who wanted to know himself and who recognized the same possibilities I did.)

Having already ascertained that Goldwater hadn't changed his mind, I wrote a story flatly predicting Miller's selection, and outlining my theory of his dual acceptability. With my neck thus on the line, I sweated for a while, until the Republicans obliged me by choosing Miller.

That may suggest the value of the sage advice I was later

offered by Edward T. Folliard, a veteran political writer for *The Washington Post*, when in 1962 I was assigned to cover the national political campaign for the *Times*. Political reporters' attention was centered that year on California, where Richard Nixon was running against Governor Edmund G. ("Pat") Brown. I made straight for California and there encountered Folliard in the bar of the Hilton Hotel in Los Angeles.

I told him of my assignment and asked him for his advice. Eddie thought the matter over for a while and then laid it on the line. "Young man," he said, "if you're going to be a political writer, there's one thing you'd better remember. Never let the facts get in your way."

At the time, I assumed Folliard was playing the cynical old hand and giving me a standard newspaper-game wisecrack. Maybe he was, but years of political writing since then—I was a principal national political correspondent for the *Times* also in 1964, 1966, 1968—have persuaded me of the basic truth of that advice. Whatever Eddie Folliard might have meant, political writing is essentially speculation.

Not that facts are unimportant, or may be ignored, or tampered with, any more in political reporting than in other forms of journalism. But in political journalism, what can be *assumed* from facts, sometimes what can be plausibly suggested *despite* the facts, is often more important than the facts themselves—which may not really be facts anyway, in the accepted sense of the word. As an obvious example, it may be a "fact" that a Democratic candidate for governor of Illinois has carried Chicago; but for someone writing the story against a deadline, it's infinitely more important to know enough to speculate that the Democrat carried Chicago by so small a margin that he could not possibly offset the predictable Republican vote downstate and win the election.

In 1962, when Edward M. Kennedy first ran for the Senate in Massachusetts, he was pitted in the Democratic primary against Eddie McCormack, the popular nephew of Representative John W. McCormack. Kennedy aroused a lot of resentment as the younger brother of the President, with no other visible qualifications for the seat, and soon found himself in a rough Irish political brawl. To most reporters, including me, it seemed likely that the primary vote would be fairly close. And when the first returns came in from Pittsfield, a voting-machine town, they showed Kennedy barely ahead.

John Fenton, the *Times* New England correspondent—a man who knew the area so well he could tell you where any New Englander came from, simply by listening to his accent—took one look at the Pittsfield result, blinked, and said with true New England phlegm: "It's a landslide."

"John," I said, "are you sure?"

"That was supposed to be a McCormack town," Fenton said. "If Kennedy's ahead at all up there, he'll carry the state by a landslide."

Which is how the *Times* came to have a front-page story in its *early* edition, flatly calling the Massachusetts primary a landslide for Edward Kennedy. Pittsfield was all the evidence Fenton and I had, but final returns bore out our story. As Eddie Folliard said, never let the facts get in your way.

A less obvious example of the speculative nature of political reporting again involves California. In 1970 I was in that state writing a piece about John V. Tunney's campaign against Senator George Murphy. My old friend Lu Haas, formerly on the staff of Governor Pat Brown but by then the Los Angeles representative for Senator Alan Cranston, suggested I might be interested in the campaign of Wilson Riles for state superintendent of public instruction.

Ordinarily, a national political writer wouldn't even look at such a race, judging it without national significance. In this case, however, the incumbent superintendent, Max Rafferty, was one of the best-known right-wing conservatives in the nation. Educationally, he was an advocate of a return to the strict teaching of the "the three R's" and practically nothing else; politically, he was the demagogue who had beaten the liberal Senator Thomas H. Kuchel in one of the most bitterly fought Republican primaries in California history (Rafferty then had been defeated by Cranston in the general election of 1968).

Riles, moreover, was black. Lu Haas—one of the most reliable political analysts I know—said he doubted Riles actually could win, but that he was running a strong campaign. Win or lose, I was intrigued by the idea of a black running against a right-wing conservative for the highest educational post in the most populous state. I got in touch with Riles, traveled with him a day or so, and saw that Haas was right, as usual. Riles was a strong, articulate, appealing candidate, who looked and sounded more moderate and reassuring than the shrill Rafferty. And he'd done so well in two debates that Rafferty had backed out of a scheduled third.

Riles then stood at only 37 percent in the polls, which is the kind of thing that too often passes for a "fact" in political writing. The conventional wisdom was surely against a black being elected statewide to such a sensitive position in 1970—the city riots and the school desegregation controversies of the sixties were fresh in memory, and President Nixon himself was campaigning hard for "law'n' order." But the *possibility*, about which I felt entitled to speculate, was that Californians would reject race and ideology and choose an apparently nonpolitical professional man who *reassured* them about schools and education.

In my article on the Riles campaign, I avoided outright prediction that he would win—I was not *that* bold—but I raised the startling possibility that he might, and in so doing acquainted readers with what I thought was one of the most interesting campaigns of the year. Riles won, ended Rafferty's California political career—Governor George C. Wallace, in a unique blending of talents, later gave Rafferty a school job in Alabama—and bolstered my slender reputation as a prophet. But my *real* achievement was to rise above the facts and open my mind to the possibilities; that would have been no less an accomplishment in political writing had Riles lost.

There is more than one way in which facts can get in a political reporter's way. They can conflict, for example, and force him to choose between contradictory conclusions. Besides, facts don't necessarily mean one thing only, or lead everyone inevitably to the same conclusion.

In July 1960 who could be sure whether John Kennedy's choice of the Texan Lyndon Johnson as his running mate meant that Johnson would "hold the South" or "lose the North" for the Democrats? To this day, it isn't clear exactly why Kennedy tapped Johnson—was he perhaps just trying to hold his party together and not thinking of sectional strategy? Did he really expect Johnson to refuse his offer? Various persons have claimed to "know" the facts—but what these persons "know" tends to be different in every case.

The ordinary difficulties of choosing among and interpreting facts, particularly conflicting facts, are magnified by an unfortunate truth of political journalism. All too often, experience is the *worst* teacher. And journalists, like generals, tend to fight the last war all over again, rather than recognizing they're in a new one with each election.

As the Democratic presidential campaign of 1972 opened, for an excellent example, the "facts" were as follows:

Two early starters, Birch E. Bayh of Indiana and Fred R. Harris of Oklahoma, had fallen by the wayside. Mayor John Lindsay of New York and Senator George McGovern of South Dakota, an early antiwar leader, were competing for the Democratic left. Senator Henry M. Jackson of Washington was running to the right of center, not only maintaining his hawkish views on the Vietnamese war and foreign policy but proposing a constitutional amendment against busing for purposes of integrating schools. The amendment was designed to steal the "busing issue" from the redoubtable George Wallace of Alabama, running again as the candidate of dissatisfaction and animosity to "the liberals," who were said to be bringing the nation bureaucrats, high taxes, the peace movement, and racial integration.

Hubert Humphrey, the nominee of 1968 who had come within a whisker of defeating Richard Nixon, was ostensibly not a candidate—but few political reporters or knowledgeable Democrats believed the effusive Humphrey was necessarily out of it. As 1972 opened, however, the leader in the polls and the clear choice of most "party leaders" was Senator Edmund S. Muskie of Maine, who had made a good impression as Humphrey's running mate in 1968.

As a consequence, Muskie had been awarded a prime political opportunity on election eve, 1970. He had been chosen to make a nationally televised speech on behalf of the Democrats. It followed, on all three national networks, a speech by Nixon, who had been stumping hard to increase Republican representation in Congress. Nixon's political managers, and Nixon himself, wrongly reading both the public temper and the nature of television, decided to run a tape of a Nixon campaign speech in which he had stridently attacked student and antiwar demonstrators.

Nixon's tape also was badly lit and the soundtrack was faulty; and the net effect of his national-television appearance was disastrous—a mean-looking, angry-sounding President, hot on a cool medium. In contrast, Muskie followed with a relaxed and temperate speech from his home in Maine—a thoughtful and impressive performance. The favorable response to Muskie's speech—written by Dick Goodwin—inevitably gave Democrats pleasant thoughts about matching a calm and reflective Muskie against a raw and ranting Nixon in 1972.

These "facts" led most of the political press to the plausible conclusion that Muskie was "the front-runner" and the "odds-on choice" for the Democrats. Other facts reinforced this view—the first primary, as usual, would be in New Hampshire, next door to Muskie's home state; he had assembled a good staff of proven political operators (always an impressive point with political reporters, who like to deal with staff people who know their way around and can manage an effective campaign swing). Muskie also had high standing in the polls.

Another set of "facts" existed, however, for anyone willing to see them. Following the controversies and conflicts of 1968, when Humphrey had won the nomination without entering any primaries, a commission had been busily at work on the Democratic party's delegate-selection rules—and the commission had been chaired by Senator George McGovern. The result was a new set of rules that made impossible two traditional political devices—the unit rule, by which the majority of a delegation cast all that delegation's votes for the majority's candidate, and the handpicking of delegates by such "leaders" as Mayor Richard J. Daley of Chicago.

In 1972 delegates would be elected by precinct, district, and state conventions, and the unit rule would not be permitted at any level.* All those endorsements for Muskie no longer meant, as they had for Humphrey in 1968, the delivery of state delegations wholesale.

No one understood that better than George McGovern, who had played a major role in devising these rules changes. McGovern, moreover, as the antiwar candidate who in a brief campaign in 1968 had been the choice of most Robert Kennedy supporters after Kennedy had been murdered, had a special position. He was acceptable, too, to those who had supported Eugene McCarthy in 1968. McGovern was heir, that is, to leadership of the antiwar movement and to the young people and other political activists, organizers, fund-raisers, and

---

*As it turned out, a unit rule was permitted in California, but nowhere else.

propagandists who had made the McCarthy and Kennedy campaigns formidable in 1968. McGovern had the potential in 1972 of *combining* what had been those two campaigns, and I was not in much doubt that if he could do that he would have put together the strongest single force in the Democratic party.

But still another set of "facts" showed that in the early months of 1968 McGovern stood so far down in the polls as to make his chances seem nil. He was, after all, only a senator from South Dakota, one of the remotest and least populous states; his candidacy in 1968 had made a good but fleeting impression; and in the Senate he was known primarily for his strong antiwar position—and on that, even many who basically agreed considered him too "extreme" and emotional.

McGovern's low standing in the polls reflected primarily the fact that he simply was not well known to the public; as the poll-takers put it, he had a low "name-recognition factor." Muskie and Humphrey, in contrast, were names that poll respondents recognized instantly. On January 18, 1971, the day he made the formal announcement of his presidential candidacy—far earlier than was then the custom—McGovern and I met for breakfast at the Mayflower Hotel in Washington. He was giving me a preview of his announcement, which he read to me from a handwritten version on a yellow-lined legal paper.

What struck me most forcefully was McGovern's anonymity. I had waited for him briefly in the Mayflower lobby; he came hurrying in and headed immediately for the coffee shop. Before I could intercept him, it was noticeable that no one else in the busy hotel lobby so much as turned a head in recognition of the senator from South Dakota. Yet, a few minutes later he was seated across from me, earnestly reading an idealistically worded declaration of candidacy for the presidency of the United States, nearly two years before the election.

Later that day one of the leading national political journalists, chatting with me, declared flatly: "George McGovern doesn't have a chance." No wonder he thought that; at the time, George Gallup was refusing to match McGovern against Nixon in a presidential-preference poll because McGovern didn't have enough name recognition even to make a showing.

I was nevertheless impressed with the *second* set of facts available to me—that McGovern had the best chance to pull the left wing of the Democratic party together, and that the new rules would then prevent him from being counted out at the convention by predatory party "leaders" using the unit rule. McGovern's anonymity, I thought, would disappear as fast as Gene McCarthy's had, if a 1968-style army of volunteers began winning primaries for him. And in this willingness to take seriously McGovern's ambitions, I was heavily influenced by a single valuable encounter dating back to 1970.

That year, McGovern had been chairman of a committee that raised funds and dispensed them primarily for the election of members of Congress who were at least potential antiwar voters. He was, at the same time, compiling mailing lists and making associations that would be invaluable in the presidential race he already was planning for 1972. I was roaming around the country, reporting on various congressional and gubernatorial campaigns, and I arranged to meet McGovern in Albuquerque and fly on with him to Denver.

At the Albuquerque airport, McGovern was still as well protected by anonymity as he later would be by the Secret Service. He was met by me and by a young advance man named Gene Pokorny, who was from Nebraska. We drove to a Holiday Inn nearby and Pokorny told me on the way that he had been a field organizer for McCarthy in 1968, although he was still a graduate student in 1970. At the Holiday Inn an hour or so later, a group of about twenty-five New Mexicans gathered in McGovern's room—and as I was introduced to them, it quickly became apparent that all had worked in 1968 for either Gene McCarthy or Robert Kennedy, and some for both.

McGovern made a modest antiwar speech, said unequivocally that he was planning to run for president in 1972, and offered his opinion that under the new rules the Democratic nominee would emerge next time from the state-primary battles. He asked them to hold themselves at least uncommitted to any other candidate until he could prove to them that he was worthy of and could handle the political leadership of the peace movement. Circulating after his speech, I found he had made a strongly favorable impression on most of those present.

Later that night, at a public rally for Senator Joseph M. Montoya of New Mexico, I heard for the first time McGovern's "Come Home, America" appeal, which was to provide the theme of his postmidnight acceptance speech at the Miami convention nearly two years later. He showed me that night something that was widely doubted in Washington—despite his flat Midwestern voice, his mild manner, and his preacherly style, McGovern could fire up a crowd, and without hiding his antiwar views.

I also carefully noted down a piece of information casually imparted by Gene Pokorny. Back home in Nebraska, he said, the Democrats were going to give Republican Senator Roman L. Hruska fits, maybe even defeat him; they'd discovered that he owned some outdoor theaters where shady movies were being shown. Since Hruska was a conservative pillar of the Senate from one of the most heavily Republican states, his defeat on such grounds would be a sensation. I passed on this tip to the *Times* national desk.

In Denver the next day I watched McGovern turn on another crowd—this time at a shopping center in suburban Boulder—and met Gary Hart, another impressive young veteran of the McCarthy campaign, by then enlisted for McGovern for 1972. Hart and Pokorny symbolized to me the kind of dedicated, innovative young workers McGovern potentially could put in the field. When the returns came in in November 1970 and Nebraska Democrats had come within a hair of upsetting Roman Hruska, I was reinforced in my high opinion of Pokorny.

A year and a half later he was the organizer of George McGovern's decisive primary victory in Wisconsin.

This second set of facts appealed to me not least, perhaps, because I was by 1972 profoundly opposed to the war myself, and therefore identified my own views and interests with the antiwar Democratic left. Besides, I was a columnist by then, free to follow my mind and write what I pleased—free as I let myself be from the bonds of both experience and objective journalism. To some degree unconsciously, I was opting for *possibilities* over what seemed to some others—such as the political writer who told me in 1971 that McGovern had no chance—the incontrovertible facts of political life (which are seldom even facts, let alone incontrovertible).

After McGovern ran a strong second to Muskie in the New Hampshire primary, which didn't surprise me much, I was reasonably confident he'd make a strong run at the nomination. Not that I thought his victory inevitable; I knew he'd need luck and good management and help from his opponents—all of which he got, as winning candidates must. I believed his nomination was *possible* and opened my mind to that possibility before it became an obvious probability.

But I was not critical of colleagues who persisted until too late in believing that Muskie or Humphrey or someone would appear to snatch the prize from McGovern. Such colleagues were the victims of experience—at a time when political experience was at least beginning to be overtaken by change; and they were the victims of objective journalism, which tended to limit both their willingness to draw bold and risky conclusions from disputed facts and their editors' willingness to print their articles if they did.

Political journalists in 1972, after all, were most profoundly aware of what had happened in 1968. Then, despite the strong showings of McCarthy and Kennedy and the rise of the peace movement, Johnson and the party power structure—men like Mayor Daley and John B. Connally of Texas—had ruthlessly used the unit rule and autocratic power over their delegations to deliver the nomination to Humphrey. What in American political history would cause experienced and somewhat cynical political reporters either to pay much attention to new rules or, if they did, to believe that a power structure still composed of such men as Daley and Connally would not find some way to circumvent or override those rules? Particularly when they saw the same power structure flocking to support Muskie, and when McGovern seemed so "far out" in his liberalism and dovishness?

As for reporters who may have suspected that in 1972 the McCarthy and Kennedy movements *combined* would be the strongest faction in the Democratic party, their backgrounds in objective journalism mostly prevented them from going far out on a limb with McGovern against the respectable political facts of Muskie's support and Humphrey's availability.

Where, anyway, were the necessary official spokesmen or the documents to certify McGovern's potential, when he stood at 3 percent in the polls—"behind Undecided," as someone said? If anything, polls and the pols had it the other way around. They said McGovern was a peacenik who had no chance. Of course, it was these same pols who continued to believe endorsements and party leaders would deliver the nomination to Muskie long after McGovern's young zealots began to take over state conventions and stack the delegations with their own men.

But if my relatively early recognition of McGovern's likely

nomination swelled my self-opinion, this euphoria did not survive 1976. In about November of 1975, in fact, I dug in to fight the last war. I had written a piece in which I casually assigned victory in advance in the Florida primary of 1976 to George Wallace, who had carried every county in the state in the 1972 primary. The next day I had a call from a young man named Jody Powell in Atlanta.

From an interview I'd had with Governor Jimmy Carter of Georgia in 1971, I knew Powell vaguely as press spokesman for Carter. In late 1975 the latter was to me merely an unlikely candidate for president, improbably running on vanity and gall.

"We think *we're* going to win Florida in 1976," Powell said, elaborating on how strongly a Georgian could run in that state, and on Wallace's organizational weaknesses.

"Oh, yeah, sure," I kept saying, *experienced* as I was in Wallace's campaign magic and as well as I knew the historical *fact* (a category no more certain than *political* fact) that a Southerner could not be elected President. Besides, I had a theory (the heaviest baggage a political reporter can carry) that Fred Harris with his Populist program and early organizational start would be heir to the Democratic left that had nominated McGovern in 1972, and would be the only candidate with an army of young workers in the field. This theory signally failed to take into account the extent to which the absence of the war issue had defanged the Democratic left *and* American youth.

Powell, apparently accustomed to such conversations with knowledgeable journalists, finally gave up on me. Months later, a week or so before the Florida primary, I went to that state and talked to various sources of information. One, an experienced Florida politician from Jacksonville, told me:

"I'm for Wallace, you know. I was a delegate for Wallace last time around. But this year I'm voting for Carter."

Why was that? I asked.

"Well, when Carter won that primary up in New Hampshire, it dawned on me. George Wallace can't get elected President. But maybe this ol' Georgia boy can."

Right *then,* it dawned on me. Jimmy Carter could be the first Democratic candidate since FDR to carry "the solid South" and its 167 electoral votes (counting border states), more than half the majority needed for election. That day, I stopped fighting the last war, just a few months too late to brag about it.

● ● ●

Many reporters, as they approached the 1976 campaign, had been as changed in their view of themselves as the public had been changed in *its* view of the press. They were more skeptical of politicians than ever before, anxious to demonstrate their skepticism and prove their independence, and in a mood to challenge every statement, question every act of those who sought the public's trust.

The long decade since Eisenhower had attacked "sensation-seeking columnists and commentators" at the San Francisco convention had had its effect on these reporters. First among recent searing experiences, of course, was their own indifference or cynicism in 1972, when most had continued to cover the Nixon-McGovern campaign routinely, despite the glacially unfolding Watergate scandal.

I believe most reporters, in 1972, at least suspected that the Watergate break-in had had its origins in the White House—if not in Nixon's office, then at least among officials responsible only to him, taking their cues from him, and for whom he had to answer. That most reporters nevertheless continued routine political coverage of the campaign, rather than digging into Watergate as they later did, reflects several factors.

One was the inability of editors and reporters alike to conceive that a mere scandal could grow to proportions as great as a presidential election. Another was the high and rather cynical acceptance in the press, by 1972, of the Imperial Presidency. Behind these attitudes lay numerous facts of life in the press and in America: the long years of the Cold War and the gathering power of the presidency, the increasing linkage of president and government, of the presidency and the man who occupied it, the promotion of this symbolic figure into imperial status—mostly by newspapers and television and the news magazines—and the desire of reporters and commentators to be part of the glittering circle of power around him. Despite Johnson's having been forced out of the race in 1968, it was widely believed in the press that if a president was clever enough, he could do just about anything, and with impunity. Admiring this power, too few were alarmed by it, so strong was the presidential mystique; and most agreed with the view that if Nixon was guilty, he would never be caught—or, if caught, held really accountable by the public.

Even after the larger dimensions of Watergate had appeared, and the bulk of the press *was* working on the story—thanks mostly to the efforts of *The Washington Post*—some reporters and editors gullibly continued to play down Nixon's personal predicament, almost to the day of his resignation under threat of impeachment. By 1976, with honorable exceptions, most reporters and editors could look back on their performances in 1972, as they concerned Watergate, only with embarrassment and anger. They were not prepared to be "burned" again.

Similarly, reporters considered themselves deceived and "used" by Spiro T. Agnew, who had so stoutly insisted on his innocence—to that very press he had so roundly attacked for its supposed bias and distortions—right up until *he* resigned under threat of prosecution on charges of accepting bribes while governor of Maryland. Many, too, had been deeply rankled by Gerald Ford's sweeping pardon of Richard Nixon—after Ford's apparent promise that he would not grant it, and the press's enthusiastic coverage of the new President's first weeks in office.

The revelation of extensive abuses of power by the Central Intelligence Agency and the Federal Bureau of Investigation, agencies with which some in the press had had virtual "sweetheart" relationships, provided still another round of disillusionment and resentment. And all these wounds had been inflicted on a press still bleeding from Vietnam and the traumatic discovery of the duplicity of American government even in the conduct of a war and in the supposed crusade against the evils of communism.

One common thread, linking all those developments, made them particularly painful for the press. That was the knowledge that from Vietnam to the unfrocking of the CIA and the FBI, the press had tended to cooperate in its own deception. The press's lack of skepticism, its unwillingness to look behind official statements and claims, its too ready linkage of the powers of office with knowledge and ability, its assumption of official virtue where rigorous inquiry would have disclosed no virtue at all—these delinquencies could only be charged to the press itself. And nothing leaves a deeper scar than the knowledge of one's own culpability or neglect of duty. If there was one thing reporters were agreed upon as the 1976 campaign developed, it probably was their determination not to be "burned" again—at least not by their own indifference.

To this newly skeptical press, belligerently ready to strike at the first hint of duplicity or scandal, generational change added another note of militance. By 1976 a few younger reporters who had grown up in the Vietnam years and never shared the Cold War-era complacency and nationalism of their elders—or the cautious ethic of objective reporting—had become sufficiently experienced to join the relatively small number of reporters covering the presidential campaign. They were skeptical of government and politicians as a matter of course, and often ready to believe the worst.

Even though Ford, by his pardon of Nixon, had helped to precipitate this mood of suspicion, Jimmy Carter predictably became its prime target. Ford *was* an incumbent, if unelected, and in his fall campaign he brilliantly adopted any incumbent's best strategy. He "played President" and confined himself until the last days of the campaign to the White House and the Rose Garden and television news conferences, while Carter dashed about the country frenetically trying to reach four media markets a day. When Ford did travel, he was shielded as all presidents are. Carter often could be surrounded by reporters with tape recorders as soon as he got off his airplane; but the Secret Service never permits such disrespectful approach to a president.

So to the normal difficulties of questioning a president—the most militant reporter cannot *demand* an answer from so exalted an official—was added the fact that in 1976 Ford mostly made himself unavailable for any questioning, except in carefully controlled circumstances of his own choosing. Most of the force of the press was turned, consequently, on Carter—who in any case, as a mere candidate rather than a president, could not as easily make or keep himself unavailable.

Carter was, nevertheless, the favorite if not the incumbent—a remarkable circumstance that had not been seen since 1948, and at that by few of those covering the 1976 campaign. As soon as his nomination by the Democrats became certain, he was viewed as likely to be the next president. That inevitably made him the center of campaign attention. And it meant that the fall campaign would be the last period in which it would be possible to get at him often and hard—the last chance, in reporter's jargon, "to smoke him out" if he was hiding anything or deceiving people, before he was enfolded in the protective environment of the White House.

Carter himself made it all the more certain that the press would put him under the magnifying glass. One reason was that except for his four years as governor of Georgia, he had no detailed political record. Nor could he be easily classified—as too many reporters simplistically try to classify any candidate—as a conservative or a liberal. He *did* have an extraordinary knack for stating his positions in such a way as to appeal to the greatest number of people of all shades of opinion. In the climate of 1976 these circumstances were translated into "fuzziness" at best and duplicity at worst.

A remarkably explicit interview in *Playboy* magazine, for example, could not dispel the fuzziness charge and—aside from the celebrated remarks on lust—was viewed in the press as minor-league duplicity. Baptist Jimmy Carter, the Sunday-school teacher, was trying to win votes in the *Playboy* belt. An honest Baptist presumably would have disdained the *Playboy* vote, in this purist view. The heightened press skepticism of 1976, I believe, blew the *Playboy* incident far out of proportion.

It pointed, however, to the second reason why Carter himself intensified the press's scrutiny. With or without the militance of 1976, reporters tend to be an irreverent lot—the kind of people who are likely to tell dirty jokes while the national anthem is being played and who ostentatiously do not stand up with the rest of an audience when a president appears on stage (except at presidential news conferences, when reporters *are* the audience). A reporter's nose for sanctimony is as sharp as a bird dog's on the trail of partridge—and sometimes sharper than his nose for news. In 1976 many reporters saw Carter as sanctimonious, owing less to his religiosity than to his emphasis on such unfamiliar political themes as love and compassion. That kind of talk from a vote-seeker, many reporters thought, had to be a "con."

Carter also made the cardinal error—with the press, *not* the public—of pledging again and again that he would never tell the voters a lie. At one level, hotly competitive reporters immediately began contending to be the first to catch Jimmy Carter in a lie; at another level, reporters who knew that "the whole truth and nothing but the truth" could not always be told in politics and government saw the no-lie pledge as still another sanctimonious "con." A man who had been governor of Georgia could not be that naïve, they reasoned with some justification; so maybe in Carter they were dealing with the kind of trickster Nixon had taught them to watch for.

Finally, from the day the fall campaign began, Carter began to slip in the polls and in reporters' estimation of his chances—who knows which having the most influence on the other? Partially because Carter's supposed early lead of 20 to 30 points on the Gallup-Harris scale had been totally unrealistic once the actual, official matchup of a little-known Southern Democrate vs. a likable incumbent president had emerged, partially because Ford and his managers waged a masterly fall campaign, the well-known foot race or game syndrome developed quickly. The underdog was catching up to the front-runner, which is the best political story of all.

If that was the case, the front-runner was weakening, stumbling, losing his speed. Why? What was wrong? The need to know *why* Carter seemed to be slipping once again focused press scrutiny on him—and probably emphasized the fact that he *was* slipping.

So a newly militant press, eager to win this time the wars it felt it had lost in the past, put Jimmy Carter under the closest scrutiny and the most stringent standards applied, in my judgment, to any presidential candidate of modern times, Barry Goldwater possibly excepted. Only once—when Ford mistakenly claimed that Eastern Europe was not under Soviet domination—did he feel anything like the same heat from the press.

Even then, the press furor was not over the facts of political life in Eastern Europe; Ford's slip reawakened the dormant questions of his intelligence and ability, and raised the possibility of slippage in his presumed support from ethnic Catholics of East European derivation. This followed the pattern of pressures on Carter, which had little to do with "issues" and was focused instead on ethics, political tactics, and personality.

Carter accurately complained in the *Playboy* interview that his press entourage was not interested in issues. He did *not* point out, however, that—like most candidates—he seldom talked of issues; his campaign themes had to do far more generally with trust, restoration of confidence, healing of wounds. Even his discussions of such issues as unemployment, welfare reform, and amnesty were more often couched in terms of love and compassion and restoring old values to American life than in programmatic details.

But it's true that the political press is not much more interested in issues than candidates are. Partly this is the consequence of a political system built on the foundation of two nonideological parties, a major function of which is to soften issues and blur ideological distinctions between candidates. That's why they so often fall back on "clear and simple" lines like Lodge's "nobody's going to take over the world" to distinguish themselves from other contenders.

Partly, in modern times, emphasis on personality results from the dominance of television and radio—instruments more useful for the conveyance of images than of issues. Reporters like to concentrate, too, on campaign tactics and devices—polls, for one good example, or Ford's Rose Garden strategy. In their usual foot-race or game perspective on politics, they and their editors see these as being both more critical to the election results than most issues, and more interesting to readers.

Political issues did not, moreover, get Nixon into trouble. That resulted from questions of trust, ethics, personality— which is exactly why Carter won the Democratic nomination, having been the only candidate to design his campaign almost exclusively to respond to those questions. Ford also made it his major theme in the fall campaign that he had restored the people's faith in government and put "our long national nightmare" behind us.

Press scrutiny of Jimmy Carter did, therefore, concentrate on such matters as his personal honesty, his candor, his personality, his political tactics. These were the questions of greatest interest about him and about the election—as Carter had brilliantly perceived—and experienced reporters could sense that, as usual, there was not *that* much difference between the two candidates on "the issues" (although a lagging economy undoubtedly worked to the advantage of the Democrats). After the election, pundits interested in "the issues" could rather accurately complain that Carter had reached the White House without ever having had to give much detail about his intentions—but that has been true of almost every new president.

It perhaps illustrated the mood of reporters in 1976 that a tempest in a teapot arose among some as to Max Frankel's part in Ford's blunder. Frankel (now the editorial page editor of *The New York Times*) was one of the second-debate questioners; he put the Eastern Europe question to Ford. When Ford's amazing answer came back, Frankel alertly inquired if that was what the President had really meant to say. Incredibly, Ford then made his mistake all over again—apparently wanting to say that he did not *accept* Soviet domination of Eastern Europe but repeating, instead, that it didn't exist.

A day or so later I wrote that Frankel had tried to get Ford "off the hook." When this appeared, I was questioned in the *Times* newsroom as to whether I had meant to be *critical* of Frankel—the furthest thing from my mind. Those who raised the question apparently thought getting Ford "off the hook" was the wrong thing for a journalist to do—that it was more useful in the new adversary approach to let him suffer from his mistake than to try to clear up the confusion as to what he actually meant.

This seems to me to be a mindless kind of opposition. It places an adversary attitude on the part of the press above its basic purpose—informing the public. No doubt those of us who have advocated a more skeptical and challenging press might bear that in mind as a cautionary tale; in journalism as in politics, reforms will almost always bring unwanted side effects. A decade after Eisenhower's attack on columnists and commentators, numerous politicians, other public figures, and even some journalists were charging the press with a tendency to opposition for opposition's sake, and too many reporters, I fear, were providing reason for the charge.

In a novel I published*—about a man who tries for the presidency and fails—an experienced political operator has this to say about the ordeal of a candidate dealing with the press:

> If you ask me, nothing in this whole business of politics is as rotten and merciless as a bunch of reporters smelling blood and closing in like a bunch of wolves for the kill.... That day the TV cameras were lined up like artillery and the writing types were sitting there just waiting to get their claws in so the cameras could show everybody the bloodshed and action. No way out of it, in this business, you live and die by the press....

But in the same novel, I put this speech in the mouth of a political "boss" talking to a reporter:

* *Facing the Lions* (New York: Viking, 1973).

You guys are a sort of nominations committee acting for everybody else. You can't be fooled all of the time, and damn few of you can be bought. Your biggest weakness is that too many of you want to believe in people and things you're too lazy to question. But in my experience your committee does manage to weed out the culls. Every now and then you do go wrong and put a good man down or a bad man up—how is that any different from anything else in life? And the truth of it is that a man who can get himself into what you call the speculation and turn it to his advantage is likely to be the kind of man who can make the presidency; on the other hand, if he can't even manage the speculation, he'd better stick to his law practice. I think political writers provide a pretty good test of whether a man's got it or not.

These passages are not, in my eyes, inconsistent. They say the same thing from different points of view. As it happened, Jimmy Carter was smart enough and articulate enough to bear up reasonably well under ordeal by press in 1976. In the case of his early mishap with "ethnic purity," he even conceded he had been wrong and apologized for the error—and promptly at that, not grudgingly and under pressure, as Ford finally did on the Eastern Europe mistake, a week after he'd made it.

In earlier elections—even unmarked as they were by post-Vietnam, post-Watergate press militance—other candidates did not fare so well as Carter under intense press scrutiny. George Romney, in the most celebrated instance, folded his 1968 candidacy as early as the New Hampshire primary, purportedly driven out by press criticism of his offhand concession that he had been "brainwashed" into his early support of the war in Vietnam. But the greater truth was that Romney had shown himself consistently unable, in news conferences and interviews, to deal with probing questions about his views on major policy questions. He lacked what eight years later Carter had—political articulateness.

Goldwater, brandishing his hawkish views, selling the Tennessee Valley Authority, and threatening Social Security, blew himself out of contention in 1964 by his inability or unwillingness to curb his tongue under reporters' questioning. Hubert Humphrey conceivably would have won the close election of 1968 had he not at first feared Lyndon Johnson's vengeance too much to give convincing answers to reporters who wanted to know how he would differ from LBJ on the war. When Humphrey, as late as September 30, 1968, finally appeared to separate himself from Johnson's war policy in a speech at Salt Lake City, the questions slacked off and the Humphrey campaign turned sharply upward, ending in a virtual dead heat with Nixon's.

Then George McGovern, telling the press one thing and doing another in the sad Eagleton affair, and unable adequately to explain under repeated questioning his $1000-per-person guaranteed-income scheme, frittered away what little chance he might have had against Nixon in 1972. Intense pressures from the press again had played a major role in a presidential campaign.

In modern times, it seems to me, the so-called "media"—television preeminent among them—provide the true arena of politics. Elections are now fought basically in public. The power and reach of television carry every round into the remotest living room, and the "writing types" follow with their detailed reports, analyses, explanations, and estimations of what the public has seen and heard—or thought it saw and heard.

The "expert" politician of today, the "real pro," is not the old-time backroom wirepuller or the ward boss or even one of the tough young "operators" who surrounded Kennedy and Nixon. He or she is rather the expert media analyst and manipulator, the person who can calculate the impression a candidate *ought* to make for best effect on the voters, and who knows how to go about creating or emphasizing that impression through the media. And the winner, more often than not, particularly for national and major state offices with enormous constituencies, is the candidate who best uses the media to convey the impressions he wants—or has been persuaded—to convey.

That is the fundamental reason for the decline of party in American politics. When the media provide the arena, the party label means far less than it did when there was almost no other way to tell candidates apart; the emphasis is, instead, on personality, style, and sometimes on their intermingling with issues. Even party organization retains, in the arena of the media, only limited importance—for registration, canvassing, and getting out the vote, all of which are complementary to, but by no means substitutes for, the impact of the media on voters' consciousness.

In today's politics, therefore, the news media are more important than the parties. For presidential candidates, the ability to win the approval, or at least the acquiescence, of the press in their purposes, ability, and integrity—or, as in Carter's case, the ability to surmount the suspicions of the press—is at least as important as the ability to win a party nomination. In fact, the first is a prerequisite to the second.

No wonder, then, that candidates spend so much time calculating and financing their media campaigns; no wonder that reporters raise all the challenges they can and push them as hard as possible. They know that it is through newspapers, magazines, radio, and—above all—television that candidates seek fundamentally to make their impressions on the public.

The results of this conflict may sometimes be unfair, even brutally unfair to certain candidates. But if the image has been substituted for the party label in American politics, as I believe it has, conscientious political reporters have little choice but to strike through the mask, in search of whatever reality there may be.

4

Friends of the President

On John Kennedy's inaugural day in 1961, I had the touchy assignment of covering Richard Nixon. Not as the defeated presidential candidate but as the outgoing Vice-President, Nixon had no choice but to attend the ceremonies at the Capitol. Washington was hip-deep in snow that day and ill-prepared as usual to cope with it; but Nixon graciously asked Don Irwin of the *Herald Tribune* and me inside for coffee. Irwin was the only other reporter who showed up, that snowy morning, at the presidential loser's house in northwest Washington.

The Vice-President—as he still would be until noon—bore up surprisingly well, even jovially, for a·man who had lost a heartbreakingly close—many believed stolen—election; and there even was some hilarity when Charlie Halleck of Indiana, who had deposed Joe Martin as House Republican leader, and Senator Styles Bridges of New Hampshire, Nixon's official escorts, arrived in the top hats decreed by Kennedy as proper inaugural headgear.

But when Irwin and I rode to the Capitol with Herb Klein and Rose Mary Woods, there was nothing resembling hilarity in the car. Miss Woods—even then the totally committed Nixon loyalist the public later came to know—wept most of the way. The next day my story on Nixon at the inaugural was played under a one-column head on the book-review page—which is as good a commentary as any on how quickly the titans of politics can fade from press and public attention. My own opinion then was that Washington had by no means seen the Last of Dick Nixon.

In June 1961, Bill Lawrence, the *Times*'s White House correspondent, quit in a huff and I was assigned to replace him. Lawrence, a *Times* veteran, Kennedy favorite, and one of the best reporters in the business, had run afoul of that deadliest enemy—the reporter's need/desire to be "in"—I had sensed on the heady day three years earlier when Eisenhower had answered my question at his news conference.

The occasion of Lawrence's departure was Kennedy's first presidential trip to Europe, on which he was to meet both Charles de Gaulle and Nikita Khrushchev. For reasons I never fully knew, the *Times* decided not to send Lawrence on the trip; James ("Scotty") Reston, the Washington bureau chief, was in Europe at the time, as were numerous *Times* foreign correspondents, and apparently no real need was seen for Lawrence to travel with the Kennedy press party.

Informed that he was not to go on the White House press plane, on which he was usually the most prestigious passenger, Lawrence promptly quit the *Times* and accepted a long-standing offer from an old friend, Jim Haggerty, Eisenhower's press secretary, who had become a vice-president of the American Broadcasting Company. ABC News just as promptly assigned Lawrence to make the Kennedy European trip after all.

This episode is worth analyzing for what it tells about reporters' mentality and the peculiarities of the White House beat. Lawrence quit, he was the first to admit, because his pride was hurt and he thought his prestige was impaired. In his particular case, this was doubly important because Lawrence prided himself on being one of the reporters most familiar with the new President and one of those closest to Pierre Salinger, the new press secretary. But Lawrence was not merely prideful; he could and did make the accurate complaint that the *Times* had seriously damaged his usefulness as its White House correspondent.

In the first place, Kennedy was off on his first big foreign venture. Being pulled off such an assignment would result in a

major gap in Lawrence's first-hand knowledge of the President
and his administration. It would signal to the powerful
foreign-policy establishment in the White House, headed by
McGeorge Bundy, that Lawrence was not the man to deal with
on the *Times*. While on major foreign-policy stories Bundy and
others at his level might in any case go over the White House
correspondent's head to Reston, the most renowned diplomatic
reporter in Washington, the *Times*'s refusal to send Lawrence to
Europe with Kennedy ran the real risk of putting him at a
competitive disadvantage with other top-ranking White House
correspondents.

. Nor was the risk limited to foreign-policy stories. In no other
circumstances do White House reporters and White House staff
rub elbows more informally than on presidential trips.
Propelled together in any case by their similar interests in
politics, government, and the man they serve or cover, reporters
and staff, freed from the constraints of the White House itself,
often quartered in the same hotel and flying on the same plane,
tend to eat, drink, talk, and—since women, too, are part of
White House press and staff—sometimes even sleep together.
This camaraderie is indispensable to any White House reporter
trying to do his or her job; it is the best opportunity to know and
evaluate the reporter's few sources of information, and to
convey to them his or her own qualities of intellect,
understanding, and trustworthiness.

To remove the White House reporter from such associations,
even temporarily, puts him or her at severe disadvantage for the
long term. It also risks the short-term possibility that the
reporter's knowledge of and familiarity with the White House
staff and routine may be sorely missed at some crucial period.
Reston, for example was on easy terms with Bundy, but not with
lower-level White House people who might have been of real
help to Lawrence; and the resident correspondents in Europe
knew none of the White House people. Some lower-level people
conceivably knew more than McGeorge Bundy ever would, not
about high policy, but about how John Kennedy, the man,
thought and reacted, even where he might be at a given moment.

A year or so later I found myself in Lawrence's shoes. The
Times pulled me off Kennedy's trip to Central America and
assigned a reporter who knew more about Latin American
affairs than I did. I thought the job was at least as much to cover
Kennedy, about whom my replacement knew little; and if I'd

had a long-standing offer from television, as Bill Lawrence had had, I might have done just what he did. As it turned out, I stayed to become Washington bureau chief, succeeding Reston, in which job one of my few accomplishments was to implant firmly on the *Times*'s management the policy that when the President travels, the White House correspondent goes with him, no matter where to cover what story.

It's easy enough, after all, to send a specialist, too, on whatever subject—arms control, China, Africa—the President may be engaged.

Replacing Bill Lawrence in 1961, I discovered that to be a specialist on a president, as a White House correspondent must be, he or she has to be a generalist about practically everything else. Sooner or later most of the government's newsworthy business passes through the White House—sometimes of necessity, just as often because the President wants to take credit. In a single week, a White House correspondent may write about weapons systems, welfare, housing, civil rights, foreign policy, the budget, taxation, politics, the President's pets, his wife's health, and the wedding of his daughter.

A large Washington bureau like that of the *Times* makes it possible to parcel this wealth of material out among semispecialists; if the President announces a decision to finance research for a new missile, the Pentagon correspondent can take over the relatively specialized story. Or the reporter covering the Justice Department may be assigned to handle some new civil-rights proposal ostensibly originating in the White House.

Smaller bureaus do not have this flexibility. The White House correspondent for such an organization has two choices. He can handle everything himself, or concentrate on the major stories and rely on the wire services to cover everything else. Either way, the advantage accrues to the White House in its never-ending effort to get the news reported as favorably as possible.

A correspondent who handles most of the tidal flow of presidential news personally, no matter how brilliant and informed and well connected he or she may be, will sooner or later be overwhelmed; more and more, he or she will have to lean on White House press releases and "briefings" rather than on independent reporting.

The wire services, on the other hand, filing as they do for every variety of news organizations—small and large, morning, evening, and round-the-clock; conservative and liberal; North, South, East, and West—and covering every scrap of official information, seldom can go much beyond that information. At best, their product tends to be swiftly moved, brief, technically accurate, cautious, and homogenized for a vast market. Wire-service White House reporters, the most general generalists of all, tend to be a telegraph editor's dream—they write fast, accurately, and in short punchy sentences that slip right into headlines. That's the way a good White House press secretary wants it, too—not too much analysis or looking beneath the surface of things.

Only newspapers, magazines, and broadcast organizations with large and semispecialized staffs can regularly provide really thorough, well-researched and reported news stories, as well as background and analyses from the White House. That's not to say that these organizations always do it, or that other organizations never do. Every reporter who sets foot in the White House press room, no matter whom he or she represents, has to develop a broad-gauged knowledge of government, politics, the institution of the presidency, the man temporarily occupying it, his program, and his associates. More than most Washington reporters, the White House correspondent has to be able, too, to file on a moment's notice; it's an action beat.

On February 10, 1962, for example, I was awakened about 1:00 A.M. and summoned to the White House by a member of Salinger's staff. I threw on some clothes, drove sleepily to the West Wing, and with the rest of the bleary "regulars" waited interminably—it seemed—for whatever was to come. At 3:20 A.M. it came, in a brief announcement by Salinger. I dashed for the phone on the *Times* desk in the press room, called our efficient dictating room in New York, and started talking:

"WASHINGTON, Saturday, Feb. 10—Francis Gary Powers has been released by the Soviet Union in exchange for the release of Colonel Rudolf Abel, the convicted Soviet spy, the White House announced at 3:20 A.M."

The long wait had been occasioned by the terms of the exchange. Powers—the U-2 pilot downed over Russia in 1960—and Abel were handed over to representatives of their respective governments in the middle of the Glienecker Bridge in Berlin, and part of the arrangement was that neither country would announce the exchange until it had been completed. Berlin time was six hours later than Eastern Standard.

In short "takes"—a paragraph at a time and no paragraph longer than the one quoted—I filed a substantial story, which ran about a column and a half in the *Times* (with some additional material added by the copy desk). The recording room sent each take, as I dictated it, straight out to the copy desk, from where it went rapidly to the composing room. I had no time to sit at a typewriter and compose a literary masterpiece; I just dictated "off the top of my head," and from my scribbled notes of Salinger's detailed announcement.

The result, that chilly morning, was that even after 3:30 A.M., we got the Powers story on the front page of the *Times* for more than a hundred thousand readers of our home-delivered editions.

I was feeling good about my performance on the Powers story until I woke up the next day to find out that *The Washington Post* had had a two-hour beat on the rest of the press. Years later, Ben Bradlee told what had happened.*

He had been attending a White House party and the President himself had given him the story at 12:30 A.M. At that hour it was of little use to *Newsweek*, for which Bradlee was bureau chief; so he phoned it to *Newsweek*'s sister publication, the *Post*. "Imagine," Bradlee recalled with pardonable wonder, "a reporter dictating an exclusive story from the best of all possible sources to the strains of a dance orchestra playing inside the White House!"

A good press secretary naturally has his job to do and while it includes considerable responsibility to the press and through it to the public, his major loyalty is and has to be to the president he serves. Press secretaries, therefore, routinely exploit the weaknesses and peculiarities of the press and ruthlessly use the considerable advantages that the White House commands.

If a president unveiling a new welfare bill provides a battery of experts from the Department of Health, Education, and Welfare to say what is in the bill and what it would do, generalist reporters not well versed in the intricacies of welfare are likely to accept the "official" explanation of the bill. Even if dissenting

Conversations with Kennedy (New York: W. W. Norton, 1975).

views quickly follow, the White House will have seized the
initiative with its own version.

John Herbers of *The New York Times*, who covered the
disastrous second Nixon administration and wrote about it in an
excellent but neglected book,* gave a good example of how
deceptive this sort of thing can be:

> On March 21, 1973, President Nixon said in a
> statement that he was pleased to report that $424 million
> in Federal funds would be made available in the summer
> for 776,000 public service jobs for youths. The statement
> went on to say that the outlook for youths in the coming
> summer was encouraging. Overall, it sounded like a very
> generous act on the part of the government to offset the
> chronically high unemployment rate among young people
> during the summer. Most of the dispatches reported it
> that way.
>
> Only because of my experience in urban affairs
> reporting [a previous *Times* assignment for Herbers] did I
> become suspicious about a portion of the statement which
> said the bulk of the funds, $300 million, would come out
> of money appropriated for the Emergency Employment
> Assistance Act, which was enacted to provide year-round
> public service jobs, mostly for adults, and it would be up
> to local officials to decide whether to use the $300 million
> for adults or youths.
>
> Under the laws then current, summer youth jobs were
> to be funded under a separate act. Informed of the
> President's statement, Senator Jacob K. Javits, Republi-
> can of New York, exploded: "Cities are left with the
> Hobson's choice of firing the father in order to hire the
> son." It was a classic case of the White House acting in a
> calculated manner, then making it appear otherwise.

Note, however, the operative sentence in this cautionary tale:
"Most of the dispatches reported it that way"—the White House
way.

In my own earlier experience, I was sitting with my
colleagues one hot day—June 5, 1963—in the football stadium
of the Air Force Academy near Colorado Springs, listening to

No Thank You, Mr. President (New York: W. W. Norton, 1976).

President Kennedy make a commencement address. Suddenly, as was not unusual for him, he veered away from the prepared text we had been given:

"It is my judgment [he said] that this government should immediately commence a new program in partnership with private industry to develop at the earliest practical date the prototype of a commercially successful supersonic transport superior to that being built in any other country of the world."

Kennedy gave no real details—adding only that there would be a design competition among aircraft manufacturers, that the government would "rely heavily on the flexibility and ingenuity of private enterprise," and that ultimate production would depend on the commercial feasibility of the plan.

When Pierre Salinger, grinning satanically around his cigar, passed among the White House reporters with a press release, it contained only a text of Kennedy's announcement. There were still no details or background—above all, no cost estimates. And no description of that "partnership with private industry" that sounded suspiciously like big federal subsidies to the aircraft makers. Here was the situation in which the White House press found itself—in which Kennedy and Salinger had *intended* to place us:

In a few minutes, we had to load into buses to be taken back to the press plane accompanying *Air Force One,* the President's jet. Then we were to fly to the White Sands Missile Range in New Mexico, where Kennedy was to be given a demonstration of that era's most advanced weapons—the likes of Honest John rockets, Sergeant missiles, the Nike Zeus antimissile missile, and a helicopter-borne battery of Little John rockets. It was afternoon already and for those of us filing for Eastern papers, there was an especially chilling note—the region was on Mountain *Standard* Time, subtracting three hours from our Eastern Daylight Savings deadlines.

Not only was there little time for writing the supersonic plane story, a major news development; not only would we have to write another story on the weapons demonstrations; but the surprise Kennedy announcement, the unhelpful press release, and a total absence of briefers had left most of us in dire need of information. The only background available was a story in that morning's *Times* business section—I had the only copy available—which reported that Pan American World Airways would order six of the supersonics being jointly developed by Britain and France. The story also contained what sounded like authoritative estimates that it would cost the United States $750 million to $1 billion to develop its own SST. I read the *Times* story over the press plane's public-address system, and that was the only "briefing" any of us had on the origins of a story that was to run for a decade of almost continuous controversy—and which may not yet be finished.

What had happened was not hard to deduce. Kennedy had said in the football stadium that his decision had been "spurred by competition from across the Atlantic." Pan American's decision to buy the British-French SST had forced his hand before he was ready; the administration had no real plans for developing the SST, no accurate cost estimates—or none it wanted to release—no idea how much time was involved, no consciousness of the environmental issues that later arose, no analysis of the commercial feasibility of an SST, none of the massive amounts of information on which a costly and important decision should have been based. Kennedy acted out of the visceral impulse of any modern president to appear on top of the game—any game—and out of a perceived political and economic necessity for the United States to remain the master of international air competition—No. 1, as always. Just as he didn't want the Soviets to lead in space exploration, he didn't want his allies to lead in aircraft development.

Kennedy thought he had to act; but he did not have the knowledge to defend his action or justify his decision against tough, explicit questions; so he made an announcement in nationalistic tones ("a . . . supersonic transport superior to that being built in any other country of the world"), in a patriotic and flight-conscious setting, and in such circumstances that the press could at best file only sketchy stories of his decision, mostly quoting him directly, and without the kind of background and analysis that might have raised serious questions about what he was doing. Development of an SST, moreover, would be given by Kennedy's approval the initiative in press and public opinion over any opposition to it that might be heard later.

Save for the cost estimates cribbed from the *Times* story on Pan Am, that was just about the way the story worked out in most newspapers. That night, in El Paso, Salinger scarcely bothered to hide his satisfaction behind a bottle of Carta Blanca.

•   •   •

In any administration, a major problem of White House
correspondents is simply getting to the sources of information.
Unlike Congress or most of the executive departments, the
White House does not permit reporters to wander around the
corridors and poke their heads into offices that interest them.
The Secret Service and the White House police patrol the place
relentlessly. An appointment must be made for the smallest
conversation, unless an official is incautious enough to appear in
the press room or on the street somewhere; if the appointment is
granted, an escort guides the reporter to the proper office,
watchful all the way.

Everything possible is done to centralize information
favorable to the administration in the press office, and to restrict
the flow of any other kind of information. Batteries of polite but
firm secretaries shield presidential counselors who do not wish
to be reached by phone or in person. These counselors park in
White House spaces, eat in the White House "mess" (one of the
really prized perquisites), travel in White House planes,
helicopters, and automobiles, seclude themselves behind White
House barriers or—nearly as impregnable—those of the
Executive Office Building next door.

The White House staff, like the President himself, is
therefore in superb position to guard itself from confrontation
with the press. Usually, the extent to which it does so depends on
the attitude at the top. Reflecting its president, the administration had been relatively open to reporters in the Kennedy years.
The Johnson White House, unpatterned and unpredictable in so
many ways, was no less so with the press. In the early years, as
Johnson himself was more accessible than any president of
modern times, so probably was his staff; later, as resistance to
the war in Vietnam turned the President sourly in upon himself,
his staff also became less friendly and informative. Herbers
found the Nixon White House all but closed to him; later,
correspondents were considerably more welcome in the Ford
White House, which was anxious to be rid of the Nixon aura.

Here is a contemporary account of how things often were
around the White House in Johnson's first years in office. In a
memo to me in 1965—I was then the *Times* Washington bureau
chief—Charles Mohr, doing his first stretch as White House
correspondent, reported at length:

• • •

Access to the President has been so abundant in recent days that it has been difficult to find time to write news stories, much less background memos. But, as things appear to taper off, I thought I would summarize for all faithful LBJ watchers. From last Wednesday to Tuesday, Johnson walked with the press every day except Sunday, went on TV almost every evening and maintained an air of excruciating suspense on all his plans (for instance, we sat in the lobby until 9:30 P.M. Thursday with bags packed waiting to be told whether we would go to Texas).

Some acute observers attributed all this activity—most of it in the evening or even late night—to the absence of Lady Bird Johnson, who had gone to Texas with Nan Robertson and other lady reporters. There is no question that Johnson gets terribly lonely when his wife is out of town, and little question that she has a restraining and calming influence on him (during the campaign it was common for her to send him notes telling him to sit down when she thought he had talked too long). Without her to keep him company, Johnson kept half the cabinet hanging around to keep him company, kept gobbling up reports from the White House "situation room" and making decisions to go on TV.

He also used the press to keep him company. There were long, two-hour walks (around the White House grounds) on Wednesday, Thursday and Friday afternoons. On Saturday there was a walk and then we all adjourned to the Truman balcony for a talk which was very lengthy, and which he continued long after his assistants began passing him notes trying to get it ended. Monday I had a day off, but on Tuesday he took a twilight walk from about 6:45 to 8 P.M. ...

He remains one of the world's great storytellers. Saturday as we passed through the upstairs oval room on the way to the balcony he recalled how, as a Congressman, he had lunch with FDR on the day when Joseph Kennedy returned from his Embassy post in London for consultations (and unbeknownst to Kennedy, to lose his job). He said that FDR took a call from Kennedy at the table and said: "Ah, Joe, old friend, it is good to hear your voice. Please come over to the White House tonight for a little family dinner. I am dying to talk to you. You have been doing a wonderful job." LBJ said that when Roosevelt put down the phone, he looked at Lyndon and then drew his finger across his throat like a razor.

Mere access obviously is not always the answer to a reporter's problems. A useful rule of thumb for any reporter is that if a White House official *asks* to see him, he probably has something to say that he wants published; if an official *consents* to be interviewed, he is at least hoping to get something favorable into print; and in either case the likelihood is that most of what he has to say will be advantageous for the administration. Of all institutions in Washington, the White House staff—clustered as it is around the president, dependent on his fortunes, organized to dominate not just Congress but the rest of the executive branch as well—is the last in which "whistle-blowers" are likely to be found (John Dean notwithstanding).

Thus, the real danger arises that a reporter is far more likely to be sold a self-serving bill of goods in a White House interview, particularly one sought by an official, than he or she is to extract useful and objective information—let alone anything damaging to or surprising about the president or the administration.

I regret—in retrospect—to say that I have on too many occasions responded like one of Pavlov's dogs when summoned to the august presence of a White House official; whatever information he had for me, I usually grabbed and ran—motivated more by the reporter's fierce desire for a good story, particularly if it's put to him as "exclusive," than by any hard and objective judgment about the material thus foisted off on me, or why it had been. Some of those stories, too—in the immortal phrase of C. P. ("Peck") Trussell, a great old reporter for *The Baltimore Sun,* later the *Times*—"remained forever exclusive." Presumably, however, they achieved whatever purpose the official had had in mind.

On assignment for *The New York Times Magazine*, I once set out to write a story about how President Johnson—then new in the White House—had organized his staff. I had the story pretty well in hand from my own observations, but dutifully scheduled numerous interviews with the staff people I was writing about. When I called Jack Valenti, who was more purely a Johnsonian creation than any of the new staff men, he was surprisingly reluctant to talk, for an ordinarily communicative person ("a pretty good word man," Salinger once said of Valenti). "Let me call you back," he said. The next day, he did.

"I've really fixed you up, Wicker," Jack said, with characteristic enthusiasm. "I'm getting you an hour with The Man."

"Great!" I lied, my heart sinking. No reporter can conceivably turn down an interview with a president, even one so omnipresent as Johnson then was. Nevertheless, I knew Johnson all too well; the last thing I needed was to have an expansive and ebullient Texan telling me what he thought about his own staff—particularly since I had learned long before, in his majority leader and my *Winston-Salem Journal* days, that LBJ had a signal failing in his dealings with the press. He believed that whatever he said to a reporter became instant truth, and if it did not appear as he had said it in the next day's paper, skullduggery and bias were unquestionably at work against him.

My fears were well founded. After I was ushered into what was *not* in those days referred to as "the Oval Office" with double capital O's—a pomposity later contributed by the Nixon administration to the Imperial Presidency—Johnson proceeded for most of the hour to fill me full of fanciful baloney about the excellences of his staff, the genius with which he had organized it, the fealty that permeated it, the profound advance in White House administration that it represented—all owing to the skills with which he had assembled and directed it.

No one man, of course, had any importance at all, other than being what LBJ once called Valenti: "A valuable hunk of humanity." Just take Valenti, for instance: I was to understand that he was only a sort of assistant to George Reedy, then Johnson's harassed press secretary. Why, Valenti was not important at all!—a ludicrous assessment of a man who was then constantly at the President's side, the first to see him in the morning and the last at night.

There was scarcely a usable line in the interview, but I couldn't ignore it. Finally, I included a passage in a long article in which I said that Johnson "believed" such and such about his staff, but that others had differing views—which I then outlined in considerable detail. After the article appeared, it was some time before I was again admitted to the presence.

● ● ●

But for the President himself to engage in high-level "back-grounding" and opinion-shaping is not uncommon in any administration, although Nixon's hostility to the press—returned with interest—limited such activities in his years in office. Kennedy and Johnson, before the latter developed a fortress mentality in response to criticism of the Vietnam war, actively sought to influence opinion through interviews, backgrounders, luncheons, and other associations with editors and reporters. But this is a process not without risk.

At the end of each of his first two years in office, for example, JFK called a group of journalists—the White House "regulars" plus a few others specially invited—into the spacious living room of the beach-front house he had rented for his year-end vacation in Palm Beach. For an hour of give and take, questions and answers, he reviewed the past year and looked ahead to the next, ranging over world and domestic questions. The ground rules were that reporters were to write two stories—one on domestic, one on foreign affairs—paraphrasing rather than directly quoting the President. This precaution was designed to give Kennedy greater freedom to speak frankly, without having to take responsibility with foreign governments or political opponents for his specific words.

In the first of these affairs, at the end of 1961, Pierre Salinger insisted on attribution of everything to "friends of the President." That is, we were to write our stories as if we had been assiduously interviewing "friends of the President" who had "talked with him recently" or who were "in his confidence" and who had given us detailed information on his views. Many of us grumbled at this awkward device, but in the reporter's usual hunger for a good story, this time augmented by the knowledge that we were getting it from the President himself, neither I nor anyone else pointed out what ought to have been obvious to all—that the "friends" device forced us to write what was not true and to cooperate in a deliberate, if not particularly harmful, deception of the public, a deception through which Kennedy wanted to get his views to the public without being held really accountable for them.

My senior colleague, Arthur Krock, then writing the "In the Nation" column three times a week on the *Times* editorial page and a veteran himself of numerous private meetings with presidents going back to Coolidge, saw through this fiction at once. In a column soon after my articles from the Kennedy backgrounder appeared, Mr. Krock—years after his death, I am unable to refer to such an impressive and formal personage in any other way—pointed out that it was perfectly obvious to any careful reader that only Kennedy himself, not his mythical "friends," could be the source of these important stories.

This revelation brought me under suspicion at the White House of having told Mr. Krock the secret. I *had* circulated to Scotty Reston and others in our bureau the official text of Kennedy's backgrounder (an official text of remarks that had to be paraphrased and attributed to "friends" perhaps suggests the more surreal aspects of this process). But Mr. Krock heatedly insisted that he had only come to a simple and obvious conclusion when he first read my stories in the *Times*; and that, anyway, since he had not attended the backgrounder, he was not required to abide by its rules or to keep Kennedy's secret.

The latter is a disputed point among reporters, but I shared Mr. Krock's view then and still do; no one need be bound by rules to which he or she has not personally agreed. It might, however, be argued that in that case the text should not have been shown to someone who did not accept the rules under which it had been compiled; but that argument could most effectively be made against direct quotation by such a person, rather than against his identifying the source. Mr. Krock had not directly quoted the text—only my paraphrases.

Actually, the real criticism ought to be against anything as deceptive as the "friends" device; with Kennedy given protection against direct quotation, there was no real reason he should not have been identified as the source—certainly by someone who had deduced that fact from experience.

At the end of 1962 Salinger—perhaps with the Krock dispute in mind—allowed a change in the form of attribution for the second year's backgrounder. We could either use the "friends" fiction or write that the information in the story was being reported on "the highest authority"—which in those days could only have been God or John Kennedy. Thus, on the morning of January 2, 1963, my lead on the *Times*'s page one was as follows:

> PALM BEACH Fla., Jan. 1—President Kennedy believes the onrush of Communist influence in the world was checked in 1962 and that the outlook for peace is slightly better in 1963.
>
> He has cautioned his associates, however, that the free world's problems remain many and

difficult, particularly in the underdeveloped areas. And he does not as yet see evidence of a softening of Soviet policy or a halt to the Communist desire for expansion.

Three major confrontations that, in the President's opinion, might have escalated into war were precipitated by the Russians in his first 24 months in office—Berlin, Laos and Cuba. Although Mr. Kennedy believes Soviet Premier Khrushchev may proceed more cautiously after his Cuban adventure, he does not beleive this one setback will prove to have reversed the bruising trend of Soviet policy.

Not until the fourth paragraph did I refer to a "source" at all:

These and others of Mr. Kennedy's views, ranging widely over the world scene, have been learned on the highest authority.

For the rest of an article that ran nearly three columns I simply reported directly—but in paraphrase—what Kennedy had said, without further attribution to any source. But the risk in this kind of story is obvious and great—misunderstanding or inept paraphrasing on the part of the reporter. And this particular backgrounder caused the Kennedy administration severe embarrassment for just that kind of reason.

Near the end of my story I wrote in reasonably accurate paraphrase:

In meeting these and other concerns as the leader of the free world, Mr. Kennedy is prepared to accept more criticism from other governments and the press if more can be accomplished. Effective policies inevitably cause friction, he believes, and while he has little hope that the United States will become more beloved, he does believe his approach may get more done in the world.

What the President actually had said at the Palm Beach backgrounder was in the context of questions about the so-called "Pact of Nassau." In it, Kennedy and the British Prime Minister Harold Macmillan had taken steps toward the

establishment of a nuclear force to be controlled by the North
Atlantic Treaty Organization.

"Well [Kennedy said] I think we are more aware probably
that we are going to incur at intervals people's displeasure. This
is sort of a revolving cycle. At least, I think the United States
ought to be more aware of it, and I think too often in the past we
have defined our leadership as an attempt to be rather well
regarded in all these countries.

"The fact is you can't possibly carry out any policy without
causing major frictions. The Congo is so difficult that no one can
predict what the results will be, but at least we have been
following a policy somewhat different [from] Great Britain, and
somewhat different from other countries, in giving the United
Nations more direct support.

"Obviously, there are elements in Europe which have
opposed that policy. We have a similar problem in the case of
India and Pakistan, where we believe that the defense of the
subcontinent can only be assured by reconciliation between
these countries, but obviously both of them get dissatisfied with
us because either the negotiations don't proceed fast enough in
the case of Pakistan, or India feels that the United States is
attempting to put too much influence into a settlement.

"So I think what we have to do is to be ready to accept a good
deal more expressions of newspaper and governmental
opposition to the United States in order to get something done
than we have perhaps been willing to do in the past. I don't
expect that the United States will be more beloved, but I would
hope that we could get more done."

This seemed sensible enough to me, and not particularly
inflammatory or controversial. The *Times*'s editors did not
question my decision to report it "far down" in my story; most
other stories from the backgrounder gave these particular
remarks no more prominence than I had.

The usually restrained Associated Press, however, based its
lead on this passage, in what I and most other reporters thought
was an overstated paraphrase. Its story went far to create the
impression that Kennedy expected to take a dictatorial stance
among the allies in the coming year:

> PALM BEACH Fla., Jan. 1—(AP)—President Ken-
> nedy intends to follow up his Cuban success by
> exerting stronger leadership over the West's Cold

War policies—even at the risk of offending sensitive allies.

This was learned today on the highest authority. The same source provided a summation of the President's view on all aspects of foreign policy.

Kennedy believes peace prospects have brightened a bit in the past 12 months, due partly to his firmness in forcing the removal of Soviet missile bases and jet bombers from Cuba.

Also, he is convinced that recent events have cost world communism its vaunted forward momentum.

Kennedy hopes to make the most of this situation by pushing harder for made-in-U.S.A. solutions to Cold War problems plaguing the West.

The President believes that if these problems are to be met and solved, the United States must assume forceful leadership and discard all thought of winning an international popularity contest. He sees a certain amount of friction with various allies as the inevitable price of progress.

This attitude doubtless had its genesis in the Cuban crisis, when Kennedy alone made the decisions. And it is demonstrated anew at last month's Nassau talks with British Prime Minister Harold Macmillan, when Kennedy accepted the ire of a substantial segment of British opinion by insisting there is no room in the U.S. arsenal for the trouble-plagued Skybolt missile.

There could hardly be a more striking example of the subjective nature of journalism, despite its pretensions to objectivity. The Associated Press White House correspondent, Frank Cormier, was an experienced and able reporter, not given to sensationalism or exaggeration. The A.P. itself is ordinarily cautious to a fault, and reluctant to go beyond the official record. Cormier later argued forcefully that his "lead" was justified by Kennedy's words.

That might have been literally true, but my view was and is that he had drawn conclusions about Kennedy's intent that were too sweeping, then stated them too bluntly. That only emphasizes the fact that fallible men and women were gathered in that Palm Beach living room to question Kennedy, and each could honestly draw different conclusions from the same words.

To be fair and honest in reaching subjective conclusions, however, is a long way from being *objective,* which by dictionary definition means "free from personal feelings or prejudice; unbiased"—not influenced in a journalistic sense by personal attitudes or views.

Not even the Associated Press can be a truth machine, and for anyone in the press to pretend otherwise—as the moguls of journalism like to do—makes the press more vulnerable to charges of deliberate bias and distortions, when problems are more often caused for it by the subjective judgments of human beings.

In any case, when the British press, particularly the sensationalist tabloids, saw the A.P. lead on the Kennedy backgrounder, they read even more into Kennedy's reported attitude than Cormier's story had suggested. Their articles, especially their headlines, blew the matter out of all proportion—as if Kennedy had decided to become dictator of the alliance. One London headline proclaimed: "KENNEDY SAYS 'I'll Decide.'"

Naturally enough, this furor, coming on the heels of the Nassau controversy, caused considerable public reaction in Britain and elsewhere, and some stiff inquiries from London and other alliance capitals were directed to Washington. Trying to put out the fire, Salinger called in British reporters and gave them the transcript of the December 31 backgrounder, ostensibly to be reported under the same ground rules as by those who had attended it.

Reporters from *The Times* of London and *The* (London) *Sunday Times*, either by misunderstanding or defiance of the rules, directly quoted Kennedy's remarks about accepting more opposition to get more done, naturally identifying him as the source—which may have been Salinger's unstated aim, since the President's actual remarks were so much less objectionable than the paraphrases and the headlines had made them seem. But this move upset American reporters who had observed the rules, particularly those trapped in the "friends" device, since the net effect was that British readers were getting Kennedy's exact words, attributed directly to him, while Americans had had to read them in paraphrase and attributed in some cases only to his "friends."

By this time Salinger had no choice but to put everything directly quoted by the London papers "on the record" for

American reporters, too. This he did on January 10, after a week of mounting tempest in the international teapot. Still, his troubles weren't over; French reporters, who also had been given transcripts but none of whom had quoted Kennedy directly, protested to Salinger that he had given an advantage to the British rule-breakers by proclaiming the passage they had quoted "on the record" after the fact of their transgression. They demanded he put "on the record" passages in the text relating to France and General de Gaulle.

In his fluent French, Salinger declined to go that far, but the "secret" was thoroughly blown. In putting any part of the transcript "on the record" the White House had to admit that the President in fact had held a backgrounder and he was therefore clearly seen to be the source of all those year-end stories on his views (including what now seems the remarkably prescient prediction that Richard Nixon, who had been defeated two months earlier in a race for governor of California, would sooner or later come back to the forefront of American politics).

Salinger sourly let it be known that because of this overheated controversy there would be no more year-end backgrounders; Kennedy was killed before reporters could test this determination. But Lyndon Johnson was very much in office at the end of 1963, and jealously aware of his predecessor's reputation for skillful management of the press.

By New Year's Eve, 1963, Johnson had not held a major news conference that could be televised live, in the Kennedy manner (although he had hung the presidential seal on a bale of hay at the LBJ Ranch and had taken questions over this improvised lectern—after which he rode off on a horse). The new President had been in Washington for years, knew its leading reporters well, its political problems even better, and had held hundreds of news conferences as Senate majority leader and later vice-president. Within days, certainly weeks, of taking office, he was mostly on top of his new job and dominating what had been the Kennedy administration. His reluctance to meet the press with television cameras on hand was not a fear of making mistakes or of being caught out by some tricky question; it was a mixture of justified political caution and his nagging inferiority complex.

Johnson believed, with reason, that Kennedy's news conferences had usually provided JFK's most effective moments in office; LBJ simply did not want to put himself in a situation where his appearance and performance could be directly compared to Kennedy's—as they surely would have been, for example, had he appeared in the State Department Auditorium, in Kennedy's familiar news-conference setting, within a few weeks of Kennedy's murder. Johnson believed—rightly, as it proved—that he would inevitably suffer by direct comparison: he did not want to risk it until the memory of Kennedy had faded somewhat and he could find a location and format more nearly his own.

Given Johnson's overwhelming force in small groups, he might have done well, however, to emulate Kennedy's year-end backgrounder. But either fearing comparison, even in private, or displaying early the arrogance which so strongly coexisted with his inferiority feelings (at least when confronted by Kennedys and what LBJ called "the Harvards"), he chose a hybrid form of backgrounding—or something—not seen before or, fortunately, since.

On January 1, 1964, he sent Andy Hatcher, the amiable assistant to Salinger, to the press room that had been set up in the Driskill Hotel of Austin, Texas, during Johnson's Christmas vacation. Hatcher came equipped with a written statement from Johnson, which set out the new President's view on East-West relations in the coming year. This view, Hatcher announced, could be attributed to "the highest authority" but not to the President by name.

As Hatcher began to read this singular document, it occurred to me and others that here was something new and dangerous—not in the substance of what the highest authority was saying, but in the fact that it was being read to us by a spokesman, not *said* to us directly by a president we could question and cross-examine. Background, deep background and off-record sessions, and the stories that grow out of them are justifiable—if at all—only because they at least afford reporters the opportunity to confront the source, look him in the eye, ask questions he might wish unasked, challenge his statements, question his facts, and gauge his motives and attitudes. It is this rewarding opportunity that the reporter seeks, and which informs him and his readers, in the most useful sense—far more than the actual information that may be imparted.

Johnson's device, on the other hand, was all take and no give. He wanted the press to convey what he told it to convey, to portray his views as he wanted them portrayed, without yielding in return what Kennedy had given reporters at the end of 1961 and 1962—an hour of close-up exchange, in which they helped set the terms of the discourse with their questions and had the chance to push and probe into his knowledge and attitudes. When this distinction dawned on me, I interrupted Hatcher and protested; so did others; and while no resolution was reached, Hatcher was forced to seek further instructions.

As a result, he announced later that the Johnson document could be attributed to "a White House spokesman." That validated the statement, since the President was entitled to have a spokesman outline his views on East-West relations; but it all but demolished the importance of the story. Here is my lead, from the *Times* of January 2, 1964:

> AUSTIN Tex., Jan. 1—President Johnson is determined to conduct "an unrelenting peace offensive" to ease the tensions of the cold war, a White House spokesman said today.
>
> Mr. Johnson is acutely aware that East and West stand upon a nuclear precipice and he does not believe that a "peace offensive" can be put off until after the American elections, the spokesman asserted.
>
> The President has made up his mind, therefore, to press for new breakthroughs toward peace.
>
> The spokesman, whose remarks were authorized by the President, did not elaborate on Mr. Johnson's intentions. He mentioned no specific new moves toward the relaxation of tensions.

The rest of my relatively brief story was almost entirely concerned with an exchange of New Year's messages between LBJ and his nearest Soviet counterparts, Khrushchev and Brezhnev. This was not just because Johnson had had little of real importance to say in his statement—the passage quoted is transparently self-serving for the first day of an election year—but because having a White House spokesman say it made the whole thing too obvious. White House spokesmen never cast the President or his views in anything but the best light.

Yet, exactly the same statement from Johnson himself, elicited by direct press questioning and accompanied by a broad recital of his views on world and domestic affairs, would have received exactly the same kind of major press attention Kennedy had achieved with his year-end backgrounders. The difference was simple—the press recognized their background sessions with Kennedy as actual *events,* in which their skill and effectiveness as reporters were challenged, as were his knowledge and effectiveness as President, no matter what the ground rules of coverage.

Johnson's document, on the other hand, even when attributed to a White House spokesman, was only one more of the endless attempts of politicians to get credit without taking responsibility. Kennedy paid his dues in 1961 and 1962, but Johnson tried to get by for nothing in 1963.

5

Standing Up to the President

At 6:00 P.M., November 20, 1962, President John F. Kennedy's forty-fifth news conference opened in the State Department Auditorium. As White House correspondent for *The New York Times,* I was in a privileged seat in the first row, directly in front of the lectern hung with the presidential seal. On one side of me sat Eddie Folliard, the venerable and humorous White House correspondent for *The Washington Post;* on the other side was Don Irwin, White House reporter for the New York *Herald Tribune.* Farther along the front row, on either side of my central seat, a White House shorthand reporter and correspondents for *Time, Newsweek,* the three television networks, the two wire services, and several other leading news organizations occupied assigned seats.

The rest of the auditorium—its size reduced by half because of screens erected across its middle—was filled with members of the Washington press seated on a first-come, first-served basis. Most were able and respected, but only those of us in the assigned seats down front could be all but assured that Kennedy would recognize us—the so-called "regulars," who represented the major news organizations at the White House.

Scattered through the crowd of reporters—over whose shoulders peered the ubiquitous television and newsreel cameras—were numerous other *New York Times* reporters, including James Reston, the Washington bureau chief and by anyone's measure the most prestigious and respected reporter in Washington. As *Times* bureau chief through most of the Eisenhower administration and all of Kennedy's, Reston had made a ritual of the *Times*'s news-conference coverage.

Eisenhower had met the press virtually every week in the old State, War, and Navy Building; JFK was only a little less regular in the new State Department Auditorium, and had permitted live television for the first time. There usually was ample warning, in those administrations, when a news conference was coming up; it remained for Lyndon Johnson later to add the element of surprise to the formidable advantages of any president in this form of managing the news to his liking.

An hour or so before each Eisenhower or Kennedy news conference, Reston would call in his White House correspondent; Wally Carroll, his news editor; and a number of *Times* reporters—some volunteers, some Reston had specifically asked for in anticipation of subjects he thought likely to arise. For perhaps an hour, the group would discuss recent developments in the news, imminent prospects, whatever seemed most of public interest at the moment.

Out of this session would come a sort of priority list of questions that the group wanted put to Eisenhower, later Kennedy, with the White House correspondent to ask the most important from his privileged seat. The other questions would be asked as various *Times* reporters gained recognition; or if someone else asked one of our questions, it could, of course, be passed over for the next subject on the *Times*'s list.

Each question would be planned, not only in its substance but for the actual phrasing that would most likely elicit a useful answer. The latter process was of considerable importance, because any skillful politican can evade almost any question; only the most tactically and semantically pointed inquiry is likely to compel him or her into a definite answer, if he or she doesn't want to give one—which is usually the case.

To say to a president at a news conference, for example— "Mr. President, would you comment, please, on reports that your policy on aid levels, particularly with regard to Africa, may be undergoing study and revision?"—is to hand him, and deferentially at that, a license to filibuster for three minutes, at the end of which probably much that is self-serving but little that is informative will have been said—unless, of course, that particular president has just been waiting for some such opening to announce for political and diplomatic effect that he is curtailing aid to Africa because, say, some African governments have been flouting American interests in the United Nations. In that case, the question—which is of the type reporters call "softballs," because they are so easy for politicians to knock over the fence—may well have been "planted" by the White House in order to elicit a prepared answer.

On the other hand, suppose for his own political or diplomatic reasons a president would rather not talk about aid to Africa. If a reporter, believing the subject nevertheless to be of legitimate public interest, framed the following question—"Mr. President, is it true that the State Department has informed the appropriations subcommittee in the House that no further aid beyond what's in the pipeline should go to Uganda? And if it is true, why did you order this action?"—he might possibly force an answer, because any president put in such a position probably would rather make his own case, however weak, than have a possibly hostile member of a House subcommittee leaking *his* version of events. So a wily reporter might ask the question that way even if he had no such "leak" from the subcommittee.

Sometimes, of course, the best-laid plans of mice and men—and reporters can be found to fit both categories—gang agley. For example, here is how effectively Kennedy once evaded a rather pointed question on a subject then of considerable embarrassment to him:

Q. Mr. President, can you say whether the four Americans who died in the Bay of Pigs invasion were employees of the government or the CIA?

A. Let me just say about these four men: They were serving their country. The flight that cost them their lives was a volunteer flight and that while, because of the nature of their work, it has not been a matter of public record, as it might be in the case of soldiers or sailors, I can say that they were serving their country. As I say, their work was volunteer.

● ● ●

After Vietnam and Watergate, probably no president could get by with such slippery stuff. He would at the least be peppered with further questions on the matter, whether or not he avoided substantive answers. In 1961 presidents still were generally considered truthful, as if the office conferred some mantle of personal honor; and anyway, before Vietnam, reporters thought they had little cause to be suspicious that even "national security" could be used for self-serving political purposes.

After long and solemn deliberations around Reston's desk on January 15, 1962, I was entrusted with a question for President Kennedy that perhaps ten *Times* reporters had honed to what we thought was a fine point. Kennedy could not entirely evade it, we were sure. So as soon as he recognized me later that day, I arose—feeling the cameras aim flatteringly at me—and demanded in my sternest voice: "Mr. President, are American troops now in combat in Vietnam?"

Kennedy looked at me—six feet away and slightly beneath his elevated lectern—as if he thought I might be crazy.

"No," he said crisply—not another word—and pointed at someone else for the next question.

He gave me no chance to follow up, and in any case I was too startled by the brevity of his answer and perhaps not well-enough informed on the matter to have challenged it. It was, we learned later, a lie—unless troops are "in combat" only when they fight by companies and battalions and not when they are acting as "advisers" in combat. That was the one kind of response we did not then expect from a president of the United States; later, we would not have been so naïve.

The fact is that presidential news conferences—particularly on television—are far more nearly instruments by which presidents manage the news in their favor than by which reporters extract from them information the public might not otherwise get. Presidents have unlimited numbers of experts and staff assistants to brief them on anything under the sun. Their press aides spend hours listing every conceivable subject that might be raised by temerarious reporters, and devising answers most advantageous to the president. By the time a president steps before the press, there is almost no chance to surprise him or trap him, and none at all to force him to answer what he does not want to answer. Any question of even remote relevance to his activities will evoke an answer carefully planned and rehearsed to serve the president's purposes to the greatest extent possible. And, in fact, the remoter the relevance, the better, as a quick answer then displays for the television audience the catholicity of the great man's knowledge.

All modern presidents regard exhaustive preparation as necessary. Television would magnify out of all proportion even the slightest mistake or political slip—as, say, it magnified Gerald Ford's *gaffe* on Eastern Europe in his foreign-policy debate with Jimmy Carter in October 1976. Besides, the modern cult of the presidency holds that no president can admit error, lest he make himself appear fallible, even mortal. It took Ford a week finally to own up to the slip on Eastern Europe, though he might have cut his political losses immediately by conceding his mistake and apologizing for it.

Carter, by promptly admitting his 1976 campaign error and retracting his "ethnic purity" statement, offered early hope that he might drop the pose of presidential infallibility. But he and his White House spokesmen soon were contorting themselves rhetorically, as so many of their predecessors had done, to avoid the ugly idea of presidential error or miscalculation.

When in April 1977, for example, Carter renounced the income-tax rebate he had proposed in December and defended at a news conference just before the renunciation, he insisted it was the economic situation that had changed—not the President who had recognized that the rebate could not pass the Senate. On another occasion, Carter said at a news conference that he had not been briefed by Attorney General Griffin Bell on the perjury investigation of former CIA Director Richard Helms. Bell later said that he *had* briefed the President and gave the date of the meeting. At least three different explanations of this contradiction, none conceding presidential error, were then offered by Carter and his spokesmen.

Elaborate preparation, however, makes error at a news conference unlikely and assures that most of what a president says is only what he wants to say; so does the skill in phrasemaking and turning questions to his own advantage without which he could not have been elected president.

It's true that the style and manners of a president often convey more than they intend—the false preachiness of Lyndon Johnson, the shifty desperation of Richard Nixon under Watergate pressures (and, even earlier, his air of being always under iron and calculated self-control). In contrast, of the other presidents I frequently saw at news conferences, Eisenhower conveyed the impression of calm, fatherly competence, Main Street common sense, and soldier's steel. Even his nomadic syntax was familiar and reassuring, like that of a Rotary Club treasurer. Kennedy's news-conference style cast him as the keen young executive of the computer generation, the cool, businesslike manager of the national enterprise—a pacesetter for a generation that believed in living well, looking sharp, and knowing all the answers.

Lyndon Johnson, who could dominate any room merely by walking into it, and whose vivid personality and salty speech may have been unique in presidential history—at least since Andrew Jackson—either couldn't or feared to convey his personal force in television news conferences. He would usually begin such an affair with one or more long and rambling announcements that his press secretary might as easily have made. If he were making public some appointment to office, he might have the sheepish appointee on hand to be displayed coast-to-coast. As much as ten minutes of a half-hour news conference might be used in this fashion, and if the opening announcements had been of sufficient substance, questions concerning them might require most of the rest of the time. By that device alone, Johnson often managed to shape more than half of a news conference to his liking.

"It gives [the President] a chance," Pierre Salinger aptly observed of the news conference, "to dominate the news once a week." As if he had no other such chances!

On the other hand, since holding a news conference is entirely a voluntary matter—nothing in the Constitution or law requires a president to do it—presidents can and do find themselves "too busy" to meet the press for periods of weeks and even months when they want to avoid embarrassing subjects. Nixon, particularly after his Watergate troubles began, was the most reluctant news-conference holder; but Johnson, in the later Vietnam years, was not much more accessible—at least for formal, televised news conferences. Following his grim confrontation in Vienna with Nikita Khrushchev in June 1961 John Kennedy held no news conference for seven weeks, after having had one almost weekly in his first months in office.

But when in 1962, for example, Kennedy found himself in deadly conflict with the steel companies on a price increase, with public opinion as the judge, the President suddenly found time in his tight schedule for a half-hour during which he could take questions before television cameras. To make sure they would be the right questions, he opened his news conference with the most scathing attack any president had made of anybody since Harry Truman called Drew Pearson an S.O.B. Kennedy's timing was so propitious, his opening statement so sensational, that the news conference of April 11, 1962, was one of the few ever devoted almost entirely to one subject—steel. The public pressure Kennedy generated that day, with reporters as his involuntary helpers, was the major factor in the ultimate surrender of the steel companies to administration pressure.

Another device Johnson and Kennedy used—as no doubt other presidents have and will—was the planted question. A compliant reporter, willing to do a favor for the press secretary in return for some imagined future news break or leak, would be told to ask the President a particular question; the President then would be sure to recognize that reporter; and the White House would have prepared, of course, an answer that was highly useful to the administration, the more so for appearing spontaneous.

I once was approached by a Kennedy administration official—not Salinger—and told that if I asked the President about a civil-rights development in the South, I would "get a good answer." I said I would ask my own questions, and was never again solicited during that administration. But at the news conference that followed I was not surprised to hear the question asked, just as it had been suggested that I ask it. And, indeed, Kennedy rattled off a "good answer"—very good for him.

One reporter I know saw nothing pernicious in this practice and agreed to ask Kennedy a question on an economics issue. He leaped to his feet at the proper moment and Kennedy pointed in his direction. But another reporter directly in front of the plant thought *he* was being recognized, and spoke first. To the plant's astonishment, the reporter who had mistakenly seized the floor asked exactly the economics question Kennedy had wanted, and, of course, got the planned answer. Taking no chances, the White House had recruited *two* plants on the same question— maybe more, for all I know.

On the other hand, presidents are adept at not recognizing anyone they dislike, desire to punish, or from whom they've learned to expect embarrassing or difficult questions—which is why, for example, the aggressive Clark Mollenhoff of the *Des Moines Register* appeared to some viewers of the last few Nixon news conferences to be about ready to attack Nixon physically. If the oversized Mollenhoff, long known to Nixon as a relentless questioner, hadn't roared and leaped around as much as he did, obviously grabbing the attention of the television audience, Nixon could and probably would have simply ignored him. Similarly, of course, presidents seldom fail to recognize those they consider friendly or whose known views are favorable.

Taking questions from an audience of editors and publishers, Kennedy once appalled Salinger by calling first on Vermont Royster, then the editor of the anti-Kennedy *Wall Street Journal.* Royster, short and feisty, fulfilled Salinger's apprehension with the kind of acerbic question for which he was well known.

"Why'd you call on *him* first?" Salinger later asked.

"The little bastard was the only one whose name I knew," Kennedy confessed.

Unfortunately, there are all too few reporters independent and assertive enough to earn such a description from any president. Besides, the sheer impact of a half-hour of presidential pronouncements on, say, 6 to 10 million home screens—more in prime time—is almost beyond quantifying, no matter what the reporters do. All three commercial television networks usually cover presidential news conferences; radio broadcasts them intensively; at least eight newspapers regularly print the complete text or extensive excerpts; and whatever is considered the top story from a news conference invariably makes every important front page—not infrequently the right-hand column, as the biggest news story of the day. In the *Times,* it is not unusual to find two or more stories from a presidential news conference on page one the next day, with the text and more stories, pictures, and perhaps an editorial on the inside.

No other political official in the world is so frequently and regularly given by a free press such an opportunity to "dominate the news"—and when President Ford seized it unashamedly on October 14, 1976, just two and a half weeks before the national election, a president's tremendous political power was nakedly exposed. Never mind equal time or campaign fairness; the networks quickly gave him the free air time, whatever the disadvantage to Jimmy Carter. Naturally, Ford had timed his news conference not to major national events but to *his* political convenience; that day, the Watergate special prosecutor had announced that he had found no improprieties in Ford's handling of campaign contributions in his days as congressman from Michigan and House minority leader. Questions on that matter gave Ford a fine chance to emphasize that he had been given a clean bill of health—certified an honest man.

To their credit, however, when Ford grabbed for more free time by scheduling another "Presidential news conference" just six days later—and with no campaign or other news developments appearing to warrant it—the networks, all acting independently, turned him down. Instead of broadcasting the news conference live, they filmed it and used appropriate excerpts on regularly scheduled news programs, as they would have with a Jimmy Carter news conference. By that action, the networks took a notable step, not just toward reducing the campaign advantages of an incumbent president but in asserting their own independence as news organizations from White House domination.

If most presidents easily turn news conferences to their own advantage—although toward the end, Nixon was in just too much trouble to manage it—reporters sometimes seem all too eager to help them, and not just by accepting planted questions (which few do). Among hundreds of clamoring reporters, only a few can be recognized, not necessarily the boldest or most thoughtful. Usually fewer than twenty questions can be asked and answered in a thirty-minute session. Not infrequently, a good question is asked so loosely or ineptly as to produce a useless answer, on which a president can then righteously stand, by referring further questioners back to it.

There is almost never any real continuity of subject matter from one reporter to the next, for the human reason that most reporters come armed with a fixed idea of what they want to ask, and insist on asking it—although the previous answer well may have opened a far more useful line of inquiry. The result is that at almost every presidential news conference too many *subjects* are raised and too little is said about any one of them.

Presidential manipulation and reportorial deficiencies produced some sort of low point in the most hostile stages of the Nixon administration. Here is John Herbers' succinct judgment on the period:

> President Nixon succeeded in making every negative aspect of the press conference worse than before, and he got considerable help from the press. He held conferences so infrequently that there was no way the subjects to which he was obligated to address himself could be covered in the short time allotted. This led to the incongruous effect of burning questions going unasked or unsatisfactory answers that were never followed up. When he chose to depict the press as an enemy unfairly attacking him, he called on reporters sure to ask the most outrageous questions. He gave long, convoluted answers to unimportant questions, thus limiting the scope of the conference. He distorted facts just enough so that the correct version never caught up with his televised account. After each press conference, much of the daily press briefings were taken up correcting Nixon misstatements.

And who can forget probably the most famous exchange of the time:

Dan Rather: "Mr. President, I want to state this question with due respect to your office, but also as directly as possible."

The President: "That would be unusual." (*Laughter.*)

Rather: "I would like to think not. It concerns..."

The President (*with irony*): "You are always respectful, Mr. Rather. You know that."

One effort to improve the reporters' performance that is sometimes suggested—usually by those outside the press— probably would be disastrous. Why shouldn't Washington reporters, it's asked, get together before a news conference, plan a concerted effort to get as much information as possible on a few important subjects, then cooperate to carry out the plan at the news conference? At least three good reasons why this isn't done, and shouldn't be, suggest themselves right away.

First, there are just too many reporters who would have to be involved—a hundred or more at a minimum. Second, reporters are, generally speaking, free spirits—sometimes prima donnas—in a highly competitive business; to expect such agreement and cooperation in action from the Washington press would be about like expecting National Football League teams to agree in August on who should be in the Super Bowl in January.

More important, such a cooperative effort would instantly open the press to the nightmare charge of Spiro Agnew—conspiracy. Indeed, when some leading reporters tried a small version of the preplanning scheme during the Nixon administration, Ron Ziegler threw the conspiracy charge at them almost before their meeting broke up. The plan obviously is open to the interpretation that the press is "ganging up" on a president, and since a good many Americans already believe the "liberal press" is a power-hungry monolith, the public confidence that would be risked would be greater than any of the gains that might result.

A far greater benefit for the press and the public for which it acts as surrogate could be attained if Washington reporters, editors, and bureau chiefs—emulating Reston's efforts during the Eisenhower and Kennedy years—were to make better preparations for challenging a president at his news conferences. Possibly realizing that, presidents since Kennedy often have announced news conferences with as little advance notice as possible—adding to the advantages that they already possess. Carter appears to be an exception, scheduling his news conferences well in advance.

Johnson, in particular, liked occasionally to revert to the television practice of Franklin Roosevelt in simpler times; LBJ would call in the reporters who happened to be at the White House and have an untelevised news conference around his desk at the White House—or, in his early months in office, while taking marathon walks around the White House grounds. In these informal sessions, Johnson was not only relaxed and more nearly his usual overpowering self; they also had for him the major advantage of including mostly White House "regulars," who are often more friendly to the President than are their non-White House colleagues, and more anxious to guard their access to and good relations with him and his staff—hence less likely to write too critically. They may also be less informed on specific subjects—say, economics or arms controls—than more specialized reporters. The latter are always shut out of informal "quickie" news conferences at the White House. They simply don't know about them in time to attend.

●   ●   ●

But the news conference is only the most public instrument by
which a really good news-managing president—by and large
John Kennedy seems to me to have been the cleverest of modern
times, with Carter promising to become almost as adept—can
color what Woodrow Wilson called "the atmosphere of events."

Suppose a new and costly urban-development program had
been announced, perhaps in a nationally televised speech by the
President. Immediately, "backgrounders" will be scheduled at
the White House and probably at the cabinet departments most
concerned. At these affairs, intensive briefings will be conducted
by high officials who can only be identified as "Administration
spokesmen"; and while the briefings will be factually accurate
for the most part, they may or may not include the whole truth
and nothing but the truth—for example, the proposal's
administrative weaknesses or its precise costs of budgetary
impact. The net result of the backgrounders, however, will
inevitably be to hand the new program to reporters in its most
favorable light; but the reporters' advantage is that they can
cross-examine the briefing officials and report what they say, as
long as they do not identify them.

This advantage is retained in "deep background"—a phrase
attributed to George Reedy, the rumpled intellectual who
incongruously served Lyndon Johnson as press secretary and
subsequently became dean of journalism at Marquette University. After a "deep background" session, the official who briefs
reporters may not be alluded to at all; and the reporter who
writes a story from "deep background" must write as if he has
gained his information from the air around him, or by
meditation, or perhaps through cosmic revelation. Others have
termed this ghostly process "legal plagiarism"—a reporter
setting forth as his own knowledge what he may not say
someone else has told him. Obviously, "deep background"
requires a relationship of considerable trust between source and
reporter, if it is to be used legitimately by both; but again,
personal cross-examination is possible.

In the hypothetical case of an urban-development program,
the chairman of the President's Council of Economic Advisers
might typically meet—singly or in a group over late-afternoon
drinks or morning coffee—with a few columnists and well-
placed reporters known to be interested in economics. He would
explain to them that while opponents of the new program were
sure to claim that it would cost too much, he could assure them
that the latest projections (copies to be provided) showed that

increased business activity would produce so much additional revenue in the fiscal years in question that even with the new urban-development program the budget could still be balanced—on a full-employment basis, of course.

Meanwhile, across town at the Department of Justice, the attorney general might well have gathered another small group in his office—the small private one for best effect, since his formal office is the size of a tennis court. Those invited would be bureau chiefs, the leading columnists, maybe a couple of network anchor men or commentators. This session would be "off the record" altogether, meaning that those present are not supposed to write or broadcast anything they hear, or even admit that there was such a gathering. What the attorney general tells them is for their private information only—although, of course, again they can cross-examine him.

His solid reports, based on months of investigation and analysis, the attorney general might say, are that unless some real progress can be made, and quickly, in fact on a crash basis, in arresting the decay of the cities, doing something about crime and drugs and bad housing, putting in some job-training and manpower-development money, maybe even a CCC-type program for the kids—in short, unless the administration can get the new urban-development program in place *soon,* well, in all candor, the cities just might blow up. ("The situation is just that bad, and you fellows ought to know it.")

A really thunderous orchestration of the press might go even further—perhaps private interviews with the President himself for, say, men at the level of Reston and—for many years—Joseph Alsop; a fan-out of cabinet officers to conduct local briefings across the country. But just those events described would get the urban-development program off to a fast start in the press. And that's where all the public and most of Congress will become acquainted with it, and get their shaping impressions of it.

The President, after all, had outlined it in prime time, committing his prestige, political clout, and presumed knowledge. Responsible officials in the "backgrounders" had thoroughly explained it, but in terms of their own choosing and without allowing disclosure of their identities—thus making press accounts seem somewhat less derived from partisan or administration sources and more nearly to reflect objective facts.

Powerful columnists and well-known reporters—both

informed and flattered by high-level "deep background" treatment—meanwhile would be lending their authority to the argument that the new program would not be too expensive. And while those gathered to hear the attorney general's dire warning could not publish it—which would be too alarming to the public, anyway, and might make the administration seem less in control of law and order than would be desirable—they would certainly be impelled to a more favorable view of the bill and might come actively to its general support. Bureau chiefs, for instance, would almost certainly pass what they had heard "off the record" from the attorney general straight to their editorial-page editors—not to be published, but to inform the editors' view of the urban program.

A few judicious "leaks" might be arranged, say, to the columnists Rowland Evans and Robert Novak, about a top-secret, hush-hush, crucial watershed meeting between the President and a high-powered group of gravely concerned urban leaders. Complete cooperation would certainly be extended to *The New York Times* in reconstructing day-by-day and meeting-by-meeting the actual hammering together of a major administration program.

Kennedy's news conference of November 20, 1962, was highly unusual, and an air of tension and excitement pervaded the State Department Auditorium as Kennedy strode across the stage to his lectern. He had not met the press since September 13, more than two months earlier, except for a special news conference on September 26, with business editors, when questions about the economy alone had been allowed. On November 6 there had been state and congressional elections in which, after unusually extensive campaigning by Kennedy, the Democrats had done marginally better than expected.

More important, on October 22, Kennedy had informed a startled American people of the installation of offensive missile sites by the Soviet Union in Cuba. In nearly apocalyptic tones, he had announced a naval quarantine against any further military shipments, and demanded that Chairman Khrushchev remove the Soviet missiles already in Cuba.

On October 28, after a period of the greatest world tension since the dawning of the atomic age, Kennedy had been able to announce the Soviets' agreement to withdrawal of the missiles.

But by November 20, he had not yet met with the press to discuss any of his actions during the Cuban crisis. Most reporters considered the delay deliberate on his part, both to avoid the possibility of some diplomatic provocation to Moscow and so that Kennedy could take the most political advantage of continuing developments in Cuba, the Soviet Union, and the United States.

So it proved. The President opened on November 20 with the statement that Khrushchev had agreed further to withdraw all Soviet IL-28 bombers from Cuba. That was the carefully stated preface to Kennedy's own announcement that he was therefore lifting the naval quarantine he had ordered on October 22. And he cautiously confirmed that if offensive weapons were kept out of Cuba and that island was not used "for the export of aggressive Communist purposes, there will be peace in the Caribbean." In short, he concluded, "the record of recent weeks shows real progress, and we are hopeful that further progress can be made."

Then—turning 180 degrees to another subject—he announced the issuance of an executive order designed to prevent racial discrimination in housing—two full years after he had promised in his 1960 campaign to sign such an order. Finally he said he had dispatched a team headed by W. Averell Harriman to New Delhi to assess India's military-assistance needs in its border warfare with Communist China.

There have been few better examples of a president using a news conference to manage the news. Already, in both parties, after the first flush of "victory" and relief in the easing of the missile crisis, critics were saying that Kennedy had been too "soft" during the confrontation with Khrushchev. Dean Acheson, the hawkish former Democratic secretary of state, was making little secret of his belief that Kennedy should have ordered air strikes on the missile sites; Republicans were arguing that in return for the removal of the missiles, Kennedy had given the Castro regime in Cuba "immunity" against invasion, a price they apparently considered too high.

So Kennedy had waited until he could announce the Soviets' withdrawal of the IL-28s before he met the press, and had seized the moment to cushion the announcement that he was lifting the naval quarantine—an act sure to arouse the hawks. He had described his part of the bargain not as a pledge of any kind to Castro but as assuring "peace in the Caribbean"—but only, of course, if Castro stayed on his good behavior. From the news conference forum, the President had forcefully taken the initiative against his critics, waiting until he could use the relatively unimportant withdrawal of the IL-28s to cast the Caribbean agreement in his own terms as—implicitly—an American triumph for which he had had to give up little in return.

Questioning began, predictably, with Cuba and even more expectably on what Frank Cormier of the Associated Press called Kennedy's "no-invasion pledge." The President immediately took shelter from that loaded phrase behind his opening statement; that set out, he said, "the position of the government on the matter." Clearly, he was not going to be drawn beyond his carefully worded description: "peace in the Caribbean."

Five of the first seven questions derived directly from the missile crisis; none of them pushed Kennedy significantly further than his opening statement. All told, ten of the seventeen questioners at the November 20 news conference asked him something about Cuba, Castro, Khrushchev, the missiles, or related circumstances—a show of interest that was only to be expected.

What might also have been expected, and probably was in the White House, was that only one question dealt with the housing proclamation—an act Kennedy had said in his campaign he could effect "with the stroke of a pen" but which, for political reasons, he had not taken during the first two years of his administration. Obviously he had chosen the missile-crisis news conference to "downplay" this long-awaited, controversial announcement; he and Salinger knew so much attention would be centered on the dramatic confrontation with Khrushchev that little if any questioning would be devoted to Kennedy's long delay on the housing order, or its effect—which later proved limited. Only one question was asked, in fact, about the mission to India, and only one about the just-completed national elections; the missile crisis dominated the half-hour, and mostly in the favorable terms in which Kennedy had cast it in his opening statement.

The news conference came to an end, as usual, with Merriman Smith of United Press International, then the senior White House correspondent, shouting "Thank you, Mr. President!" after Kennedy had answered a final question with the judgment: "I think this is a very climactic period."

Wire-service reporters and those with immediate newspaper or broadcast deadlines sprinted for the bank of telephones in a corridor outside the State Department Auditorium. The rest of us began drifting out, talking over what had been said, what "the lead" was; no one doubted it was the withdrawal of the IL-28s and the lifting of the quarantine.

I recall no discussion of some important questions that had *not* been asked that day or of the answers to them that might have been given. Just seven weeks before, on the night of September 30, 1962, seventeen days *after* his last news conference, Kennedy and Attorney General Robert F. Kennedy had used federal marshals and twenty thousand federal troops to force the registration of James Meredith, a black, at the previously segregated University of Mississippi. Before the troops arrived to disperse an unruly white mob and put an end to a rock-throwing, shotgun, and tear-gas battle between the mob and the marshals, more than a third of the 160 marshals were injured, 28 by gunfire. A French reporter, Paul Guihard, and a bystander were killed, in one of the biggest pitched battles ever waged between the American government and a group of its citizens.

The Kennedy brothers—it could be seen in hindsight—had over-estimated the reliability of the Mississippi state police, failed to arm, equip, and organize the marshals adequately, midjudged Governor Ross R. Barnett's willingness to compromise, and waited too long, allowing the situation in Mississippi to become inflamed before acting forcefully. No doubt a lot of Americans, however, and not just in the South, thought in 1962 that the administration was moving too far and too fast to force integration. On the other hand, Meredith's entry into the University of Mississippi, a temple of segregation, was one of the great symbolic triumphs of the civil-rights struggles of the sixties. Yet none of the questions that *might* have arisen, let alone those that *ought* to have been asked, had been put forward in the first news conference the President had had since the bloody night of September 30, fifty-one days earlier.

Of course, there had been ample time between that night and October 19, when Kennedy had been alerted to the missile crisis, for a news conference at which the events at Ole Miss surely would have been central. But the President had used the handy excuse that he was then campaigning hard for the election of Democrats to Congress; and it's altogether likely that even without the missile crisis intervening, the canny Salinger would have kept Kennedy out of the State Department Auditorium for a long time after the Ole Miss battle. However that may be, there can be but one place to fix the responsibility for an astonishing failure to question Kennedy about the Mississippi drama.

That place, of course, is on the press itself; not even the kind of careful preparation that was then the practice of the Washington bureau of the *Times* had prevented a signal failure. No minutes of our planning meeting were kept, and I don't remember if we actually listed a question about the Mississippi incident and failed to get it in. More likely, another element of journalism and modern life—what I call "dailiness"— intervened. In the seven weeks after the battle at Ole Miss, the onrush of events in a world of omnipresent communications had pushed the battle too far into the past for it to retain significant presence in the minds of journalists preoccupied with the world's narrow escape from nuclear war and whose attention had been focused on the missile crisis by the President's opening statement.

So no one asked Kennedy, for example:

"Mr. President, if you had it to do over, would you have handled Governor Barnett differently in the Ole Miss crisis?"

No doubt Kennedy was just as happy no one raised the subject. My own failure to do so gives ironic point to an exchange between Kennedy and my wife at a White House dinner. It was the first time we had been invited to such an affair and we were naturally excited. When we were walking from the East Room along the long corridor to the State Dining Room, my wife almost fainted when Kennedy himself came up beside her, grinning, and took her arm.

"What's it feel like when you see your husband on TV standing up to question the President?" he asked.

"I'm always terrified," Neva said.

Kennedy laughed out loud. "I am too," he said, but even then I knew better.

6

Camelot

One Sunday evening in 1963 the White House press plane—
chartered by the White House transportation office, paid for by
the news organizations of the reporters aboard—was returning
routinely to Washington from a presidential weekend at
Newport. Unexpectedly, the plane landed in New York—
following President Kennedy in *Air Force One*—and the
disgruntled press corps was bused into the city where, for hours,
we hung about in the lobby or in the close vicinity of the Carlyle
Hotel.

President Kennedy maintained a suite there and—as I
remember it—the reporters were tipped by White House aides
that he was using it that evening for an informal meeting with
Adlai E. Stevenson, the ambassador to the United Nations. But
no meeting with Stevenson had been scheduled or announced
before *Air Force One* and its trailing press plane had taken off
from Newport. No one saw the ambassador arrive at or depart
from the Carlyle. There was no later announcement concerning
any business transacted or decisions reached. There was no
known international or U.N. business likely to have caused
Kennedy to interrupt his flight to Washington for a sudden

meeting with an official of little influence whom he was reported not even particularly to like.

By midnight or sometime thereafter, when weary reporters piled back into the bus for the airport, most of us believed—or professed to believe—that Kennedy had been meeting a woman in his Carlyle suite. It was an article of faith in the White House press room that the young President was a "swinger"—a reputation dating back to his good-time days in the Senate and to some hazily reported escapades during his campaign. A report that he had had a secret first marriage annulled through his father's financial power had been so widespread that the White House had had to issue an official denial. Certain White House staff women were widely believed to have more than an official position with the President.

At the time, however, the supposition that Kennedy was involved with women other than his wife, in and out of the White House, rested on evidence about as strong as that presented by the Carlyle Hotel stopover. The implausibility of the supposed meeting with Stevenson was what set the rumors going on the press bus; in fact, however, there could have been reasons why Kennedy wanted to see Stevenson and why the latter entered and left the Carlyle privately; or there could have been any number of legitimate reasons for the President to visit his private suite for a few hours, then put out the Stevenson story as a cover. Just for one example, he might have been meeting secretly with a prospective appointee to high office, with neither man wishing the possible appointment to be known at that stage to the press.

The notion that Kennedy was meeting with a woman arose because of his reputation. But that reputation, in 1963, might as easily have been myth, and part of it undoubtedly was. It was bruited about in the White House press room, for instance, that Jacqueline Kennedy, while showing a French photographer through the presidential mansion, had pointed to a staff woman and remarked: "She's supposed to be having an affair with my husband."

That Mrs. Kennedy would have said such a thing is inherently implausible. As I heard it, the story suggested that if she did say it, she too might have been listening to rumors rather than fact. Nor did I ever hear anyone say he had heard the story directly from the French photographer. Long after the first time I heard this bit of "evidence" about Kennedy's swinging life, I heard it again, but with *another* woman who worked in the White House pointed out as the supposed inamorata.

That—plus such suggestive "facts" as that Kennedy went to parties at Frank Sinatra's house when the President took an occasional bachelor weekend in Palm Springs—was the kind of evidence we mostly had that Kennedy was a "swinger" with women. I never heard, on the other hand, even the name of Judith Campbell, before she became known in 1975—as an indirect consequence of the Church committee's investigation of the CIA—for apparently having had an affair with Kennedy, including visits to him in the White House. At the same time, by her own statements, Miss Campbell—by then Mrs. Exner—had been involved with two Mafia leaders through whom the CIA had scandalously sought to arrange the assassination of Fidel Castro.

Nor did I ever hear a whisper about an affair Kennedy was reported—in 1976—to have had during his presidency with Mary Pinchot Meyer, the former wife of a high CIA official, who was in 1965 the victim of a famous unsolved Washington murder. The question here is not so much whether the Campbell and Meyer stories, or any of the others about Kennedy's sex life in the White House, are true; but whether the White House press in the Kennedy era—as is now frequently charged—covered up or conveniently ignored Kennedy's sexual escapades.

My judgment—self-serving though it may appear—is that we did not. I can't conceive of a reporter in his right mind, for example, who would not have broken his neck to get into print a story that would have had a lead something like this:

"President Kennedy has been having intimate meetings in the White House, apparently with the connivance of the Secret Service, with a young woman known to be personally involved with two Chicago leaders of organized crime."

That's a story any reporter would have given anything to write, even if it were personally distressing for him to do so. It's absurd to suggest that, instead, the White House press corps generally refrained from pursuing such a sensation, either out of regard for Kennedy or owing to some kind of preference he showed the press in return. On the other hand, to anyone who has done time in the White House press room, and who knows the reach and zeal of the Secret Service, it's not too far-fetched that Judith Campbell could have come and gone numerous times in absolute secrecy. That Kennedy would have taken such personal and political chances is harder to believe, but not impossible.

I doubt seriously, and inquiries among colleagues and former colleagues support my view, that anyone in the press at the time knew of Miss Campbell's visits, if they took place as she says they did—at least that anyone knew enough about them to write a documented story. As for Mary Meyer, the report concerning her is far more nebulous and unsubstantiated than the Campbell story, even today; again, during Kennedy's lifetime no whisper of Mrs. Meyer's relationship with him, if any, ever reached me or any reporter I knew.

My assertion is supported also by the strenuous efforts numerous news organizations made during the Kennedy administration to prove and print the first-marriage story— "John's Other Wife." This tale derived from a private history of a certain Blauvelt family, a volume available in the Library of Congress. The genealogy flatly stated that one Durie Malcolm, a Blauvelt descendant, had married "John F. Kennedy, son of Joseph P. Kennedy, onetime ambassador to England." From this document had sprung a thicket of rumors, suggesting that Kennedy had married Durie Malcolm in Fort Lee, New Jersey, but that the marriage had been annulled and all records of it bought up and hidden by Jospeh P. Kennedy, acting to protect his son's political future.

If that sounds more like a Taylor Caldwell novel than real life, the melodramatic yarn was nevertheless lengthily investigated by numerous major news organizations well aware that if it could be proven that the first Roman Catholic president once had been married secretly to a twice divorced woman, the results might ruin him politically.

Wallace Carroll, the news editor of the *Times* Washington bureau in those years, assigned Ben Franklin, an experienced rummager among records and documents, to dig into the story. Franklin bored in with characteristic zeal but got about where all other reporters had gotten—nowhere near publishable proof. When this came to the attention of James Reston, the bureau chief, Reston erupted—not at Franklin's failure but that he had been working on the story at all.

"I won't have *The New York Times* muckraking the President of the States," he declared—a pre-Watergate attitude not then uncommon in Washington, or on the *Times,* but one which had not deterred most editors and bureau chiefs from hot pursuit of John's Other Wife. None of them ever published the story, but it kept popping up in right-wing hate sheets, supported only by the excerpt from the Blauvelt genealogy.

In his book, *Conversations with Kennedy,* Ben Bradlee—then *Newsweek* bureau chief and a close friend of the President's—tells how the hate-sheet publications finally led to the scotching of the story. Using the fact that the story was appearing in such journals for a pretext, *Newsweek* also printed a strong White House denial and the results of its own research casting heavy doubt on the yarn's accuracy. After that, the story more or less died, although to this day John's Other Wife occasionally bobs up—still unproven. The point here is that the press's interest in it during Kennedy's time does not bear out the notion of a concerted cover-up of his sex life. Rather, there was a considerable effort to find supporting evidence for a story that finally could not be proven.

Besides, the Washington press in the Kennedy era was by no means solidly pro-Kennedy, despite his skill at managing the news. As has been the case with all presidents, there were news organizations whose editorials opposed his administration; there were reporters who disliked or mistrusted him personally or politically; there probably were some who felt aggrieved at having little part in the glamorous life the Kennedys were supposed to lead. Many then in the upper echelons of Washington journalism—men like Richard N. Wilson of the Cowles bureau and Walter Trohan of the *Chicago Tribune*—were inherently, if to varying degrees, conservative.

In 1961-63, therefore, it was not really possible that "the press" could cover up for Kennedy on some large scale, nor was it likely that all Washington reporters would manage to look the other way—particularly as to stories of the magnitude of the Judith Campbell affair. The press is not that monolithic, and the truth is that no reporter or news organization knew enough, at the time, to have exposed Kennedy's White House sex life, whatever it may have been like.

But that only raises the question: *should* we have known? Should the press of the time have probed far more deeply than it did into the atmosphere and the inner activity of the Kennedy White House? And if it had discovered proof of damaging sexual episodes *would* it have printed them?

Those questions, of course, only suggest the real problem: how much is the press and the nation entitled to know about a president's private life? Put the other way around, how much *ought* a democratic society to know about the persons who seek and hold its highest office?

With all due regard to my colleague Reston, for example, I disagree with the stand he took in the Blauvelt matter. The press had a duty, I believe, to seek the truth of a story that would have told so much about Kennedy's background and character. Besides, since printing it—if proven—clearly would have had damaging impact on Kennedy's political prospects, a decision *not* to print it—if proven—would amount to protecting Kennedy from that impact. Similarily, there seems to me no question but that the Judith Campbell story should have been published, had it been known and proven; no president should be accorded the personal privacy to have links that close to the Mafia, even if he did not know of those links.

But suppose the apocryphal story—as I believe it to be—of Jacqueline Kennedy's remark to the French photographer were true, and suppose I, at the time, as White House correspondent for *The New York Times,* had conclusive evidence that Kennedy—or Johnson or Nixon or any president—was having an affair with a woman on the White House staff? If she had no criminal or other disreputable connection, there was no security breach, and the matter appeared entirely private, what should I have done?

On one hand, it could be argued that this would be a president's personal affair, with no effect on the national interest, and therefore would be none of the public's business; while to publish the story might seriously embarrass the President politically and perhaps diplomatically, even to the point of ruining his political standing and impairing his ability to lead the country.

On the other hand, it could be as strongly argued that everything a president does speaks to his character and integrity, and therefore *is* the public's business; that a president's extramarital affair would be offensive to millions of Americans, who would have a right to know that their leader was involved in such a relationship; and that a reporter would have no right to decide for himself *not* to publish such a story if he knew it to be true—that he would have as much of an obligation to print what he knew about the President's private life as, say, *The New York Times* had to publish, in the Pentagon Papers, what it knew of the secret conduct of the war in Vietnam. Besides, a reputable newspaper has no more right *not* to publish adverse information about a president than it would have to write puff or propaganda stories on his behalf.

To these ethical and professional questions, any sensible reporter would have to add consideration—that if he or she had found out about the President's affair, some other reporter could find it out, too, or it could come to public notice in a number of other ways. Aside from such a reporter having sacrificed a competitive advantage, political opponents of the President would be entitled to charge that a reporter who had known the story and decided not to publish it must have been covering up for the President, for political or less reputable reasons. Personal credibility, as well as that of a reporter's newspaper—and neither has a more vital asset—could well be damaged or destroyed.

My personal instinct would be to accord a president, in such a matter, as much privacy as any other person should have. But my better judgment persuades me that, on balance, distasteful as such a story might be, and recognizing the possibility of exceptions, a presidential love affair would not justify deviation from my Second Law of Journalism, perhaps the most important rule of all—that a reporter should write and his newspaper should print what they know.

Nevertheless, I believe the press of the Kennedy era, if it did not cover up for him, or knowingly look the other way, did not put him or the White House in his time under as close and searching scrutiny as it should have. This, of course, is hindsight, and certainly concedes some personal culpability.

Defenders of Richard Nixon and other critics of the press are essentially right, I believe, in asserting that the press was much more rigorous in its probing of the Nixon White House than it had been in the Kennedy or the first Johnson years. (They are *not* right, I think, if they suggest that, therefore, the press had no right to investigate Nixon and was only showing its partisanship when it did so.)

For two basic reasons, the press did give Kennedy more of a free ride than any of his successors have had. One was—I think unquestionably—the man's wit, charm, youth, good looks, and general style, as well as a feeling among reporters that he probably liked us more than he liked politicians, and that he may even have been more nearly one of *us* than one of *them* (an impression that tends to be confirmed by Bradlee's *Conversations with Kennedy*). And the impression was the stronger because it was made hard on the heels of the staid and elderly Eisenhower administration; even among some reporters who differed with Kennedy politically or doubted him personally, there often was a sense that *their* generation and *their* style had come to power at last.

Hence there was at the least an unconscious element of good wishes for Kennedy—the hope that he would vindicate either a style or a political view or a generation of all three—that was at war with reporters' normal mistrust of politicians and muckraking instincts. But more important in my judgment was the fact that in the Kennedy administration, the Imperial Presidency reached a sort of apogee—not to be attained later in the grandiosities of Johnson or the abuses of Nixon.

For most of their incumbencies, Johnson and Nixon were under heavy critical fire; moreover, much of what they did in Vietnam and Nixon did in Watergate that we judge harshly today were *corruptions* of the imperial style that had developed in the White House since the second Roosevelt. It was a style Johnson and Nixon inherited but one that had reached its highest level in the Kennedy administration—and to which Kennedy himself had made a unique contribution.

He was the first president to meet the press on live television, and the televised news conference proved to be a perfect forum for his looks, his wits, his quick brain, his self-confidence. Kennedy gave millions of Americans their first look at a president in action, and it was a memorable view of him meeting challenges and answering questions. He may have been better at this art form than at anything else in his presidency—the model of the brilliant young executive up to any demands of circumstance or policy. Together with Eisenhower's father image, Roosevelt's political magic, and the supposed transformation of Harry Truman from middling senator to great president, JFK's news-conference performances surely were among the important factors in the public's elevation of the presidency into awe and myth.

Johnson, struggling to avoid the appearance of defeat in Southeast Asia, Nixon with his plumbers and tappers, trying to shore up the supposed infallibility of "the President," seeking desperately to lose his own tormented persona in the splendor of the office, should be seen as desperately trying to hold the

Imperial Presidency together past its time. Both talked often of their determination to leave the office no weaker than they found it, although both did.

But in Kennedy's time, the ghastly casualties and divisions of Vietnam were far in the future. *His* little war in Southeast Asia was hardly noticed in the grandeur of the world-wide struggle against communism he had proclaimed and welcomed.

Nixon's desperate power grabs were highly visible—the impoundment of appropriated funds, the attempted elevation of a dubious doctrine called executive privilege into holy writ. Few such divisive issues of legitimacy and power troubled Kennedy's presidency, although he was constantly at political odds with a conservative Congress. He looked rather like a hero during the missile crisis and manfully accepted public responsibility for the Bay of Pigs, not long before he fired its CIA masterminds. The several offenses of *his* administration—the wiretapping of Martin Luther King, Jr., CIA outrages in Cuba, Africa, and elsewhere—only came to light long after his death. So did Judith Campbell Exner.

Kennedy reigned at the height of the Cold War, in the echoes of Khrushchev's pounding shoe and brutal threat: "We will bury you." With memories of World War II's glories relatively fresh, the martial spirit of Kennedy's inaugural address found immense favor as an eloquent expression of America's determination to play the major role in world affairs required of it by destiny; and *Ich bin ein Berliner* seemed at the time the true watchword of his administration, and of Americans.

At the end, after the missile crisis and the nuclear test-ban treaty with the Soviets, Kennedy appeared to be moving cautiously toward détente with Moscow, possibly even disengagement in Vietnam. But for most of his presidential lifetime, he was the true knight of the Cold War. Had he not picked up the torch, this young liberal who was prepared to press relentlessly what he liked to call "the cause of freedom" in the world, no matter where the pressure might lead? And was it not he who gave the nation its emotional charge to "support any friend, oppose any foe" in the name of liberty?

In that sense, John Fitzgerald Kennedy was the last president the American people looked up to, in the old, unquestioning way. He was our young emperor, before the throne became bloodied and the cause tarnished by its own excesses. After his years, the Imperial Presidency may have gathered power—

mostly by illicit means—but it could no longer inspire the people or symbolize their spirit. Kennedy was the last leader in a time when Americans were eager to follow. And his may have been that moment of all the postwar years when reporters, long schooled in the near-religious attitudes of the Cold War and the supposedly transforming powers of the presidency, were least likely to "muckrake the President."

So John Kennedy is perhaps the most fascinating might-have-been in American history, not just for what he was in his time but for what Americans made of him—not because of what we were but because of what we thought we were, and know now we'll never be. Merely that he was cut down as he was, on a sunlit day, in the bloody mess of his mortality, might have been enough to establish him forever as the symbol of all our uncompleted selves, spoiled dreams, blasted hopes. Even Americans mindful of the limitations of John Kennedy's thousand days, and of the later revelations of his follies and fallibilities, look back upon him as to their own lost dreams.

But if disillusionment is enlightenment, after his death—in Vietnam, Cambodia, the streets of Chicago, Watergate—the rest of us, as no doubt he had, began to learn the lessons of power and its limitations. The shots ringing out in Dealey Plaza marked the beginning of the end of innocence.

I think I was in the first press bus. But I can't be sure. Pete Lisagor of the *Chicago Daily News* says he *knows* he was in the first press bus and he describes things that went on aboard it that didn't happen on the bus I was in. But I still *think* I was in the first press bus.

I cite that minor confusion as an example of the way it was in Dallas in the early afternoon of November 22. At first no one knew what happened, or how, or where, much less why. Gradually, bits and pieces began to fall together and within two hours a reasonably coherent version of the story began to be possible. Even now, however, I know no reporter who was there who has a clear and orderly picture of that surrealistic afternoon; it is still a matter of bits and pieces thrown hastily into something like a whole.

It began, for most reporters, when the central fact of it was over. As our press bus eased at motorcade speed down an incline toward an underpass, there was a little confusion in the sparse crowds that at that point had been standing at the curb to see the President of the United States pass. As we came out of the underpass, I saw a motorcycle policeman drive over the curb, across an open area, a few feet up a railroad bank, dismount, and start scrambling up the bank.

Jim Mathis of The Advance (Newhouse) Syndicate went to the front of our bus and looked ahead to where the President's car was supposed to be, perhaps ten cars ahead of us. He hurried back to his seat.

"The President's car just sped off," he said. "Really gunned away." (How could Mathis have seen that if there had been another bus in front of us?)

But that could have happened if someone had thrown a tomato at the President. The press bus in its stately pace rolled on to the Trade Mart, where the President was to speak. Fortunately, it was only a few minutes away.

At the Trade Mart, rumor was sweeping the hundreds of Texans already eating their lunch. It was the only rumor that I had ever *seen*; it was moving across that crowd like a wind over a wheatfield. A man eating a grapefruit seized my arm as I passed.

"Has the President been shot?" he asked.

"I don't think so," I said. "But something happened."

With the other reporters—I suppose thirty-five of them—I went on through the huge hall to the upstairs press room. We were hardly there when Marianne Means of Hearst Headline Service hung up a telephone, ran to a group of us and said, "The President's been shot. He's at Parkland Hospital."

One thing I learned that day; I suppose I already knew it, but that day made it plain. A reporter must trust his instinct. When Miss Means said those eight words—I never learned who told her*—I knew absolutely they were true. Everyone did. We ran for the press buses.

Again, a man seized my arm—an official-looking man.

"No running in here," he said sternly. I pulled free and

---

* After this was published, Marianne Means told me she had called her office in New York and had heard the news from there. The New York office had heard a radio bulletin. By that roundabout route, the motorcade press learned what had happened.

ran on. Doug Kiker of the *Herald Tribune* barreled head-
on into a waiter carrying a plate of potatoes. Waiter and
potatoes flew about the room. Kiker ran on. He was in his
first week with the *Trib*, and his first presidential trip.

I barely got aboard a moving press bus. Bob
Pierrepoint of CBS was aboard and he said that he now
recalled having heard something that could have been
shots—or firecrackers, or motorcycle backfire. We talked
anxiously, unbelieving, afraid.

Fortunately again, it was only a few minutes to
Parkland Hospital. There at its emergency entrance,
stood the President's car, the top up, a bucket of bloody
water beside it. Automatically, I took down its license
number—GG300 District of Columbia.

The first eyewitness description came from Senator
Ralph Yarborough, who had been riding in the third car
of the motorcade with Vice-President and Mrs. Johnson.
Senator Yarborough is an East Texan, which is to say a
Southerner, a man of quick emotion, old-fashioned
rhetoric.

"Gentlemen," he said, pale, shaken, near tears. "It's a
deed of horror."

The details he gave us were good and mostly—as it
later proved—accurate. But he would not describe to us
the appearance of the President as he was wheeled into the
hospital, except to say that he was "gravely wounded."
We could not doubt, then, that it was serious.

I had chosen that day to be without a notebook. I took
notes on the back of my mimeographed schedule of the
two-day tour of Texas we had been so near to concluding.
Today, I cannot read many of the notes; on November 22,
they were as clear as 60-point type.

A local television reporter, Mel Crouch, told us he had
seen a rifle being withdrawn from the corner fifth- or
sixth-floor window of the Texas School Book Deposito-
ry. Instinct again—Crouch sounded right, positive,
though none of us knew him. We believed it and it was
right.

Mac Kilduff, an assistant White House press secretary
in charge of the press on that trip, and who was to acquit
himself well that day, came out of the hospital. We
gathered round and he told us the President was alive. It

wasn't true, we later learned; but Mac thought it was true at that time, and he didn't mislead us about a possible recovery. His whole demeanor made plain what was likely to happen. He also told us—as Senator Yarborough had—that Governor John Connally of Texas was shot, too.

Kilduff promised more details in five minutes and went back into the hospital. We were barred. Word came to us secondhand—I don't remember exactly how—from Bob Clark of ABC, one of the men who had been riding in the press "pool" car near the President's, that he had been lying face-down in Mrs. Kennedy's lap when the car arrived at Parkland. No signs of life.

That is what I mean by instinct. That day, a reporter had none of the ordinary means or time to check and double-check matters given as fact. He had to go on what he knew of people he talked to, what he knew of human reaction, what two isolated "facts" added to in sum— above all on what he felt in his bones. I knew Clark and respected him. I took his report at face value, even at second hand. It turned out to be true. In a crisis, if a reporter can't trust his instinct for truth, he can't trust anything.

When Wayne Hawks of the White House staff appeared to say that a press room had been set up in a hospital classroom at the left rear of the building, the group of reporters began struggling across the lawn in that direction. I lingered to ask a motorcycle policeman if he had heard on his radio anything about the pursuit or capture of the assassin. He hadn't, and I followed the other reporters.

As I was passing the open convertible in which Vice-President and Mrs. Johnson and Senator Yarborough had been riding in the motorcade, a voice boomed from its radio:

"The President of the United States is dead. I repeat— it has just been announced that the President of the United States is dead."

There was no authority, no word of who had announced it. But—instinct again—I believed it instantly. I sounded true. I knew it was true. I stood still a moment, then began running.

Ordinarily, I couldn't jump a tennis net if I'd just beaten Gonzales. That day, carrying a briefcase and a typewriter, I jumped a chain fence looping around the drive, not even breaking stride. Hugh Sidey of *Time*, a close friend of the President, was walking slowly ahead of me.

"Hugh," I said, "the President's dead. Just announced on the radio. I don't know who announced it but it sounded official to me."

Sidey stopped, looked at me, looked at the ground. I couldn't talk about it. I couldn't think about it. I couldn't do anything but run on to the press room. Then I told others what I had heard.

Sidey, I learned a few minutes later, stood where he was a minute. Then he saw two Catholic priests. He spoke to them. Yes, they told him, the President was dead. They had administered the last rites. Sidey went on to the press room and spread that word, too.

Throughout the day, every reporter on the scene seemed to me to do his best to help everyone else. Information came only in bits and pieces. Each man who picked up a bit or a piece passed it on. I know no one who held anything out. Nobody thought about an exclusive; it didn't seem important.

After perhaps ten minutes when we milled around in the press room—my instinct was to find the new President, but no one knew where he was—Kilduff appeared red-eyed, barely in control of himself. In that hushed classroom, he made the official, the unbelievable announcement. The President was dead of a gunshot wound in the brain. Lyndon Johnson was safe, in protective custody of the Secret Service. He would be sworn in as soon as possible.

Kilduff, composed as a man could be in those circumstances, promised more details when he could get them, then left. The search for phones began. Jack Gertz, traveling with us for AT & T, was frantically moving them by the dozen into the hospital, but few were ready yet.

I wandered down the hall, found a doctor's office, walked in and told him I had to use his phone. He got up without a word and left. I battled the hospital switchboard for five minutes and finally got a line to New York—Hal Faber on the other end, with Harrison Salisbury on an extension.

They knew what had happened, I said. The death had been confirmed. I proposed to write one long story, as quickly as I could, throwing in everything I could learn. On the desk, they could cut it up as they needed—throwing part into other stories, putting other facts into mine. But I would file a straight narrative without worrying about their editing needs.

Reporters always fuss at editors and always will. But Salisbury and Faber are good men to talk to in a crisis. They knew what they were doing and realized my problems. I may fuss at them again sometime, but after that day my heart won't be in it. Quickly, clearly, they told me to go ahead, gave me the moved-up deadlines, told me of plans already made to get other reporters into Dallas, but made it plain they would be hours in arriving.

Salisbury told me to use the phone and take no chances on a wire circuit being jammed or going wrong. Stop reporting and start writing in time to meet the deadline, he said. Pay anyone $50 if necessary to dictate for you.

The whole conversation probably took three minutes. Then I hung up, thinking of all there was to know, all there was I didn't know. I wandered down a corridor and ran into Sidey and Chuck Roberts of *Newsweek*. They'd seen a hearse pulling up at the emergency entrance and we figured they were about to move the body.

We made our way to the hearse—a Secret Service agent who knew us helped us through suspicious Dallas police lines—and the driver said his instructions were to take the body to the airport. That confirmed our hunch, but gave me, at least, another wrong one. Mr. Johnson, I declared, would fly to Washington with the body and be sworn in there.

We posted ourselves inconspicuously near the emergency entrance. Within minutes, they brought the body out in a bronze coffin.

A number of White House staff people—stunned, silent, stumbling along as if dazed—walked with it. Mrs. Kennedy walked by the coffin, her hand on it, her head down, her hat gone, her dress and stockings spattered. She got into the hearse with the coffin. The staff men crowded into cars and followed.

That was just about the only eyewitness matter that I got with my own eyes that entire afternoon.

Roberts commandeered a seat in a police car and followed, promising to "fill" Sidey and me as necessary. We made the same promise to him and went back to the press room.

There, we received an account from Julian Reed, a staff assistant, of Mrs. John Connally's recollection of the shooting. Most of his recital was helpful and it established the important fact of who was sitting in which seat in the President's car at the time of the shooting.

The doctors who had treated the President came in after Mr. Reed. They gave us copious detail, particularly as to the efforts they had made to resuscitate the President. They were less explicit about the wounds, explaining that the body had been in their hands only a short time and they had little time to examine it closely. They conceded they were unsure as to the time of death and had arbitrarily put it at 1:00 P.M., CST.

Much of their information, as it developed later, was erroneous. Subsequent reports made it pretty clear that Mr. Kennedy probably was killed instantly. His body, as a physical mechanism, however, continued to flicker an occasional pulse and heartbeat. No doubt this justified the doctors' first account. There also was the question of national security and Mr. Johnson's swearing-in. Perhaps, too, there was a question about the Roman Catholic rites. In any case, until a later doctors' statement about 9:00 P.M. that night, the account we got at the hospital was official.

The doctors hardly had left before Hawks came in and told us Mr. Johnson would be sworn in immediately at the airport. We dashed for the press buses, still parked outside. Many a campaign had taught me something about press buses and I ran a little harder, got there first, and went to the wide rear seat. That is the best place on a bus to open up a typewriter and get some work done.

On the short trip to the airport, I got about five hundred words on paper—leaving a blank space for the hour of Mr. Johnson's swearing-in, and putting down the mistaken assumption that the scene would be somewhere in the terminal. As we arrived at a back gate along the airstrip, we could see *Air Force One*, the presidential jet, screaming down the runway and into the air.

Left behind had been Sid Davis of Westinghouse Broadcasting, one of the few reporters who had been present for the swearing-in. Roberts, who had guessed right in going to the airport when he did, had been there too and was aboard the plane on the way to Washington.

Davis climbed on the back of a shiny new car that was parked near where our bus halted. I hate to think what happened to its trunk deck. He and Roberts—true to his promise—had put together a magnificent "pool" report on the swearing-in. Davis read it off, answered questions, and gave a picture that so far as I know was complete, accurate and has not yet been added to.

I said to Kiker of the *Trib*: "We better go write. There'll be phones in the terminal." He agreed. Bob Manning, an ice-cool member of the White House transportation staff, agreed to get our bags off the press plane, which would return to Washington as soon as possible, and put them in a nearby telephone booth.

Kiker and I ran a half-mile to the terminal, cutting through a baggage-handling room to get there. I went immediately to a phone booth and dictated my five-hundred-word lead, correcting it as I read, embellishing it too. Before I hung up, I got Salisbury and asked him to cut into my story whatever the wires were filing on the assassin. There was no time left to chase down the Dallas police and find out those details on my own.

Dallas's Love Field has a mezzanine running around its main waiting room; it is equipped with writing desks for travelers. I took one and went to work. My recollection is that it was then about 5:00 P.M. New York time.

I would write two pages, run down the stairs, across the waiting room, grab a phone and dictate. Miraculously, I never had to wait for a phone booth or to get a line through. Dictating each take, I would throw in items I hadn't written, sometimes whole paragraphs. It must have been tough on the dictating room crew.

Once, while in the booth dictating, I looked up and found twitching above me the imposing mustache of

Gladwin Hill. He was the first *Times* man in and had found me right off; I was seldom more glad to see anyone. We conferred quickly and he took off for the police station; it was a tremendous load off my mind to have that angle covered and out of my hands.

I was half through, maybe more, when I heard myself paged. It turned out to be Kiker, who had been separated from me and was working in the El Dorado Room, a bottle club in the terminal. My mezzanine was quieter and a better place to work, but he had a TV going for him, so I moved in too.

The TV helped in one important respect. I took down from it an eyewitness account of one Charles Drehm, who had been waving at the President when he was shot. Instinct again: Drehm sounded positive, right, sure of what he said. And his report was the first real indication that the President probably was shot twice.

Shortly after 7:00 P.M., New York time, I finished. So did Kiker. Simultaneously we thought of our bags out in that remote phone booth. We ran for a taxi and urged an unwilling driver out along the dark airstrip. As we found the place, with some difficulty, an American Airlines man was walking off with the bags. He was going to ship them off to the White House, having seen the tags on them. A minute later and we'd have been stuck in Dallas without even a toothbrush.

Kiker and I went to the *Dallas News*. The work wasn't done—I filed a number of inserts later that night, wrote a separate story on the building from which the assassin had fired, tried to get John Herbers, Don Janson, Joe Loftus on useful angles as they drifted in. But when I left the airport, I knew the worst of it was over. The story was filed on time, good or bad, complete or incomplete, and any reporter knows how that feels. They couldn't say I missed the deadline.

It was a long taxi ride to the *Dallas News*. We were hungry, not having eaten since an early breakfast. It was then that I remembered John F. Kennedy's obituary. Last June, Hal Faber had sent it to me for updating. On November 22, it was still lying on my desk in Washington, not updated, not rewritten, a monument to the incredibility of that afternoon in Dallas.

7

Deep Stroke

By February 25, 1964, it was clear to the White House press corps that Lyndon Johnson, who had been in office only about three months, already was beginning to backslide on his promise to meet frequently with the press. In January he had used informal news conferences adeptly to dramatize his presentation of a budget he had kept just below the "magic number"—$100 billion. But for about a month he had not personally been "available" to the press.

Depending on the administration, the press secretary usually conducts two White House news briefings a day, at which whatever public business has been transacted in the executive branch can be duly announced. Most briefings are dull affairs, productive of little real news; but sometimes when the press secretary is trying to surmount a touchy issue, the briefing resembles a bear-baiting. That February 25 Salinger—still on Johnson's staff—was busy elsewhere and the briefing was conducted by Andrew Hatcher, another holdover from the Kennedy press office. Unobtrusively standing at the edge of the crowd of reporters jammed into Salinger's office—where the briefings were then held—was Bill Moyers, the bespectacled young assistant to LBJ and at age thirty suddenly one of the most important men in government. I decided on the spur of the moment to make a fuss about a news conference.

As soon as I could, I asked Hatcher whether, in view of the weeks that had passed since Johnson had met the press, the President had changed his announced policy of holding frequent news conferences. I phrased it that way for a reason; in government, it must be understood, the idea of conceding a "change of policy" strikes terror to the heart of officialdom and bureaucracy. The idea of change implies that something was wrong with the old policy, and government never wishes to admit *anything* is wrong with government, or needs to be changed. So Hatcher denied vehemently that there had been a policy change: of course, the President would meet with the press as soon as he could.

This barren exchange went on for a while, going nowhere, until I was sure that I had made my point—not so much to Hatcher as to Bill Moyers. Some of my colleagues also joined in and I was satisfied the word would reach Johnson, although it was not then suspected, as later was the case, that the ubiquitous LBJ listened to the news briefings through the intercom system on the press secretary's desk.

The briefing finally broke up indecisively, and the reporters not on deadline wandered out to the "press lobby" in the West Wing—then dominated by numerous brown leather sofas on which our more relaxed colleagues snoozed away much of the day, and by a hideous round table in the center which had for a pedestal an arrangement of water buffalo legs and hoofs. The table was said to be a gift from the Philippines to the White House; if so, it should have been rejected as an international insult.

I was chatting with a few reporters when one of the women from the press office approached. Mr. Moyers, she said, would like to see me in his office. Amid much hooting and jeering from colleagues—the connection with my protest to Hatcher was obvious—I was led past guarded doors and gimlet-eyed Secret Servicemen and down quiet corridors to Moyers' office near the President's.

I'd known Moyers since he'd been Johnson's youthful (26) campaign manager in 1960, and he was cordial. He could tell, he said, that my exchange with Andy Hatcher had not been satisfactory. He wanted me to know that the President really had not changed his news-conference policy; he'd actually been too busy with the budget, legislation, a new congressional session, controversies with Castro and about the Panama Canal. And, of course, there was Vietnam, where the second new government since the fall of the Ngo Dinh Diem regime had just taken over, but was only beginning to take hold.

I understood all that, I told Meyers. I had just tried to remind the press office and the President that it was a long time since the press had met with him.

Both he and Johnson realized it, Moyers said. And Johnson particularly wanted me to know that he'd see me anytime I asked.

As it happened, I felt I knew LBJ from his majority leader days and from the 1960 campaign, and in his brief administration he'd already seen me—the *Times* White House correspondent—privately on two occasions. I told Moyers I had no complaint about that, but since he'd raised the subject, I told him also that I'd asked Salinger two weeks before to arrange another appointment for me with the President. Nothing had happened since.

Moyers pondered this, took a phone call, looked grave, hung up, and told me he had to go inform the President that Herbert Hoover had been taken sick; he'd be right back. I don't know whether Hoover was really all that sick, but when Moyers came back he said LBJ would see me right away—which I believed probably had been the point of Moyers' original summons. Johnson, in his usual proprietary manner, was trying to answer my complaint not by holding a news conference as requested but by "buying off" with a personal interview the reporter who had made the complaint.

That day, Johnson kept me in his office for an hour—while Clark Clifford, I later learned, waited more than half of that time for a previously scheduled appointment. I may have asked one question during the hour, which would have been about par for a Johnson interview in his ebullient early days in the White House; from that question, he took off on one of his lengthy, fascinating, informative, boastful monologues—from which, I already knew, it was vital to be able to separate the few nuggets of real information from the fog of bombast.

Ranging over Vietnam, Panama, Cuba, Cyprus, Zanzibar, the foreign leaders he'd met, Latin America, differences with de Gaulle, his White House staff and organization (I still have the notes I made on my return to the *Times* bureau) Johnson nevertheless managed to tell me several times that it was *his* business alone how and when he held news conferences. Up to then, he'd kept them informal, in his office, without live television; he might or might not change later. Meanwhile, the press had better beware of references to what the President "was thinking" or "had decided"; no one knew such things about the President but the President himself.

That early in his administration, Johnson already was displaying—as I realized later—attitudes that would mark his relations with the press, and with the public. For one thing, he pointed to a story in the *Times* of that day which said on the authority of unnamed sources that he was studying a new plan for solving American differences with Panama over the canal. But, Johnson complained, he didn't even have the plan in front of him to study, so obviously the leaked story had come from some "kid"—he used the term contemptuously—at a low level who wanted to be taken as important and who was therefore acting as if he knew something. But he didn't.

Now very likely that study was on Johnson's desk or in channels on its way to him; I knew the *Times* had been told about it by a responsible official; and Johnson's denial that he was "studying" a new plan probably rested on the thinnest technicality. But throughout his presidency, Johnson exhibited an extraordinary animosity to anyone who held himself out to the press as knowing what "the President thinks" or "the President believes" or "the President has decided." He was even known to cancel nominations to public office or change his mind on major questions of policy because leaks appeared saying that he was about to name someone or "had decided" something.

In 1966, for example, numerous reporters, including me, were told by Democratic officials in California that Johnson would make a late congressional-campaign appearance there. Some White House correspondents were told the same thing by Bill Moyers. I actually saw bleachers being erected in a West Coast shopping center in preparation for the appearance; but when stories appeared that Johnson "had decided" to campaign in California, he canceled the trip and angrily denied he ever had "decided" to make it. I suppose one doesn't finally *decide* to make a trip until one irrevocably makes it; but this was again a technicality and a transparent one. Johnson's propensity for such deceptive denials—the word "deniability" first began to be heard in his administration—was not the least of his problems with the press on Vietnam and other matters far more serious than the aborted California trip.

Even Moyers—who in 1965 became LBJ's press secretary—tripped over this Johnsonian idiosyncrasy. Thoroughly familiar with Johnson's plans, programs, attitudes, and thought processes, he began going further than LBJ wanted anyone to do in telling reporters what was in the President's mind, how he looked at certain issues, how he regarded certain men, what he was likely to do in certain circumstances. This was a major reason why Moyers, one of Johnson's ablest assistants, finally left the White House, not altogether voluntarily.

That February 25 Johnson also flourished before me a sheaf of polls from virtually every available source—most public, some private. All were favorable, but LBJ was particularly pleased with a Mervin Field poll from California that showed him defeating any Republican in 1964, and leading all Republicans, except Henry Cabot Lodge and Richard Nixon, even among Republicans only. He flashed at me an editorial from the London *Daily Telegraph* that compared his State of the Union message to one of FDR's. Then he flicked across his desk an approving cartoon. All the time, he was insisting that he paid no attention to the press, didn't intend to, would do just what was right, do his job, no matter what was written about him. The contradiction was plain, and worrisome.

I was shown out of the President's office, all but engulfed in Johnsonian warmth—the arm about my shoulder, the assurances that I could call him or see him anytime of day or night. Clifford, on the way in, eyed me balefully. Moyers was eager to hear about the conversation.

Perhaps because as a Southerner myself I was sympathetic to Johnson and privately hoped for his continuing success, I took it on myself to tell Moyers that the President should relax, stop pushing an "image," stop promoting himself, actually do what he claimed to be doing—the best he could, without worrying too much about what the press said about him. If he performed well, his image would take shape favorably without Johnson having to worry about it every minute; and the more he *did* worry about it and try to shape it—particularly the more he relied on opinion polls as if they were Holy Writ—the more trouble he was likely to get himself into.

Nodding agreement, Moyers asked me if I'd told Johnson as

much. I said something craven about not having been able to get
a word in, but the truth was that it hadn't occurred to me to talk
to the President as I was talking to his aide and at that I was only
telling Moyers the quick conclusions I'd drawn from Johnson's
rather compulsive behavior with the polls and the clippings.
Johnson was not an easy president, in any case, for a reporter to
address that candidly and toughly.

The President had begun to question, Moyers then
confessed, his early determination to be open with the press.
Some of the people he'd counted on most had even caused him
trouble. Johnson was beginning to wonder, in fact, if it was
possible for a president to have "personal relations" with anyone
in the press. This, I quickly saw, was the true reason he had not
recently held a news conference.

I walked back to the *Times* bureau, then at 17th and K
streets, N.W., pondering Johnson's question. I thought decent
"personal relations" between a president and the press were
possible if that phrase meant a genuine give-and-take between
mutually respectful parties.

But if, as I suspected, Lyndon Johnson really only wanted the
kind of "personal relations" that would bring him what he
called a "friendly press," and if he was going to seek such a press
by heavy manipulation—flattery, threats, favoritism, favor-
swapping, boasting, and the like—I believed he would get the
opposite of what he sought. And he did.

Later, Johnson explained in detail to Doris Kearns the
attitude that I sensed in him that day:

> Reporters are puppets [Johnson told her]. They simply
> respond to the pull of the most powerful strings. . . . Every
> story is always slanted to win the favor of someone who
> sits somewhere higher up. There is no such thing as an
> objective news story. There is always a private story
> behind the public story. And if you don't control the
> strings to that private story, you'll never get good
> coverage no matter how many great things you do for the
> masses of the people. There's only one sure way of getting
> favorable stories from reporters and that is to keep their
> daily bread—the information, the stories, the plans, and
> the details they need for their work—in your own hands,
> so that you can give it out when and to whom you want.*

*Doris Kearns, *Lyndon Johnson and the American Dream* (New York: Harper &
Row, 1976).

• • •

Few intelligent men have ever been so tragically wrong about a subject that obsessed them. Johnson's conviction that if he just pulled the right strings he would get "favorable coverage" from puppet reporters was not the least reason for his ultimate downfall.

All presidents, of course, complain about how badly they're treated in the press—and it certainly must be difficult for these nearly imperial figures, surrounded by sycophants and catered to in every way, to find themselves nevertheless so nearly under constant, total, not always friendly scrutiny from people who do not usually know as much as they ought to, let alone as much as they think they know. But however presidents may pity themselves, except in extraordinary circumstances, like those of Vietnam and Watergate, they have overpowering ability to manage the news and shape it to their interests.

Aside from such devices as the backgrounder, the presidency's vast array of powers, its control of foreign affairs, its initiative in domestic legislation, its influence in the national economy and on the atmosphere of American life—all these mean that the presidency is constantly *making* the news, causing it to happen. No one else approaches a president's ability to make things happen.

In October 1976, for example, Gerald Ford believed he had come off poorly in his second debate with Jimmy Carter on what the Ford administration had done—actually, had *not* done—to counter the Arab boycott of American companies dealing with Israel. So Ford ordered a quick shipment of sophisticated new weapons to Israel, without customary staff work or clearance. The press had literally no choice but to give headlines to this act taken in Ford's role as commander-in-chief, but in fact designed for domestic political recovery.

Some newspapers and columnists did question editorially whether the arms shipment was justified, at least in the fall of 1976, but immediate headlines always have more impact than later editorials. That is the major advantage any president has in trying to present himself favorably through the press; and before the ink was dry on the headlines about Ford's arms shipment to Israel, he was capitalizing on the publicity by campaigning heavily through Jewish neighborhoods in New York.

Despite such advantages, sometimes the news just won't stay

managed by those who supposedly only make it. Obstreperous reporters raise difficult questions. Experienced eyes spot the holes in presidential programs, or the discrepancies in presidential statements. Out of the bureaucratic woodwork comes an unwanted leak that some hot-eyed reporter speeds into the headlines. A dogged investigator keeps piling detail upon detail until he has combined them into some story the press secretary never would have announced. Even with these irreverent happenings—and they occur, with embarrassing frequency—the White House has its means of coping.

The press secretary might speak to the offender with disapproval, only just barely implying that some further punishment or withholding of favor could be forthcoming. Or an uncooperative reporter might experience severe difficulty for a while in getting White House officials to accept phone calls. His or her turn to fly as a "pool" reporter on the President's plane might be mysteriously passed over; Ron Ziegler was particularly zealous in this form of punishment during the Nixon administration. Directing the next good "leak" to the culprit's most important competitor is a sure way to deliver the message of official displeasure. On one occasion LBJ discovered that Douglas Kiker of the *Herald Tribune,* who had displeased Johnson frequently, had taken time off rather than make a presidential trip to Texas. The President at once ordered his press aides to find an important leak for Kiker's replacement— that would touch up Kiker a little bit, teach him to show some respect.

Theodore C. Sorensen, the White House counsel under Kennedy, complained to me once about some *Times* editorials critical of the administration, and added: "Our relations with you can get very sour if this sort of thing keeps up."

Knowing I had nothing to do with the editorials, Sorensen probably had a more collective "you" in mind than just the *Times* White House correspondent, but at the time he seemed pretty specific to me. In any case, I did what he probably had expected me to do; I sent his comments through Reston to the *Times* editorial board, on which the effect, if any, was no doubt subliminal.

John Herbers, covering the Robert Kennedy presidential campaign in 1968, wrote a story about a Kennedy-Johnson meeting. Later, while filling in one day for Max Frankel, the *Times* White House correspondent, Herbers was summoned by loudspeaker to Press Secretary George Christian's office. Christian enumerated errors he thought Herbers had made in the Kennedy-Johnson story and announced portentously: "You are writing about the President of the United States," as if to say that any reporter as impudent as that had some special responsibility to uphold the President's majesty.

Herbers, who believed his story had been accurate and fair, was annoyed, not intimidated. He wrote later: "I did not believe I owed Christian any explanation. It was the idea of being summoned to stand accused that offended me." Later he saw the practice become commonplace with Ron Ziegler.

Not all such efforts are necessarily serious. Kenneth O'Donnell, Kennedy's appointments secretary and political operative, once called in Bill Lawrence after a news conference and handed him a dagger. "After that question you asked today," O'Donnell said, "the President wanted you to have this." Lawrence took the dagger as a joke, which it probably was.

But presidents and White House press secretaries do tend to see themselves as affronted by a press that sometimes refuses to concede their infallibility. "I have called in reporters and pointed out factual errors in their stories," Salinger conceded to Fletcher Knebel, *Look* magazine's Washington correspondent. "Why is there any obligation on me to be perfectly speechless?" Knebel theorized that Salinger saw it much like a baseball player who yells at the umpire after a strike call; he has no chance of changing the call but hopes to sway the umpire's judgment on the next pitch.

Sometimes this kind of thing can backfire. Even if David Halberstam, for example, were not one of the best American reporters, he would have become something of a folk hero to young people in the sixties after it became known that Kennedy had urged Arthur O. ("Punch") Sulzberger, publisher of the *Times,* to pull Halberstam off coverage of the war in Vietnam. At about the same time, White House staff men were whispering to me the slander that Halberstam was a Saigon bar-hopper who had never been to the front. When Kennedy so blatantly intervened in the *Times*'s business, however, Sulzberger had no choice but to rebuff his suggestion; when the incident became known, it made Kennedy, not Halberstam, look bad.

All this suggests what can sometimes be the most important instrument—the reporter himself—by which presidents and other high officials manage the news. Reporters, it can be reported on the highest authority, are more or less normal human beings, with about as much ambition, competitive fire, desire for status and affluence, fear, caution, ethics, honesty, and guile as the rest of the human race. Therefore, they can be and often are manipulated, threatened, rewarded, punished, cajoled, and conned into doing what their news sources want them to do—sometimes without even realizing that they have been any of the above.

I did not receive a sizable package of deer-meat sausage from the LBJ Ranch one Christmas morning merely because Johnson was being neighborly. My wife and I were not invited to the White House dinner mentioned in an earlier chapter because the Kennedys had decided we would be a charming couple to know. We were put on the list by the press office, as numerous other reporters and their mates have been before and since, for the purpose of what was known inelegantly but graphically in the Nixon administration as "stroking."

I was also being stroked when Salinger sent me a telegram informing me that JFK thought mine was the best story on the first year-end backgrounder he had had with White House reporters. Stroking, like threatening, can take many forms, but both are always prime instruments of news management. Particularly in the Kennedy era, with the glamour of the White House and the supposed glitter of administration social life, reporters faced the danger of being stroked by inclusion—which carried two accompanying problems.

A reporter who was included at high social levels—say, in a party around the swimming pool at Robert Kennedy's house—might be *suspected* by the public and his colleagues of having been seduced, whether it was true or not; thus he could lose journalistic credibility if nothing else. And one who was, in fact, included at such levels was vulnerable to the threat of suddenly being excluded—as even John Kennedy's closest friend in the press, Ben Bradlee, was for three months after being quoted as mildly critical of JFK in a *Look* magazine article. If inclusion had value to a reporter, exclusion obviously could be used as a threat against him.

But I believe the danger that a reporter's news judgment and honest coverage could be seriously influenced by social preference, or lack of it, is overrated. The desire for inclusion, which can be powerful and disorienting, most often drives a reporter not to Georgetown cocktail parties but to seek private access to the mighty and the knowledgeable. A reporter's Grail is to be confided in, to know what's happening at the top, to be able to reach the highest sources, to be first with the news and most complete with the background of the news. The drive for such access is by no means the same as the drive to be invited to parties and embassy receptions and state dinners. James Reston, for an excellent example, has never been in the forefront of Washington social life, nor tried to be.

I doubt if many reporters have sacrificed any of their independence to obtain an invitation to a White House social function. On the other hand, many might yield to a bit of independence or stretch an ethical point or do a dubious journalistic favor in order to get an interview with a president, a favored position in his confidence, an important leak, or a chance to sit in on some closed-door meeting. The reporter's drive can be as excessive as anyone else's—but it's usually for a story, not for an engraved invitation.

Of course, social affairs can facilitate access to news. That's why reporters take news sources to expense-account luncheons. That's why Washington dinner parties usually mix journalists and officials. It's easier to talk to people with whom a social relationship has been established. A friendly personal association, particularly between people of differing views and responsibilities, makes a relationship of trust more likely.

I once attended a luncheon at the splendid table of Katie S. Louchheim, an assistant secretary of state in the Johnson administration and a leading Washington Democrat. I was the only journalist among numerous important political figures, including Hubert Humphrey before he became vice-president.

As the luncheon talk progressed, each of the notables began to preface his remarks with phrases like "This is off the record, Tom, but..." or "Of course I can't say this for publication, but..." Having been under the impression that luncheon was a social affair, I began to get a little hot under the collar and finally interrupted some such comment to say:

"Well, of course I'm not going to get up from this table and dash for the phone. But it's all grist to the mill, you know. Everything you say goes into my head and stays there, for what it may be worth."

That slowed the chatter no more than a minute or two, but I hope it made the point that nothing is ever finally off the record if it's said within the hearing of a reporter, no matter what the social circumstances.

But social occasions and associations, while often useful, are neither vital nor necessarily corrupting to reporters. I have known few news sources on more than a casual social basis, and seldom suffered for it; and the few sources I have known well have not been, on the whole, fountains of information. None has ever sought special favor from me.

If friendships with sources become more valuable to a reporter than his journalistic obligations, of course, he's professionally crippled. If a reporter somehow becomes obligated more than casually—accepting, say, the use of an official's weekend cottage or a congressman's houseboat—he runs a real risk of the debt being called. Huey Long probably was only half joking when he asked Arthur Krock, the day after the banks were closed in 1932, if any of the boys in the *Times* bureau needed a loan from the Kingfish.

Mr. Krock himself came to a kind of grief through Lyndon Johnson's untiring efforts at flattery and cajolery in his early years in the White House. A Krock article, written before President Kennedy's death, appeared after that event in *Fortune*. It discussed in stern tones what Mr. Krock saw as Kennedy's efforts to win the press by wining and dining reporters and otherwise soliciting favor by appealing to journalistic vanity—a commodity Mr. Krock well knew to be in oversupply.

President Johnson, then reaching out as rapidly and as often as possible to anyone who might be of assistance to him, called Mr. Krock to the White House one day for an interview. As then often happened, the "interview" turned into a luncheon in the private presidential quarters, rambled on for three or four hours, and ended in what was then a typical White House ceremony. Mr. Krock found himself standing at attention and being crowned with a pearly white, five-gallon LBJ hat with the brand of the LBJ Ranch emblazoned on the interior band.

The next day I was summoned to Mr. Krock's office. "Mr. Wicker," he informed me gravely, "I am in deep trouble. You must help me."

I was only too happy. "Mr. Wicker," Mr. Krock said, after telling me of the luncheon and coronation, "I could not refuse the President's gift. But I could only think of those men sitting out there in the press lobby. I could only think of them watching me pass through, wearing my LBJ hat. Or carrying my hat box. Mr. Wicker, after my article in *Fortune,* I could not do it."

In desperation, Mr. Krock had found his way through the White House corridors to a secretary's desk. Presenting her with the explosive hat box he had said, "Young lady, you must hide this for me. And you must never let your boss know." Now, he informed me, it was my duty to an elder to get the LBJ hat out of the White House in deepest secrecy. I was only too glad to do it, having an LBJ hat of my own hidden in a closet at home.

Gifts like that are hard to turn down. But I believed it unwise of some Washington newspapermen to accept weekend flights to Cape Cod, at about the same time, on the Kennedy family's privately owned plane, the *Caroline*, even though it was going to Hyannis anyway and even though I never heard of an instance when Robert or Edward Kennedy demanded anything in return.

Robert Kennedy did once inquire of my wife at a party why I never flew to Cape Cod on the *Caroline*, since we were then taking summer vacations at Plymouth. She told him I thought I shouldn't accept hospitality, however well meant, from someone I was supposed to write about.

Kennedy looked puzzled and a little irritated. "Suppose I offered to buy him a drink. Would he take that?"

My wife replied that the two things seemed a little different to her—and properly so, since what was really being offered was the price of a round-trip airline ticket, Washington to Cape Cod and return. And conflict of interest, for a reporter as for anyone else, is as much in the appearance of things as in the actuality.

Manipulating access, not granting or withholding social preference, is the most standard means of stroking and threatening, and by all odds the most effective, even against bold and independent reporters. A reporter who was a State Department correspondent, for example, while Secretary of State Henry Kissinger kept the reins of power and policy closely in his own hands, had little value to his editors unless he had reasonably good access to Kissinger himself and to the exceptionally close circle around him.

Since Kissinger is a man of high vanity and no small vindictiveness, sensitive both personally and politically to press accounts of his activities, it behooved correspondents trying to cover him regularly to watch their steps. By refusing to accept their phone calls, invite them to backgrounders, favor them with an occasional "leak" or "fill-in"—even on occasion by denouncing them to their editors—the Kissinger circle had an exceptionally "good stroke" on the State Department press corps. It's no accident—aside from his considerable achievements—that for so much of his time in office Kissinger received an excellent press; and when criticism began to come, it was rarely if ever from the correspondents who covered him regularly.

No hasty judgments about that should be made. Many a reporter and editor would argue forcefully that the State Department reporter's job in the Kissinger years was precisely to maintain access, stay close, at least get the official version of events as clearly and in as much detail as possible. Criticism could and did come, eventually, from journalists who did not have to maintain regular daily relations with Kissinger and his aides; but much of that criticism was based on analysis of the raw material that only the State Department press could have reported from its sources, including Kissinger himself.

In some cases, such as the Kissinger State Department, a reporter's livelihood may even depend on access. Even if that's not the situation, his or her professional status can be deeply affected in some circumstances. If, for example, a correspondent for a competitive organization is consistently getting more favorable access and therefore is scoring "beats" on important news stories, a reporter's pride, standing among his or her peers, and the good opinion of his editors may all be damaged—not to mention that his or her readers or viewers also are being shortchanged.

The other side of that coin is that reporters can be tempted into cooperative relationships with news sources on the promise or the fact of favorable access. How much cooperation for how much favor is a balance every reporter must constantly strike for himself or herself, always with an eye to that right of the public to know, the service of which alone should be—but all too seldom is—the reporter's guide.

When President Nixon nominated and President Ford renominated Earl Silbert to be U.S. attorney for the District of Columbia, much criticism resulted. Silbert had been one of the team of attorneys who originally prosecuted the Watergate case, a team widely believed to have been either pressured or deceived by the Nixon administration into limiting the investigation. Numerous Washington reporters, despite such criticism, staunchly supported Silbert's nomination, either in articles or in conversation; and it was therefore suspected that they had been the beneficiaries of Watergate information from Silbert when it had been hard to come by.

Similarly, a professional eye can almost always detect the major but unnamed sources of books such as *The Final Days* or

The Best and the Brightest, Reporters do not usually depict in a harsh light those who have provided them valuable information, just as district attorneys are likely to arrange favorable sentences for defendants who have been cooperative and provided information useful in other cases. Such major sources also tend to cast themselves in the best possible light; that's often *why* they're sources.

There's nothing pernicious in this—sometimes quite the opposite—so long as the reporter can be satisfied that he's getting the best of the bargain or at least coming out even. In almost any walk of life, useful action is accomplished only at some substantial price; a senator, for only one example, may be able to get a useful piece of legislation passed only if he agrees to cast his vote for some other legislation not quite so admirable.

When I was the *Times* Washington bureau chief, I formulated still a Third Law of Journalism—a not-very-helpful rule that at least suggests the problem. "Be neither in nor out," I told the reporters when the question would arise, "but decide for yourself just where that is." A reporter obviously can't be "out" with necessary news sources and do his or her job properly; but a reporter should not be so far "in" with sources—particularly the high and the mighty—that he or she would be inhibited in writing honestly about them, or in letting the chips fall where they may.

A reporter might ethically, for instance, delay publishing or broadcasting a story for a short time, even if doing so provided some advantage to a news source, if that source had pledged in return to provide more information, documentation, and details. This would require a judgment (subjective again) by the reporter that there was nothing unethical in whatever advantage the source would receive—perhaps he wants a Friday-night or Saturday-morning release, so that the stock markets will be closed for two days before they can react to the news—and that the additional information is of sufficient value to warrant the deal. The more a source may try to persuade a reporter, however, to alter his story significantly, leave parts of it out, or put in ameliorating material, the less ethical room the reporter has for accommodation. An obvious and vital factor in any such arrangement would be the degree of trust between reporter and source.

This is one of the major variables in a business that is at best imprecise and *ad hoc.* Most reporters insist on having a "fact" imparted by one source confirmed by another source, or several others, before they'll accept the "fact" as a "fact." But I have known, and I suspect most reporters have, news sources I trusted so fully that I would write important stories on their testimony alone. Never yet, in such a case, has my trust been misplaced—for the good reason that it had been well tested long before. On the other hand, I've known some stories "confirmed" by three or four reputable people to turn out wrong or incomplete. Even good sources, well informed, may not have known as much as they thought they did.

That suggests still another variable for the reporter. When does he stop reporting, confident that he knows the relevant facts? Some real pluggers—the most assiduous I have known is Neil Sheehan, formerly of the *Times*—literally never want to start writing. They always feel the need to interview two or three more people, take another few days of checking. Obviously, those extra interviews may produce the *real* story or give it new dimension and direction. On the other hand, the news business has its deadlines, limitations, competitive requirements, and while it seeks the truth and nothing but the truth, sometimes the *whole* truth is beyond practical reach. At some point, even the most diligent reporter reaches what Professor Phillips Russell called "that ghastly moment" when he or she *has* to start writing the story, and at that point the story—right or wrong, complete or not—inevitably becomes frozen in time and type. Perhaps there was one more person, two more, who *should* have been interviewed, another document that should have been sought— once again, there can be no surety in a subjective field, only fair and honest effort.

The most perplexing question, however, and the one that most affects a reporter's work remains: how far should he or she be "in" or "out" with news sources? Over the years, with considerable hesitation and owing to the bitter experiences of having been both too far in and too far out, I think more often than not—something on the order of eight cases out of ten—the news source needs the reporter more than the reporter needs the source. People who have information to confide are dealing in a commodity not much different from any other, and they want to market their wares at a profit—rarely, in the case of information, for money but usually for some personal or professional or policy advantage in politics, government, business, any field of public interest. The staff aide seeking a good word in the Washington press for a senator is not much different from the public-relations director seeking favorable mention in a travel magazine for some resort hotel. They want the news shaped and timed to their advantage.

My experience has been that, therefore, an independent and courageous reporter can almost always get whatever information he or she needs on adequate ethical terms, without paying too high a price in advantage to the source or in restraint on himself or herself. If sources do not want to "deal" on that basis, the reporter can do surprisingly well without them. Sometimes—usually, I'd say—instinct, experience, a good memory, a sharp eye, careful attention to surrounding detail, a skeptical sense of the way things work, a wary regard for human nature yield far more useful information and insights than any number of self-serving news sources and official spokesmen.

In the dark and suspicious Nixon White House—"a beat without sources"—John Herbers found that "covering the White House became a matter of trying to perceive through sight and sound what was happening and build stories on that perception. To my surprise, it turned out to be more reliable than any official word from those strange men who held Washington in their grip."

Not so incidentally, it seems to me, the most respected reporters, and usually the best professionally, are those who most strongly assert their own independence and are willing to rely heavily on their own qualities of intellect and experience.

8

After the Trench Coat

One day in the winter of 1952 Wallace Turner, a young reporter for the Portland *Oregonian,* was browsing through some letters referred to him by an editor. At thirty years of age, Turner—a Missourian transplanted to the West Coast by marriage—had won local renown and a few journalism prizes as an investigative reporter. But nothing in the letters piqued his interest until he came upon one signed "S. O. Newhouse."

Turner might not even have read the letter carefully had it been signed "Smith" or "Jones." But once he learned that it had *not* been written by the newspaper magnate—S. I. Newhouse— but by a lumber broker from Oregon, his reporter's eye spotted the makings of a story. Newhouse had written the editor of the *Oregonian* to complain that something appeared to be wrong in the regional offices of the Bureau of Indian Affairs.

A small businessman who bought timberland on commission for others, or occasionally for himself, Newhouse had spotted an 800-acre tract of nearly virgin forest—Douglas fir, hemlock— not far from Gold Beach, Oregon, near the mouth of the Rogue River in what was then wilderness country. Investigating title, he found that he was eying "Indian trust land"—a parcel of five

160-acre grants made by the federal government early in the twentieth century to "non-reservation" Rogue River Indians.

When Newhouse checked further, he found the land was owned by two Indian descendants of the five original grantees. One was Harold Thornton, who was one-legged, and the other was elderly Jasper Grant; neither was looked upon in the Rogue River country as ever having amounted to much.

Newhouse knew that "Indian trust land" actually was subject to the trusteeship of the Bureau of Indian Affairs; so neither Thornton nor Grant could sell without BIA approval. He wrote the regional office to find out if there was a chance that he could buy the 800 acres. The regional office replied that regulations would not permit the land to be sold to a non-Indian—too bad, but no deal. Newhouse dropped the matter regretfully.

But in the autumn of 1951, routinely pursuing his land-buying business in the old two-story frame courthouse of Curry County, Newhouse had come across papers filed with the register of deeds that roused first his curiosity, then his ire. The documents showed that the BIA regional office, acting for the two Indian heirs to the 800-acre tract that Newhouse had coveted, had approved its sale to one Ernestine Seneschal for $135,000. *That* might have been all right because she was part Indian. But Newhouse had understood from the BIA that because of the fractional interests of the heirs to the land, an auction sale was required by regulations—and the sale to Ernestine Seneschal had been negotiated by the BIA's regional office realty department.

Worse, the Seneschal sale had scarcely been completed when she sold the land again, this time to three men—Fred Marsh and William Brenner were two of them—for $160,000, a quick profit of $25,000. None of the three second-round buyers was Indian, so far as Newhouse could learn. But what most outraged him were the sums involved; an experienced landbuyer, he calculated that an 800-acre tract of virgin timberland was worth far more. Newhouse fired off his letter to the *Oregonian*, together with some poorly reproduced photostats of the documents and letters that he had exchanged with the BIA.

Wally Turner—studying that material in the *Oregonian* newsroom—saw that the crucial document was the one that transferred title to Ernestine Seneschal. That transfer removed control of the land from the BIA, which then had no power to stop or influence the resale of the 800 acres. One other fact also stuck solidly in Turner's memory. A letter from the BIA to Newhouse had been signed by Clyde W. Flinn, the area realty officer; Turner had never seen what he thought of as "Flynn" spelled "Flinn."

Not unaware that for decades the BIA had been accused of exploiting rather than protecting Indians, Turner drove down to Gold Beach—an all-day undertaking in 1952—checked the records in the old courthouse, looked over the land, ordered a professional appraisal, and learned that the 800 acres, true to Newhouse's estimate, were valued at at least $500,000 to $600,000. He began to see a real story behind the timberman's outrage at losing the tract; and the next step was obvious. He needed to know more about the three second-round buyers.

Records showed that Marsh lived in Lebanon, the other two men in The Dalles. Working routinely, Turner got in touch with George Lindsey, the *Oregonian*'s stringer in The Dalles, and asked him what he knew about the buyers who lived there. Not much, Lindsey said. Nothing unusual. He did know that William Brenner was a builder. Turner told him to check all available records—at the courthouse, city hall, the police station, the funeral home—any records that might shed some light on the men's part in the Rogue River land sale. He put a similar check in motion on Fred Marsh in Lebanon.

Lindsey soon called back with the information he'd gathered on Brenner. Among other things, he said, Brenner's wife's mother had died not too long before. A lady named . . .

"How do you spell that?" Turner asked.

"F-L-I-N-N," Lindsey said.

Turner wanted to make sure. That was with an "I", not a "Y"? Right. F-L-I-N-N. And among William Brenner's mother-in-law's survivors was her brother, one Clyde W. Flinn, spelled the same.

A more excitable reporter than Wally Turner might have been jumping up and down with excitement as he hung up the phone. But there was much more work to do and Turner got at it. He set up an interview in Portland with E. Morgan Pryse, the regional director of the BIA. Pryse insisted that the 800-acre land sale in the Rogue River valley had been legal and in the best interests of Harold Thornton and Jasper Grant; what was more, the regional realty officer, Mr. Flinn, had handled that particular transaction himself.

Could he speak to Flinn? Turner asked—and as he recalled it

twenty-five years later, "in came Flinn, looking innocent." Turner asked him about the Rogue River land sale; Flinn repeated the assurances Pryse already had offered. The sale to Ernestine Seneschal had been legal and proper.

Well then, Turner asked Pryse, did he happen to know a man named Fred Marsh?

Pryse did not.

William Brenner?

No again.

What about Flinn? Turner asked. Did *he* know Marsh?

Flinn did not.

Well, did Flinn happen to know a William Brenner?

No. Clyde W. Flinn said he did not know William Brenner.

Wally Turner had come to believe in his young career that at some point in every investigation, the investigator needed to make a "quantum leap" from information to conclusion. When he heard Flinn deny knowing Brenner, he knew he had made the necessary leap.

"Well, that's goddamned strange," Turner said, "since Bill Brenner's married to your niece."

Better men than Flinn have been confronted by Wally Turner, and come apart at the seams. Not unnaturally, Flinn began to hem and haw. What he had meant to say, he tried to explain, was that it had been a long time since he had seen or talked to Brenner.

How long? Turner demanded.

Oh, a long time, Flinn tried to assure him. Blunt as a billy-club, Turner kept hammering away, bullying Flinn and intimating at the same time that he knew the truth anyway. Undone, Flinn finally blurted that he had last seen Brenner on a stopover in The Dalles at Thanksgiving, only a few months before. The admission supported Turner's conclusion that Flinn was lying about the land sale, too.

But conclusions, however firm, are not courtroom evidence. When Flinn crept chastened out of the director's office, Turner told Pryse he intended to report the whole story, but Pryse did not agree to take corrective action. Even when Turner ran a full account of the Rogue River transaction in the *Oregonian,* with emphasis on the Flinn-Brenner connection and the flouting of BIA regulations requiring an auction, there was at first no response.

Then Jasper Grant, one of the Indian heirs to the 800-acre tract, alerted by Turner's story, retained a lawyer. In consultation with Turner, the lawyer filed a federal court action to nullify the sale of the land. Eventually, Judge Gus J. Solomon, a jurist with a reputation for strong-minded honesty, set the property sale aside and ordered a new sale—this time at auction.

When the auction was held, Harold Thornton and Jasper Grant sold their 800 acres of virgin timber for $1,050,000.

If that were all the story, Wallace Turner still would have cause to consider it one of the most satisfying of a distinguished career. But Interior Secretary Oscar Chapman, made aware of the land fraud that had been abetted by the BIA regional office, dispatched William J. Hoppenjanss, a federal investigator, to Oregon. Hoppenjanss, building on Turner's original investigation, so thoroughly probed into the Rogue River land sale that, more than a year after Turner's *Oregonian* story, Clyde W. Flinn and Fred Marsh pled guilty to criminal charges and went to prison (others involved evaded imprisonment for a variety of reasons).

The day Marsh and Flinn were to start serving their terms, Turner went down to the U.S. marshal's office to see them off.

"You son of a bitch," Marsh said, as he was led off in handcuffs. "I hope you're satisfied."

And Wally Turner was... even when, some time later, he encountered Harold Thornton at the New Eastman Hotel in Portland. Thornton, by then a rich man, was somewhat the worse for the bottle that day and, as Turner recalls it, he "reared back on that one leg and called out to me: 'Hey, what's your name? Haven't I met you somewhere before?'"

Turner went on to win a Pulitzer Prize for stories that helped expose Dave Beck and the Teamsters Union scandals of the 1950s. Later he was a Nieman Fellow at Harvard, briefly an assistant secretary of health, education, and welfare in the Kennedy administration; since the early sixties, he has been West Coast bureau chief for *The New York Times*, its ranking expert on the tangled affairs of Howard Hughes, and the investigator who disclosed most of the strange financial involvements surrounding Richard Nixon's purchase and renovation of the San Clemente estate.

Turner's Rogue River land story is recounted here in detail

not just because it is one of my favorite investigation stories. In the new popularity of the investigative reporter, it also makes a few useful points about the breed and their work.

In this relatively small matter, for example, just as was the case when Woodward and Bernstein were tracking down their Watergate stories, checking out small facts was the essence of the thing. Any good reporter also will alertly capitalize upon a good piece of luck when it comes his way—as Turner did with the unusual spelling of "Flinn."

Still, it's the dogged pursuit and accumulation of facts, perhaps unimportant in themselves, that most often pay off. If Turner had not pushed Lindsey, the stringer, to turn up everything the records disclosed about William Brenner, the crucial family connection between Brenner and Clyde W. Flinn might never have been turned up in a funeral home guestbook.

The Rogue River story, moreover, suggests what many a journalism student may not quite realize—that it is not just at the Pentagon or the White House or in Wayne Hays's committee rooms that the investigative reporter is needed. Hands get into the till in the smallest businesses, the most obscure city halls; and the public can be as surely bilked by a sticky-fingered county treasurer as by a tax loophole for a multinational corporation or an open-ended Pentagon weapons contract. A local sheriff can be as big a threat to civil rights and liberties as the FBI or the CIA, and he often is; and along any Main Street there's likely to be as much scandal, exploitation, and cover-up, relatively speaking, as at either end of Pennsylvania Avenue, or on Wall Street.

Those who may want to be "investigative reporters," therefore, with an eye to national fame, or rescuing the Constitution, or some other such glamorous objective, should reflect that inquiry begins at home; and at any level, from the *Sandhill Citizen* to *The New York Times,* journalism has need of reporters with inquiring minds, skeptical attitudes, and the patience and assiduity to add one small fact to another, until the sum discloses a larger meaning. That—not merely cultivating a cabinet officer in search of a leak—is the real job of the investigative reporter. And there are more ways to protect the public interest than challenging the high levels of the federal government.

The Rogue River story also tells much about the investigative reporter—that is, the specialist in the field. Note that Turner did not *have* to follow up the Newhouse letter, or take any of the further steps that broke the story. Neither he nor his newspaper would have been disgraced had he thrown the letter in the wastebasket and forgotten it. But Turner has, and every successful investigative specialist must have, a prosecutorial zeal, an urge to seek out the wrongdoer, a rather cynical conviction that determined search will always find a wrongdoer.

This kind of bulldog approach obviously can reflect a passion for justice—and just as obviously a self-righteous desire to smite those perceived as wicked, whether or not investigation bears out the charge. In newspaper as in police work, zeal is a quality it is sometimes necessary to restrain. Even at its best, it can take an investigator down wrong or unrewarding paths, far past the point most reporters would have pursued a story, so that the investigator must be prepared sometimes to see six months' or a year's work come to naught. Often, a difficult decision has to be faced—is there no story here after all, despite all my hard work? And sometimes the even tougher problem arises—is this story really worth publishing or am I just fascinated or outraged by it?

Determination to get the story, to keep searching until the links at last fall into place, and the patience to surmount disappointment and frustration are nevertheless the investigator's greatest strengths. Most reporters—I include myself—do not have the zeal or the patience or the resourcefulness to ferret out, say, the truth about Howard Hughes's last years, or the connections between organized crime and certain "legitimate" businesses. And journalism offers plenty that's useful to do other than the investigative story, although little that's more important.

I. F. Stone, once a journalistic pariah for his leftist political views, now one of the most respected of American reporters, was a somewhat different kind of investigator, one whose example ought to be more widely followed. Partly because of his natural skepticism, partly because deafness made interviewing difficult for him, partly because Establishment officials gave him short shrift, Stone turned early to the microscopic perusal of the mountains of documents that are stacked up—mostly to gather dust—in Washington.

They proved a gold mine of information much of which officials had never expected to be publicly exposed. Hearings, reports, studies, regulations, legislative histories, surveys of all kinds—for years in *I. F. Stone's Weekly*, Izzy Stone printed what he had culled from them, damning facts and quotes, contradictions, disclosures of all sorts, conflicts, telling statistics. It was only one of his feats that he virtually demolished Air Force claims for the bombing of North Vietnam by quoting the "World War II Strategic Bombing Survey."

Government records may not be as romantic as meeting Deep Throat in a parking garage but Woodward and Bernstein would be first to agree that such records often contain the most vital kinds of information. Doubtless the same is true of corporation and other institutional archives.

With all due respect to Woodward, Bernstein, Seymour Hersh, and Jack Anderson, of course, investigative reporters like Stone had been on the scene for a long time before today's heroes made them newly famous. One of the best I have known was John Seigenthaler, before he became publisher of the *Nashville Tennesseean;* Jim Phelan, an authority on Howard Hughes, is another; in New York, Jack Newfield was scourging assorted rascals in the columns of *The Village Voice* long before Dan Schorr leaked anything to it.

And although Wally Turner, even in 1952, was beginning to specialize in such investigations as that of the Rogue River land sale, he was then and is now as good a general reporter as any editor could wish for—which makes the most necessary point of all, that *every* reporter in a real sense should be an investigative reporter, if not a committed specialist in the field; else, what is journalism's excuse for its constitutional protection from those who would silence inquiry if they could?

In that sense, the current fad of editors and publishers—hiring reporters or teams of them entitled "investigators" and even printing their work under special labels—smacks faintly of exploitation of the public's infatuation with the *idea* of the investigative reporter. That idea probably got a considerable lift from the Redford-Hoffman movie of *All the President's Men,* restrained and factual though it was. It just doesn't often happen that the investigative reporter's target is the President; more often, it's somebody like the purchasing agent at city hall, who's got three kids, big hospital bills, and a rakeoff from the asphalt company.

There's no question, however, that the investigative reporter has become—rather like the foreign correspondent in his trench coat used to be—the most idealized and romanticized figure in journalism today. The only rival, if my mail and the questions of journalism students are any guide, is the columnist.

During the 1968 Democratic National Convention, I emerged one day from the air-conditioned Tribune Tower in Chicago to find a long line of demonstrators marching past on the sun-blistered sidewalk of Michigan Avenue. *The New York Times* was using rented office space in the Tower as its center for convention coverage and I was on my way to an early session at the Stockyards Amphitheater.

The marchers—all youthful, but not all bearded, most of them neat, but some in old fatigue jackets and overalls—were not protesting the *Chicago Tribune*. They were on the way to the front, farther along Michigan Avenue across from the Conrad Hilton Hotel, the convention headquarters. They carried posters with messages like "End the War," "Trade Hubie for the *Pueblo*," "Stop the Bombing," "Dump the Hump," and "Vote No for President." The McCarthy peace dove was emblazoned on many of their placards. I nudged my way through the long line and headed for a rented car at curbside.

Then someone in the orderly line shouted at me. "Hey, Mr. Wicker," he called, rather politely, "come on and march with us!"

All is vanity and I was pleased to be recognized. But others in the line took up the shout: "Come on, Mr. Wicker! March! March with us, Mr. Wicker!"

I just waved and stood there. Traffic went past. The line moved on, the shouts weakened, and one last call came back to me above the sounds of tires and horns, and is with me still:

"March, Mr. Wicker! Put up or shut up!"

So I stood there a while longer, and the picketers went on past, until those who had called to me were far up the avenue; and in the wilting heat I felt sad and old and out of shape. I had believed always that I belonged with the young and the brave and the pure in heart; but in the end I got into my rented car and went on out to the Stockyards and up to the press gallery. And there I sat, not unlike William Allen White's memory of himself after he had voted for Harding at the 1920 Republican convention: ". . . ashamed, disheveled in body and spirit, making a sad, fat figure while the bands played, the trumpets brayed and the crowd howled ... a sad spectacle I made, and time has not softened the shabby outlines of the picture in all these long years."

The first "column" I wrote for *The New York Times* appeared in the summer of 1965, when I was asked to fill in for James Reston, who was on vacation; my beginning effort was an absolutely undistinguished piece favorably analyzing a rent-subsidy program put forward by the Johnson administration. I happened to be in the New York office that day, rather than the Washington bureau, where I normally worked, and I was not even sure with whom to "file" my copy. When I had done so, I worried for hours as to whether my article would be acceptable for such an exalted purpose as a column on the *Times* editorial page.

It must have been, because it appeared the next morning on schedule—July 2, 1965—and I never heard a word of praise or criticism or advice from anyone. I continued to fill in for Reston, and later that summer for Arthur Krock, and while a trickle of fan mail gladdened my heart, there was nothing but silence from the *Times* editors and officials I had imagined scrutinizing my every word.

In the summer of 1966, upon the retirement of Mr. Krock, I was appointed a regular columnist to succeed him, again receiving no instructions save a stern admonition from Executive Editor Turner Catledge—"Now don't stand around sucking your thumb!" Translated out of press jargon, that meant he wanted a reporter's column, not "thumbsuckers," as pieces that contain more reflection and speculation than documentable facts are apt to be termed by newspapermen. Taking heed, I wrote my first official column—July 12, 1966,—from Billings, Montana, a reportorial account of a rather typical American political rally in that city's Pioneer Park.

I never heard anything about that one, either, from Catledge or John B. Oakes, the editorial-page editor, or Arthur Sulzberger, the publisher. Nor did I get lectures or letters of sage counsel or grave warning, as the months wore along and I settled into the columnist's relentless routine—for me, three articles a week, at the fixed length of 750 words each (about the equivalent of writing a magazine article every week), the three pieces due on certain days of the week, rain or shine, ideas or no ideas, hangover or no hangover. Gradually, I learned what has been the most important fact of my work as a *New York Times* columnist—I have about as much independence as any person in any line of work could ever hope to have.

In more than ten years at that inexorable schedule—allowing a month for vacation each year, I calculate it at just over 1500 articles, at this writing—I have never been told what to write, or what not to write; I have never been told, after the fact, not to do something again; I have never had an article or any part of one killed, for policy or any other kind of reason; I have never had to submit an article for prior approval; I have never even heard it seriously suggested that someone in authority on the *Times* would be pleased if I did or did not write something; and I have never felt the slightest pressure to conform to *New York Times* editorial policy—indeed, *Times* columnists are *not* members of the *Times* editorial board precisely because the columnists are considered independent of *Times* policy.

On several occasions that I recall, a *Times* editorial has been written to *answer* something I had written. In one such case, having to do with the death of George Jackson in San Quentin prison in 1971, the assistant editorial-page editor, A.H. Raskin, courteously called to tell me that an editorial was being written to take issue with my view that American blacks would not believe the official account of Jackson's death. Nor have I been inhibited in publicly disputing *Times* editorial policy in my own articles.

When the *Times* officially called for Richard Nixon's resignation more than a year before he did it, I wrote a piece the next day urging impeachment instead, on grounds that the nation had had too much irregular procedure—that was the substance of Watergate—and needed to follow the constitutional route of formal charges against Nixon and a trial on their merits.

I cite these instances not to suggest that either one was right, or that either was possessed of more wisdom than the other, but to demonstrate that the intellectual and political freedom of *Times* columnists is virtually unlimited, and that the consequence is a wide range of views even within the pages of a newspaper considered "liberal." The only case I know in which a *Times* columnist was specifically restricted came during the unusual circumstances of a New York newspaper strike that lasted more than a hundred days in 1963.

James Reston, a man to whom the morning newspaper is more vital than breakfast, wrote a strong criticism of the Printers Union for keeping the *Times* from publishing (he was filing for what were then the West Coast and European editions of the *Times* and for the Times News Service). Orvil E. Dryfoos, then the publisher, was at a crucial stage of negotiations with the union and killed the column for fear that it would delay a settlement—surely a permissible infringement of Reston's accustomed independence.

Too much cannot be made of that independence, of course; for it exists only within well-understood if never stated limits. I doubt I would last long if I consistently called for the overthrow of the government, or advocated Marxist Leninism, or blatantly advanced my personal financial interests or political ambitions—if I had any—or those of friends. But those are proscriptions of good sense, common values, and ethical behavior that I find neither abhorrent nor chafing. Useful political, social, and economic discourse can easily be carried on within such limits, and in great depth and range. No metropolitan American newspaper, needing minimum public acceptance for its financial survival and journalistic credibility, could be reasonably expected to propagate revolution. Nor have I ever wanted to.

Nevertheless, I suspect some of my articles have caused my employers discomfort and embarrassment, which they have manfully swallowed in silence. And my journey from Pioneer Park in Billings to a position as something of a dissident—if not a marching demonstrator—within the Establishment symbolized by the *Times* took place in no small part because at a critical period I *was* a *Times* columnist, and frequently a thumbsucker, endowed with the independence cited, and given a responsibility to meet, not to mention a reputation to make and maintain.

No one lightly places his or her ideas and opinions on controversial matters publicly on view, three times a week, in a medium so widely and closely read as *The New York Times,* by such an impressive audience as it reaches in every center of national thought and action. The inherent personal risk of being laughed or stoned out of the marketplace of ideas forces a reasonably careful self-examination of a columnist's stock in trade—his own knowledge, ideas, assumptions, and attitudes.

But it is precisely these things—their own knowledge, ideas, assumptions, and attitudes—that *reporters* theoretically are supposed to keep out of news stories (as if they really could). That is the difference, not always recognized by readers, between a reporter and a columnist.

A reporter basically reports what happened and what was said, and delves into reasons and meanings only to the extent that they can be documented or attributed to persons in a position to know. Only recently and in a limited number of news organizations has the reporter's role been expanded even to the extent that he or she might openly draw on his or her own knowledge and experience to supplement what can be learned from others.

Writing earlier about political reporting, I confessed that when an interpretation of events is attributed to "political observers" or "experienced observers," the reporter in most instances is offering his or her own view—but wording it to meet the requirements of editors and of "objective journalism." It may also be reasonably supposed that most "diplomatic observers" or "veteran analysts" or "well-placed persons" in any field are semantic inventions; the rule of thumb is that the more general the attribution, the more probably it is a front for a reporter who is not permitted to write "I believe" or "I think" or "I have concluded"—much less to state the opinion or conclusions on no authority save his or her "by-line."

The result is that news stories are restricted primarily to facts, as they should be; but opinion columns necessarily deal also with ideas. I learned early that I could accumulate a lot of facts on a given subject, and still not be able to put together a useful column on that subject. I learned too that mere advocacy is not much of an idea. To delineate the facts of a bill before Congress, then to write a final paragraph supporting or opposing it, even for a reason, is not really to write a useful column—rather such an article usurps the editorial writer's function, which is basically that of reasoned advocacy.

An opinion column needs an *idea*—rarely more than one, given length restrictions—whether complex or simple, original or conventional. In journalism as in any other form, an idea does not require acceptance to justify its existence; nor does it necessarily exist to achieve anything other than an intellectual end. An idea *is*; and an informed, opinionated, argumentative person—all of which an opinion columnist must be—will put forward ideas, defend them, modify or abandon them, attack or analyze or even accept those of others, as *concepts,* intellectual speculations, without much regard to their general popularity or immediate utility or relevance to a given situation. An idea in itself is of interest, and offering ideas is the task of the opinion columnist at his infrequent best.

For example: an article detailing how the two-party system works in America is a factual report; if the writer states that he is for it or against it or favors modification, it is an editorial; but if the article assumes that everyone knows what the two-party system is and that most Americans favor it as an instrument of political stability and moderation, then goes on to argue nevertheless that the two-party political system is an instrument of the economic status quo—that's an opinion column. Wrongheaded, maybe; certainly not aimed at some specified reform; rather an *idea* calculated to offer a different perspective on some known facts, arouse intellectual interest, produce discussion, maybe even affect thought and attitudes.

Obviously, then, making himself into an opinion columnist may offer some difficulty to the experienced *reporter,* indoctrinated as he is to be fundamentally a fair and accurate recorder of what other people do and say. In the simplest terms, as a columnist he must begin to think for himself and express his own ideas, rather than seeking and transmitting the ideas—at least the assertions—of others. The opinion columnist's job is not to report faithfully the views of, say, Henry Kissinger on Rhodesia; of course, he or she may permissibly be informed and influenced by Kissinger's ideas, as by those of anyone; but the columnist's job, finally, is to offer an idea of his or her own—if no more than a personal perspective on what Kissinger or Andrew Young or Kenneth Kaunda may be saying on Rhodesia.

My own transition from reporter to columnist coincided roughly with the immense American political re-evaluation that sprang in the sixties from the Vietnam war and the movement against it, from the ghetto riots in the major cities, and from the brief flowering of the counterculture. My experience as a *journalist* in that period paralleled the experience of many an American as a *citizen*—we began to think for ourselves, to put forward our own ideas rather than accept what we were told.

•   •   •

While a Washington reporter in 1965 and 1966, I had not much questioned the developing war in Vietnam. I was a child of my time, seized by the lesson of World War II that "agression" had to be met with force wherever it occurred, steeped in the Cold War mentality of the fifties and early sixties, and profoundly influenced by the dominant political idea of my lifetime up to then—the primacy, almost the omnipotence, of the presidency in the American system, particularly in foreign affairs.

All these ideas worked together to persuade me, even against some obvious evidence, that *the President* was right *to resist aggression by a Communist power* against a free nation allied with the United States. All my reporter's training at the same time led me to confine my stories mostly to what I was told by official persons, and what the President said, and what was contained in the official documents—such as the State Department's white paper "Aggression from the North."

As White House correspondent, for example, I was called in to the office on the night of August 4, 1964, to cover President Johnson's speech announcing that he had ordered retaliatory air strikes against North Vietnam, following an attack on American ships by North Vietnamese torpedo boats in the Gulf of Tonkin. Later it developed that the facts of the Tonkin Gulf "attack" were unclear at best, that they did not certainly justify retaliation, and that LBJ welcomed an opportunity to demonstrate a muscular military response at a time when his Republican opponent, Barry Goldwater, was denouncing a "no-win" policy in Vietnam. But that evening, while the political advantage to Johnson was apparent (he adeptly seized the occasion to spring the celebrated Tonkin Gulf resolution on a gullible Congress), it never occurred to me that the facts were in question or that Johnson was deliberately manipulating events or that the air strikes were uncalled for; and no such unseemly doubts crept into my story, which "led" the *Times* the next morning (that is, it appeared in the right-hand column on page one).

Johnson spoke in prime time, on short notice, long after our regular deadlines. Working from a White House text and a television set, I had to crank out my story virtually as Johnson spoke, in "short takes" and at unholy speed. A reporter able to deliver a smoothly written story under such conditions and in time to make most of the press run may be highly valued in the trade; but the truth is that if I or any other reporter had had doubts about the validity of Johnson's speech or actions, we would have had no chance to check them out that night—which meant that television and the morning headlines gave *his* version of events the initiative in the public's consciousness. No other version would ever quite catch up. Thus, the press magnified the impact of what Johnson told the nation, instead of acting as a check on or a balance against the actions he was taking and the policy that was emerging; and it could hardly have been otherwise.

By the summer of 1965, however, I was acting not only as a reporter but as a fill-in columnist. The resulting necessity to think for myself forced certain seeds of doubt—at least of caution—into my mind. For July 23, 1965, I recalled in my column space that President Kennedy, after the Bay of Pigs, had asked himself, "What is prestige? Is it the shadow of power or the substance of power?" and had decided that "We are going to work on the substance of power." Then I noted that President Johnson and his advisers were conducting a full-scale review of the question whether to expand the war in Vietnam.

> ... the real problem for them [I wrote] is to distinguish between the shadow and the substance of power.
> No doubt Mr. Johnson would be assailed now if he stopped short of committing the nation to a full-scale ground war in Southeast Asia—just as Mr. Kennedy would have been attacked had he canceled the Cuban invasion. No doubt anything less than such a war would be considered in some quarters of the world as weakness—just as disbanding the exile brigade would have been in 1961....
> These things may be true but it is certainly true that a full commitment of American power—even non-nuclear power—to a war in South Vietnam could in an instant become another Frankenstein's monster....
> President Johnson's task now is to cut through graver shadows and find the substance of what is required of this nation in Vietnam. If that should prove to be something less than bloody war, he will enhance—not impair—the true strength of American by recognizing it.

In the years that followed, as my emphasis gradually shifted from reporting to my own column—as bureau chief, I was still doing some writing for the news columns—the necessity to think for myself as a columnist, to develop my own ideas rather than report the actions and assertions of others, began to have profound intellectual and political effect on me. I found that the analytical and conceptual lobes of my brain had been like old pieces of machinery long abandoned in a vacant lot, covered with rust and moss. Gradually, resisting all the way, complaining and screeching, this almost forgotten equipment creaked back into service, greased and polished by the efforts I had to make in those years to fill that yawning space three times a week with something more than facts or advocacy. Despite Turner Catledge's admonition about thumbsucking and my prudent early efforts to meet it, I believed from the start that my real job as a columnist was to deal with ideas.

The search for ideas, however, is a risky business, like opening locked rooms. It's possible to stumble into almost anything. As I struggled to do my work well, at precisely the time in American history when the war in Vietnam was growing into a reeling ruinous giant—a Frankenstein's monster indeed—and at home American youth was rising in rebellion against its heritage and the ghetto blacks were turning cities into chaos, the necessities of my professional life led inevitably to a root-and-branch re-examination of the dominant assumptions of my intellectual and political lives. I could no longer ignore the contradictions and discrepancies in what I was *told* or accept the bland explanations of officials with a personal or bureaucratic interest at stake.

So far from keeping myself "uninvolved," as reporters are instructed to do, as a columnist I *had to be* involved, not as marcher or demonstrator but as a seeker after ideas I could support—ideas that fitted perceptions rather than assumptions. I could not believe, much less support, what Lyndon Johnson and his aides were trying to tell me about the war in Vietnam in 1966 and 1967 and 1968 because my perception of that war (no small thanks to television) was too far at variance with the assumptions they urged me to make.

Had I been a doctor or a businessman entering the same epoch with the same views, the dislocations and disillusionment of the time might have forced a similar revision; I don't know. But as a columnist necessarily searching for ideas, I quite literally had no choice.

For the most explicit example, I came to see the presidency

not as an inspired office that broadened and ennobled its occupants, thus justifying its powers, but as something of a Frankenstein's monster itself, out of control and uncontrollable, more the illicit creation of mad genius (American imperialism) than a work of necessity. That idea, too, was exaggerated— particularly as to a president's rather limited power in domestic affairs; but in the years of Kennedy, Johnson, Nixon, and Kissinger, it was a needed corrective idea as against an aggressive and Imperial Presidency. In my life, it was a perception arrived at in some pain and only in defiance of the assumptions of a lifetime, the failed gods of an era.

So, too, with my ultimate understanding that the war was a fraud except to the dead—the "aggression from the north" a civil war, the "free nation" neither a valid nation nor all that much freer than its Communist rival, the American role a blundering, destructive juggernaut carried on past any sensible dimension for the shabby political goal of avoiding the appearance of defeat.

All that is commonplace to say today, but in 1967 and 1968, to a patriotic World War II and Korean War veteran rigidly conditioned to be an "objective reporter," opposition to the war on such grounds was deeply unsettling, disorienting—if he had been so wrong about *that,* how much else must he have been wrong about, too, or at least naïve and ill-informed?

The civil-rights movement was a case in point. As a Southern liberal and a veteran of school-integration battles, I had long favored "civil rights" for blacks. The ghetto riots and "long hot summers" of the sixties forced me, however, to a new conclusion—a relatively simple idea, but fecund; it was to spawn a hundred offspring in later years. I saw that "granting" rights to blacks, a process reasonably advanced by 1968, would never solve the racial problem in America, because that problem was the *inequality* of blacks in white eyes.

Those who have to be granted rights by others are not made truly equal by the grant; not until generations pass and granted rights become as inherent as anyone else's does something like equality result. More important, it was not just "rights" in which the blacks were disadvantaged but income, wealth, status, and power—in none of which were whites ready to "grant" even the opportunity for equality, much less the fact of it. *That* would have to be wrested from unwilling hands, made the more so by white shock and disillusionment that blacks were not particularly grateful for having been "granted" rights by those who had for so long deprived them of the same rights.

That idea no doubt offended a lot of complacent white assumptions. But then ideas always challenge assumptions, not necessarily successfully; and that may be as good a description as any—"challenging assumptions"—for the work of the opinion columnist. First, of course, he must challenge his own.

Challenging people's assumptions, however, is an endeavor that wins few thanks and fewer converts; it obviously requires independence, which *The New York Times* has provided me for more than a decade; and it renders a good many Americans uneasy or angry or both—judging by the number who've asked me in person or by mail something like the following question (which was actually put to me after a speech in 1977 at Lafayette College in Easton, Pennsylvania):

"What gives you the right to tell the American people what to think?"

The short answer, of course, is that I *don't* tell people what to think; and the proof is that if I did, this would be a different world. Joe Kraft and Scotty Reston and George Will don't tell people what to think, either; they say what *they* think, usually bluntly, which is quite a different thing. Even Walter Cronkite doesn't tell people what to think, although so great is the impact of television news that he does tell a lot of people most of what they *know*; but that's still another thing.

The broader meaning of the question, however, is in its first half: "What gives you the right . . . ?"

What *does* give me or Mary McGrory or William F. Buckley the right to do what we do—challenge people's assumptions with our opinions, wrongheaded as all of us and every other columnist have shown that they can sometimes be? Again the shorter answer—our publishers give us the right—doesn't reach the point, which is what *qualifies* columnists for the independence they have to use the powerful forums at their disposal? And the point takes on a poignant double meaning if—as I believe—most of the American people themselves are aching to be heard, to have an impact, to raise their voices above all the others in the indistinguishable cacophony of a mass society. No wonder they want to know of any columnist *What gives you the right?* Implicitly, of course, they are adding *instead of me?*

There may be no final answer other than the imponderable chances of life. But I'd suggest at least the following:

Experience: not the short-term knowledge of what happened yesterday or last year that leads reporters and politicians and generals to prepare to fight the last war, but a broad-scale experience of public persons, public institutions, public processes. Most columnists have spent a lifetime in journalism, politics, or both—or some more specialized calling, such as economics—and have learned much about the way things work, the things people do, the effects of power, the limitations of politics, that events control people more often than the other way around. Policies and programs can be seen differently by different writers, but most of them know, or at least sense, what Arthur Krock once wrote from a vacation house in Newport:

"...a shore from which the ocean stretches unbroken to an unseen landfall in the other hemisphere is perhaps the place where a vacationing Washington observer of the ways of Government is most likely to keep them, however unwillingly, in mind. For, like the ocean as seen from such a shore, only their surface changes. In the depths, there is no change."

Access: if nothing else, journalism provides the practitioner a privileged seat in the arena. To continue the sports metaphor, not only does the journalist have a seat behind home plate, he's privileged to go to the locker room after the game and interview the manager and players. The privilege in itself doesn't yield wisdom or even knowledge, but it provides opportunity to learn something about this year's players to people who already understand the game. Combined with the opinion columnists' independence, the opportunity gives them considerable ability to speculate knowledgeably about motives, relationships, influences, ambitions, fears—the proximate causes of action.

Knowledge: the basic equipment of any columnist includes knowledge about a variety of things, or—perhaps as important—the ability to obtain and absorb such knowledge on short notice. Here there's a useful cycle at work—a columnist needs the knowledge of, say, an economist; because he or she *is* a columnist blessed with a forum, the economist usually is willing to impart the necessary information; published or drawn upon in a column in *The Washington Post* and syndicated nationally, that knowledge enhances the ability of the columnist to obtain even more knowledge when he needs it. A columnist, therefore, must be a skillful and voracious brain-picker, as well as an assiduous student of documentary sources—remembering always that in obtaining *knowledge* from others, the object must be to stimulate his or her own *ideas*.

Experience, access, knowledge—maybe they don't give anyone the *right* to preach ideas from a pulpit like that provided by *The New York Times* or *Newsweek* or a syndicate of hundreds of newspapers; they do tend to give legitimacy to someone who does so. For example:

An intelligent man, living in the borough of Queens, working at a middle-income job, raising a family, coping with life, is afraid of crime. He *should* be afraid of crime—of robbery, assault, rape, theft, illegal drug sales, unreasoning violence. He may have three locks on his door, walk his teen-age daughter to school every morning and worry all day about her safe return, never take the subway after dark, and belong to a pistol club in the belief that marksmanship will help him protect his family. Quite naturally—and whether he's white or black—he probably wants more people sent to prison and kept there for longer terms.

That appears to be a plausible, sensible, and justified way to deal with the crime that engulfs Queens, and most American cities. But is it? The man from Queens knows a lot about the crime on his doorstep and is entitled to his view about how best to deal with it; he can hardly be expected, however, to have a sophisticated knowledge of criminology, penology, the criminal justice system, economics, the causes of crime—he merely wants something drastic done and wants it done fast, which is natural but not always the best way to proceed.

The columnist writing about crime has the obligation, however, to look beyond the immediate fear of crime—which he may well share, and should if he lives in Washington or New York. He should know or be able to find out whether putting more people in prison for longer terms is really the best thing to do, even in the immediate self-interest of the man in Queens—whether it will really diminish crime, or perhaps actually increase it; what the prisons are costing the honest citizen in taxes and social pathology; whether there may not be deeper causes of crime that might better be attacked; whether the police are being used to best advantage; whether the courts could handle more criminal cases if it were possible to bring them; and a host of other questions, which it is the columnist's opportunity and obligation to *raise* even if he can't answer all of them.

The columnist has the ability, with his or her experience, access, and knowledge, to put forward ideas about crime, why there's so much of it, what can be done. That is what makes him or her different from—not better than—the man in Queens. That is what gives him or her "the right" to tell people, not what to think, but what can be knowledgeably suggested.

Within the enormous latitude allowed me as a *Times* columnist, I have had to evolve some useful guidelines for myself—the most important of which, I believe, is "Don't be afraid to be wrong." Being wrong too often obviously would ruin any columnist's credibility. On the other hand, infallibility can be achieved only by limiting oneself to the narrowest and most obvious range of opinion, which would rule out bold and imaginative dealings in ideas. The higher value is to risk wrongheadedness in the search for illumination; and the obligation I feel is not so much to be *right* as to be provocative.

A willingness to be wrong cannot, of course, extend to facts; and it should include a readiness to concede error, not just as to fact but in judgment as well. It wouldn't matter too much if I made the factual error of writing that in 1976 there were eleven thousand Cuban troops in Angola when there were thirteen thousand; but it would matter a great deal if I offered readers the judgment that these troops offered no threat to Rhodesia, only to find them later in combat with Rhodesian forces. In either case, it seems to me, and particularly as to errors of judgment, I would owe readers an accounting to "set the record straight." So I periodically publish pieces in which I confess error—although not necessarily *all* the error readers may charge to me out of their differing views of things.

Of almost equal importance is my determination not to write a column merely to achieve some definable end. Getting a bill passed by Congress, that is, or a particular person elected, or some policy adopted by a president, does not seem to me really the business of the columnist. Some such results might flow from his or her work, combined with other forces moving in society; but if the columnist's purpose were first and foremost to achieve a particular consequence, he or she would become—and might better openly be—a politician.

For example, in 1972, it surely was not hard for readers to deduce from my articles that I was more likely to vote for George McGovern than for Richard Nixon. Yet, when I touted McGovern's $1000-per-person scheme as an appropriate plan for the redistribution of income, then learned that the idea not only didn't "cost out" but had been misrepresented to me and to the public, I believed I had no choice but to write an article denouncing it as unsound and oversold. I did, and was astonished at the volume of mail I received from irate McGovern partisans who apparently believed that his election over Nixon was sufficiently important that he was entitled to sell a bill of goods—I think from his own lack of understanding of the proposal—to the voters, and that I should not expose his having done so.

Audiences sometimes react in disbelief when I insist that I am not trying as a columnist to *achieve* anything other than the intellectual stimulation of readers. But it's true. If I wanted to get bills passed or defeated, I'd run for Congress or take a lobbyist's job. It's not my responsibility to force President Carter to reduce unemployment to 4 percent; it *is* my job to argue in print—vigorously—that unemployment not only takes a vicious social toll in crime and welfare costs and human misery but that it also runs up the federal budget deficit and holds down productive capacity and hence causes inflation, too.

Another guideline I try to follow is frequently to challenge the conventional wisdom; put another way, I try to keep an open mind even on what may seem to be the most obvious proposition. It's axiomatic that the more general agreement there may be on something—the Viet Cong can't hold out; LBJ can't be dumped; McGovern can't be nominated—the more there's likely to be a kind of peer-group psychology at work, in which no one wants to be "far out" or "not with it" or "emotionally involved," and the safe place to be is with the crowd. Columnists seldom belong with the crowd.

Any consensus, in fact—Jimmy Carter is "fuzzy" on the issues; openness in foreign policy won't work—is fertile ground for the columnist in search of ideas. It isn't so much that a consensus is right or wrong but that, either way, it dulls thought and stifles independence—exactly the opposite of the columnist's ideal. A consensus, after all, is merely a widespread assumption, a crowd with a notion.

Let me not leave the impression that all my columns put forward provocative ideas, in defiance of popular views, without concern for consequences and with fearless disregard for the possibility of misjudgment. Alas! Caution inevitably creeps in, facts dominate concepts, immediate attitudes on policy questions find expression, human weakness prevails.

Just as Detroit sometimes has to recall its cars, not everything I or any columnist turns out is up to scratch. For myself, I estimate—and talks with colleagues suggest that my experience is not untypical—about one-third of my columns come reasonably close to meeting my personal standards. I don't mean one of every three or one a week, either; sometimes a long period of intellectual aridity afflicts anyone who has to keep turning out articles week in and week out. It's easy, too, merely to react to the morning's headlines. I mean roughly a third of the total over the years may have been the kind of work in which I could take real satisfaction.

As for the rest, some aimed high but missed the mark, which is neither surprising nor deplorable; but more have been the kind of hackwork any demanding schedule is likely to produce—compilations of fact without illumination, old ideas rehashed, easy pieces of advocacy, slick repackaging of someone else's news story. Ideas worth writing about don't come all that easily or often; or maybe they just aren't recognized.

But the search is exhilarating and the occasional discovery well worth the cost. It might be more comforting on occasion to march with the crowd, and the temptation is always there to move out on the picket lines; and sometimes even yet, I feel myself "a sad, fat figure" while the trumpets are braying elsewhere. In the main, however, a columnist's work has yielded me the independence I cherish, and provided me the opportunity to circumvent some of journalism's most profound limitations.

9

Who Elected the Press?

In the late fall of 1967 General William C. Westmoreland, the Army Commander in Vietnam, and Ambassador Ellsworth Bunker came home from Saigon to tell the nation that its unpopular Southeast Asian war slowly was being won. In public statements and private sessions with reporters, businessmen, members of Congress, the two officials delivered the message— the corner was being turned, light was visible at the end of the tunnel.

Some time after these couriers had returned to Vietnam, I had a visitor in my corner office at the *New York Times* bureau in Washington; I was then still the bureau chief. He was brought in by Neil Sheehan, the *Times*'s Pentagon correspondent in 1967, and I vaguely remembered him—Dan Ellsberg, the militant young ex-Marine I had first met when following Hubert Humphrey around Saigon in 1966. He explained that he was working in the Pentagon as an employee of the Rand Corporation, a "think-tank" heavily involved in defense research.

"You guys have been conned," Ellsberg told me. When I asked him what he meant, he laid out in some detail what I thought was an appalling story.

Westmoreland and Bunker, he said, had come to the United States strictly for propaganda purposes. What's more, the figures they had publicized—villages under control, Viet Cong killed, captured, or defecting, all the then-familiar lists of Vietnam quantifiers—had been hoked up for best effect.

"You should have seen what they *wanted* to tell you," Ellsberg said. The first figures Bunker and Westmoreland had cabled to the Pentagon were so wild, he said, no one in Washington would have believed them for a moment. Whereupon, he went on, Pentagon officials aware of the rising skepticism of the Washington press had cabled back to Saigon that the figures had to be revised downward if they were to have any credibility at all. As Ellsberg told the story, the cables had flown back and forth until agreement had been reached on what the traffic would bear—the level of statistical claims Bunker and Westmoreland could foist off on the American public with plausibility. These, of course, were the figures those of us in the press had been reporting in good faith as representing the factual situation in Vietnam, as described by the commanding general and the ambassador.

I had been skeptical of the Westmoreland-Bunker performance anyway and I could see right away the significance of Ellsberg's story; so could Sheehan. If we could print documentary proof of the deception Ellsberg was alleging, the pretense that the war was being won would be shattered, an administration already lacking basic credibility would be in deep political trouble, and the war might even become insupportable.

"Can you get copies of those cables for us?" I asked Ellsberg.

A slender, intense young man, looking then much as he did when he later became famous, Ellsberg seemed almost to recoil from my suggestion. Of course not, he said; the cables were Top Secret.

"But they'd prove the government's been lying," I argued.

Ellsberg said he could vouch for *that*. He'd seen those cables; from them and from other evidence, he knew what he was talking about.

"Your word's just not enough," I told him. "It wouldn't prove anything by itself. They'd just call you a liar, or too emotionally involved. And the *Times* wouldn't print a story making a charge that serious unless we could document it."

This seemed to surprise Ellsberg, who'd apparently thought a "leak" of this magnitude would produce immediate headlines.

Still, he would not agree to procure the cables. He thought he could go to jail if he did—that releasing Top Secret material was against the law.

In fact, releasing the cables probably would not have been against the law, so far as the law is clear; but in that relatively innocent period, neither Ellsberg nor I knew it. We both thought that classification of documents was a serious matter and believed that anyone violating the rules controlling such documents obviously was breaking the law. As a young Navy officer, I'd briefly been in charge of classified materials—code books and the like—at a base in Japan; and I remembered the rigorous logging and checking procedures for which I'd been responsible and the solemn warnings of superiors that I could be court-martialed for mishandling or losing any of those weapons manuals, code books, and other documents. At the least, I believed, Ellsberg could lose his security clearance, hence his job, by producing those cables for us and getting caught at it; at worst, neither he nor I then doubted, he might go to prison.

Nevertheless, and recognizing that it was he who would take the risk, I made him a strenuous argument that if (a) the government was lying and (b) he could produce the cables as irrefutable proof of it, then (c) maybe the war he and I had come to abhor could be greatly affected, even brought to an end. So (d) he had a duty as a concerned citizen to try to put those cables in our hands. For my part—it was easy to promise—I could guarantee prominent play in the most prestigious newspaper in the country, plus absolute, unyielding protection of the identity of the source of the documents.

Long afterward, Dan Ellsberg told me this argument had impressed him, perhaps even started him on the road to release of the Pentagon Papers three years later. Looking back on it, in the light of all that's transpired since, I'm not sure I'd argue as strongly as I did then. It's just too easy to urge someone else to take such risks as I then thought were involved; and I have a clearer sense now of the lengths to which the government may go in tracking down such leaks and punishing the culprit. In any case, even the Pentagon Papers didn't stop or materially affect the course of a war two administrations were determined to wage. I think I overstated to Ellsberg both the possibilities of publication and his duty to bring it about. Worse, the likelihood is that my zeal for a major story out of our bureau was a greater influence on me at the time tjan I recognized.

Ellsberg eventually produced one cable, from Saigon to

Washington, apparently the first in the series he had told us about; and while it tended to bear out his story, the crucial need was for the whole series of cables showing how the fake figures for publication had been bargained out between the two capitals. Ellsberg couldn't get hold of the rest of the cables, and ultimately the story eluded us—only to be subsumed in the Tet offensive, which soon did more to turn the public against the war than any newspaper story could have.

The story of the cables we couldn't print provides at least one kind of answer to a question that in one form or another is frequently heard nowadays: Who elected the press?

Put another way—if the press can decide for itself what to publish, whether the government wants it published or not, what check *is* there upon the power of the press?

Because of its constitutional sanction in the First Amendment, on one hand, and because of its supposed power to affect public opinion, on the other, many people have come to believe that the press—more often "the media"—is the least checked and controlled of all American institutions. It has been called "the fourth branch of government," which is largely true, and sensible men believe that its power is sufficient to overcome or shake the powers of the other three. Such power, if it existed would be ominous indeed.

As I have said, my belief instead is that—in my lifetime at least—"despite the freedom conferred by the Constitution, the American press operated under severe limitations, inherent in it nature and that of the country, which effectively restrained the power derived from freedom."

These limitations may not be readily seen—particularly by those who feel their privacy invaded or their policies inhibited by a sometimes bumptious press. They exist, nevertheless Sometimes, as in the case of the widely accepted "Eastern press conspiracy" popularized first by Goldwater, than by Nixon and Agnew (and more or less credited by Lyndon Johnson), the situation is the reverse of the common view.

The publishers and editors of, say, *The New York Times, The Washington Post, Newsweek, Time,* and *The Boston Globe* together with the chieftains of the television networks, *may* have generally similar political and social views—although even that is a dubious proposition, considering the range of attitude among executives like William S. Paley of CBS and Andrew Heiskell of Time Inc., and editors like John B. Oakes of *The New York Times* (until December 31, 1976) or Osborn Elliott, formerly of *Newsweek*. It's true that Katharine Graham, as head of the Washington Post Company, publishes both the *Post* and *Newsweek,* and that Heiskell is married to the former Marian Sulzberger Dryfoos, a member of the board of directors and the sister of the publisher of *The New York Times.*

To make a "conspiracy" out of such thin stuff is ridiculous; even Agnew usually charged no more than a "fraternity," and that, among other things, slighted Mrs. Graham. But even the idea of a fraternity—a sort of publishers' club—falls of its own weight as soon as the sometimes savage competition between the television networks is realized, or in any analysis of the *Post's* determined drive to equal or replace the *Times* as the nation's leading newspaper. Does Macy's conspire with Gimbels? Neither do Ben Bradlee and Abe Rosenthal. To suppose, as Richard Nixon did, that such hard-charging competitors together "decided that they would have to take that particular line"—to "get Nixon," he meant—is simply paranoid. If the "fraternity" ever made such a decision, why did the rest of the members leave it mostly to Bradlee and the Post to try to "get Nixon" for Watergate during the crucial months from June 1972 until the election in November?

But the real point is that the exact opposite of "conspiracy" or "fraternity"—competition—is a major limitation on the power of the press in America. Agnew was not wrong to assert that because of closings and mergers of newspapers over the years. "Many, many strong independent voices have been stilled in this country." Obviously, the nation is the poorer for the loss of the New York *Herald Tribune, Life,* the *Saturday Evening Post.* The twelve dailies that were being published in New York City before the long newspaper strike of 1963 have been sadly reduced to three. But there is much evidence that the trend toward newspaper failures has been reversed and that newspapers are flourishing in America—at last count 1768 dailies plus any number of weeklies and semi-weeklies. However, 97.5 percent of the dailies have no in-town competition and there are fewer than fifty American cities with competing daily newspapers.

Newspaper independence also has been diminishing in another sense—the growing prevalence of chain ownership. In

1930, only 16 percent of American daily newspapers, with 43 percent of total daily circulation, were chain-operated. By 1960, 30 percent of all dailies, with 46 percent of newspaper circulation, had been brought into chains; today, 60 percent of all dailies, with 71 percent of circulation, are controlled by chains. The biggest in number of newspapers—73—is the Gannett chain; the most circulation—3,725,000—is claimed by the 34 papers of the Knight-Ridder chain, itself the product of a merger between two chains.

Worse, 52 percent of national circulation is supplied by the twenty-five largest chains, and the bigger chains are beginning to swallow the smaller chains—as Samuel I. Newhouse did in 1976 when he added the eight Booth newspapers in Michigan to the twenty-two he already owned, making his chain second in circulation nationally, with 3,530,000 readers.

But Newhouse does not impose editorial unanimity on his newspapers and most chain operators grant their individual newspapers considerable editorial autonomy. Chain formation and expansion seem mostly a financial rather than a journalistic or a political operation. The disappearance of so many weak competitors has made surviving dailies attractive to purchasers, combined operations offer many opportunities for cost reductions, and most mergers and acquisitions turn out to be advantageous stock operations rather than cash transactions aimed at journalistic and political power.

Some chain proprietors may even agree privately with Lord Thomson of Fleet, whose international chain controls fifty-seven American newspapers, mostly small ones, and who once described his operations as follows:

"I buy newspapers to make money to buy more newspapers to make more money. As for editorial content, that's the stuff you separate the ads with."

That attitude surely does little for the quality of newspapers so published. But some other chains—that of *The New York Times* is one I know about—have tended to interfere with local editorial control only to *improve* the quality of some of the newspapers they own. As to newspaper quality, therefore, chain ownership is a mixed bag, and some of the best American newspapers—*Newsday,* for instance, and the *Philadelphia Inquirer*—are chain-owned.

And there are a lot of chains; if 60 percent of dailies are chain-operated, it is not by two or three but by 168 multiple ownerships. Thus, while financial ownership of newspapers certainly is concentrated in fewer hands (although often available publicly in the stock markets), it still is rather widely dispersed; and within the chains considerable diversity of editorial opinion and news coverage usually exists.

Representative Morris Udall of Arizona is sponsoring useful legislation to help preserve independent local ownership through tax incentives. The profitable Nashville *Tennesseean,* for example, is principally owned by Mrs. Lucile Evans, widow of the late Silliman Evans, Sr., who was in her seventies in 1977. Her son, Amon C. Evans, president of the company, would be better off financially to arrange an exchange of stock with a major chain than to pay estate taxes at his mother's death; but the notably independent *Tennesseean* would pass out of the family's hands into chain ownership. The Udall bill would permit trusts to be set up to absorb some of the current revenues of such a newspaper to pay future estate-tax liabilities and avoid tax-forced sales to chains.

The weeding out of so many once-competitive newspapers and the trend toward chain operations have not yet eliminated competition from the American press—far from it. Competition flourishes, and it limits the theoretical power of the press in at least two powerful ways.

Most important, competitive editorial control of various organs of news and opinion rather effectively inhibits any one of them—or any "fraternity" that might actually form among some—from distorting and coloring the news to its own liking. There are just too many other publications and broadcasters who would not go along and who would act as counterweights in public opinion.

If, for example, *The Washington Post* had really set out to "get Nixon" with unfounded or ill-supported Watergate stories in the fall of 1972, such stories could have been refuted by the administration, and other newspapers surely would have printed any documented refutations available to them. The knowledge of that in itself would have deterred the *Post* or any newspaper from such a reckless and unethical course. As it was, the Nixon administration could *not* refute—only deny and denounce—most of what the *Post* printed, and gradually other newspapers began following in the *Post*'s footsteps.

On at least two occasions, however, this sort of "negative competition" helped scotch two potentially explosive stories concerning the Nixon administration that had appeared in *The New York Times*. One, printed years before his ultimate disgrace, reported that Spiro T. Agnew, just before becoming governor of Maryland, had been involved in questionable land dealings involving the approaches to a new bridge over the Chesapeake Bay to the Eastern Shore, and that as governor he had remained as a shareholder and member of the board of a bank over which he had some regulatory authority. The other story reported that Secretary of the Treasury John B. Connally, Jr., while governor of Texas, had received payments from the Sid Richardson oil interests, which he previously had served as counsel and estate executor.

Connally and Agnew—and, in Agnew's case, Richard Nixon—strenuously protested the articles, denied wrongdoing, produced plausible accounts to explain the facts reported by the *Times*, and found ready access to other publications and broadcasters to make their case. Other news organizations, if they investigated these reports, apparently could not take the stories beyond the *Times*'s disclosures. Thus, competitors' reluctance or inability to "match" or "top" these stories, as well as their hospitality to Agnew's and Connally's explanations, limited to the point of negating the effect of the *Times*'s publication.

During the 1976 election campaign, for another example, *The Washington Post* printed an exclusive dispatch, shortly before the Republican National Convention, that Ronald Reagan and his supporters had all but given up hope of defeating President Ford for the nomination, and were only going through the motions of challenging him. That didn't jibe with what other political reporters were hearing; no one else followed the lead of the *Post*'s prominently displayed exclusive; and the Reagan camp's persuasive refutations were widely published and broadcast. The *Post* rapidly—in newspaper jargon—"climbed down" from its exposed position. Reagan's strong challenge at the convention subsequently bore out other papers' reluctance to accept the *Post* story.

Such cross-checking will happen less often locally, where many press and broadcasting monopolies exist, than among the larger newspapers. William Loeb's outrageously slanted *Union-Leader* in Manchester, New Hampshire, is a case in point. But even in that instance the *Boston Globe*'s sizable circulation in

New Hampshire, as well as vigorous competition from the *Concord Monitor* and other local publications, acts as something of a balance to Loeb's fulminations.

The Federal Communications Commission is requiring the breakup—at least the diminution—of local communications monopolies where they involve the ownership of both press and broadcasting outlets by the same person or company. Even in such monopolies, of course, some publishers and broadcasters can be sensitive to all shades of opinion. When I worked in Winston-Salem, for example, the morning *Journal* supported the "wets" in a hotly fought liquor election. But the editorial-page editor of the afternoon *Sentinel,* Santford Martin, a devout "dry," was at the same time permitted by the owner of both papers, Gordon Gray, to oppose liquor stores in the city.

Years later, when Gray sold the *Journal* and *Sentinel* to a chain—sad day for their alumni!—a television station operated by the company had to be separated from the newspapers and sold to still a third party. The FCC rule is that such monopolies cannot be sold; thus, when Joe Albritten bought *The Washington Star,* he was faced with the necessity to sell its prosperous television station, Channel Five in Washington. But without Channel Five revenues, the *Star* probably could not survive. Albritten solved the problem brilliantly by trading Channel Five for a television station in Oklahoma City, preserving revenues but not monopoly.

The FCC rule, too, is helping preserve useful competition in American journalism. But the second manner in which that competition limits the supposed power of the press is not so constructive. The sad fact is that many of the worst sins of newspapers and broadcasters are committed under the pressures of competition. If one newspaper or magazine or broadcaster comes up with an "exclusive"—even more so if there is a series of them—its competitors come under intense pressures to match or top the story. This is particularly characteristic of the top levels of the socalled "Eastern Establishment press"—between the *Times* and the *Post,* for instance, among the networks, or between *Time* and *Newsweek.*

Under such pressures, many a story with insufficient documentation or carelessly written or violating some nicety of privacy or ethics, or that is simply incorrect, has been rushed into print. Without fierce competitive pressure, it might never have been published or at least not until it had been whipped into proper shape.

When faulty stories do get into print, and turn out to be false or misleading or overstated, not only their unfortunate subjects are damaged; so is the general credibility of newspapers. Lack of credibility with readers, of course, is a profound limitation on the power of the press; if people don't believe what they read or hear or see, then the supposedly prodigious ability of the press to shape public opinion comes to little. To the extent that the press discredits itself with inaccuracies and wild swings, it ironically limits its own theoretically vast powers—and those inaccuracies and wild swings often are the direct result of competition.

An example was the 1977 race between the usually sensible New York *Daily News* and the *New York Post* to be first and most colorful with the news of the search for—later the arrest of—"Son of Sam," the so-called ".44-caliber killer." The *Post*'s acquisition in 1976 by Rupert Murdoch—publisher of some of Britain's and the United States' wildest tabloids—had set off circulation and news wars between the two New York dailies; the "Son of Sam" case turned this competition into perhaps the hottest headline scramble since the long-gone days of "yellow journalism" and the "extra" edition.

The two newspapers featured star reporters urging the killer to surrender to them; fevered speculation as to when and where he might strike next; such largely unsupported yarns as the *Post*'s breathless announcement that outraged Mafia hoods had taken up the hunt for the murderer, whose victims were mostly young women; a *Post* headline screamed that "No One Is Safe from the Son of Sam!" After the arrest of one David Berkowitz—as a suspect generally assumed to be guilty—both papers purchased letters from his former girl friend; the letters suggested mental instability. Local television joined this saturnalia with some equally hard-breathing coverage.

So much publicity obviously endangered Berkowitz's right to a fair trial. Floyd Abrams, one of the country's foremost First Amendment lawyers and a strong advocate of press disclosure, said flatly that "if [Berkowitz] asks for a change of venue from this city and doesn't get it, that's reversible error in my judgment." Endangering the suspect's rights thus endangered the community's right to have him convicted, if found guilty.

The "Son of Sam" coverage raised other questions, too—about reporters becoming "part of the story," about "buying" news, even about reporters violating the law to obtain information, since one reporter and two photographers were arrested after apparently having made a surreptitious entry into Berkowitz's sealed apartment. Sadly, the episode reinforced the doubts of those who had believed all along that the press lacked restraint, balance, a sense of fair play, ethical standards. Along with David Berkowitz's rights, press credibility suffered a damaging blow.

In 1976, for another example of competitive excess, after exposure of the fact that Representative Wayne Hays of Ohio had placed a woman on the government payroll, in return for which she mainly gave him her sexual favors, a positive eruption of "sex in Washington" stories followed. The trend was spurred by the coincidental arrest in Salt Lake City of a Utah congressman on charges of soliciting a prostitute—who turned out to be an undercover policewoman. This story was inevitably linked with the "sex in Washington" pieces, although it had nothing whatever to do with Washington. For weeks, the impression was created that the nation's capital was a veritable sinkhole of sex and iniquity—although in the end, Hay's case was about the only one of real significance.

Again, when Bob Woodward of the *Post* reported in 1977 that King Hussein of Jordan had been on the payroll of the CIA for many years, and had received millions of American dollars, other newspapers rushed to get in on *that* story with revelations of their own about other world leaders who had been allegedly on the take from the CIA. None of these charges was proven true, although some probably were; President Carter complained that the episode had kept him busy writing letters of apology to foreign leaders who contended they were falsely accused.

In the early sixties, in the Washington bureau of the *Times*, the period around 9:00 P.M. used to be known as the Maggie Higgins Hour. The *Herald Tribune* came out about an hour earlier than the *Times,* and Marguerite Higgins was its star Washington reporter. By *Times* standards, perhaps somewhat stuffier then than now, she tended to be freewheeling, but was an able reporter indeed. Her frequently exclusive stories obviously had to be checked out, and the Maggie Higgins Hour arrived when the bureau phone would start ringing with calls from New York on the latest Higgins headlines, just out in the *Herald Trib.* Could the bureau match?

Obviously, after 9:00 P.M., with only a night staff on duty and many sources of information unavailable, that kind of competitive pressure can have any of several results, not all of them desirable. Maybe an exclusive story can't be checked out sufficiently to prove it right or wrong; if it's of sufficient importance, the paper trying to catch up may have to print a cautious repetition of the story, attributed to its rival. This is not only embarrassing but risks spreading a faulty story. To ignore the whole thing risks missing a true story to which readers were entitled.

If the opposing paper's "exclusive" checks out wrong, what should the other paper do? To print a correction of someone else's story may only give the yarn more notoriety; not to do so lets stand an inaccuracy or a misunderstanding. Neither course is particularly helpful to journalistic credibility.

If the story checks out properly, the real trouble may follow. The editors of the paper that didn't originally have the story may bring heavy pressures on its reporters not just to catch up but to "top," or "find another angle"—improve on the original in *some* way. That kind of pressure can produce serious errors, overstatements, and faulty conclusions. Not that a reputable editor would knowingly publish an inaccurate story; the almost certain exposure of the inaccuracy would make that risky as well as improper. Rather, under the pressures of competition, hasty judgments can replace meticulous editorial standards.

Just as the urge to compete—that is, to win—can lead a football player to jump offside or even slug an opponent in the heat of battle, so the urge to compete—to get ahead—can cause newspapers and broadcasters to breach their standards in ways that would never happen in conditions of calm reflection and unhurried judgment.

I can recall with pleasure one minor triumph over competitive pressure. I was in Hyannis, Massachusetts, with the White House press during one of the innumerable weekends President Kennedy spent there. Having filed a "Kennedy's day" story I believed to be accurate, I passed a bibulous evening with colleagues and turned in happily. But the phone rang about midnight; a nervous editor informed me that the Associated Press had filed a somewhat different version of my story. What should be done about it? (Had he sent me a telegram instead, it would have inquired, after setting forth the conflict, in supercilious cablese: "How please?")

I had long since learned that editors feel safer when their stories conform to those of the A.P. After all, *everybody* gets the

A.P. and if your story conforms to everybody else's story, you can't get into trouble over it—not alone, anyway. But I knew, too, that the generally admirable wire service was not a "truth machine"—far from it that particular weekend.

"Don't worry about it," I told my editor. "My story's right and anyway, I just left the A.P. It's down in the bar, drunk."

Competition is not the only built-in limitation on the powers of the press. Another is what I call "dailiness" and my colleague James Reston once called "catching history on the wing."

Both phrases refer to the inexorable onrush of diverse events that swamps modern news organizations. The communications revolution has only poured more information into the hopper, and the resulting problem is not unlike the proverbial difficulty of putting ten gallons of whisky into a five-gallon jug.

Immense areas have been added to expected news coverage—more than twice as many governments as the number that founded the United Nations, for example; outer-space exploration; energy and environment; consumerism; and many others. No part of the world is too remote for coverage. *The New York Times,* for one, doesn't even try anymore to be what it was founded to be—"the newspaper of record." The record of events has become too extensive for any one news organization to keep.

All sorts of problems derive from the avalanche of information—the raw material from which newspapers and news broadcasts are fashioned. Selection is, of course, the first of them—a process that boils down to deciding what's important and what isn't, within the limited means available for publishing or broadcasting. For television, the selection of news to present is further complicated by the question of what film is available to complement information.

But even a reasonably intelligent reduction of the avalanche to "all the news that's fit to print" leaves a greater problem—how to fit the selected news into the continuing stream of history, make sense of it in the light of yesterday's news, and prepare readers for what may therefore be coming tomorrow. Compared to this problem, merely selecting what's most important on a given day is simple, although never easy; and most news organizations, in my judgment, don't do well at this sensitive and subtle task of putting yesterday's events in longer and deeper perspective.

The avalanche metaphor is useful to convey the magnitude of

the dailiness problem; but a more accurate general comparison is to waves pounding one after another upon the beach. The waves of information never stop coming; each day a new one rolls in—each hour, really; and before the recipient picks himself up from one he or she is bowled over by another. The result is that yesterday's wave often gets short shrift, while a news organization copes with today's and keeps an eye out for tomorrow's.

There's not enough time to absorb and analyze news coming in in such an overwhelming fashion; if there were, there are not enough columns in the paper or minutes in the broadcast to present it, fully rounded and clearly explained. Yesterday's sensation is old news today—and never was properly dealt with. And anyway, the rigidities and rituals of news presentation, whether in print or on the air, tend to make each day's news seem about as important or as unimportant as any other day's news, unless closely analyzed. Whatever is on the *Times* front page, or leads the Chancellor-Brinkley report, automatically becomes important—at least as important but probably no more so than what was there yesterday, or will be tomorrow.

All the problems of dailiness are compounded further by human failure—inadequate preparation, unqualified personnel, slipshod methods, paralyzing attitudes and traditions—as well as by the subjectivity of the process. It is not unusual to find a *Times* front-page story played down in *The Washington Post* and not played at all in some other paper; my judgment on the Howard Unruh story all those years ago in *The Robesonian* may have been a little out of the ordinary, but editors can and do see things differently, there are no real rules to guide them, and much of the time the news is not so obvious as a man biting a dog, or Hitler invading Poland.

Dailiness is the process by which a Cuban missile crisis wipes out press and public consciousness of a racial battle at Ole Miss. Dailiness causes an election in one country to be all but ignored because of a revolution the next day in another. Dailiness, shrewdly seized upon by press manipulators, can erase the memory of a damaging headline—Ford Accused/On Boycott—by the manufacturing of a helpful headline soon after—Ford Approves/Arms for Israel. The second is all too seldom placed in proper context with the first. Dailiness turns an editor's attention to an earthquake in Turkey before he or she has really dealt with yesterday's hurricane in Guatemala. Dailiness, as exemplified by my coverage of Johnson's Tonkin Gulf speech, often creates news impressions that seriously mislead the public.

As a limitation on the power of the press, dailiness functions by restricting the intellectual coherence, if any, of daily news presentation. With rare and honorable exceptions, news organizations must run hard merely to pass along the daily surface events of a war in Lebanon, a political campaign in the United States (actually hundreds of them), an incipient revolution in South Africa, an economic slump in Britain—each following upon the other relentlessly, or occurring more or less simultaneously. As a result, a newspaper's explanations and analyses of these events, why they happen, what they mean, what could or should have happened instead, are almost sure to be limited and shallow. Moreover, the coverage itself often tends to be confusing rather than clarifying; it lacks the capacity to distinguish the importance of one event from that of another, and thrives on oversimplification. Such coverage earns the deserved scorn of authorities on the subject matter and leaves much of the general public dissatisfied or exasperated, partially informed at best, misinformed at worst.

Dailiness therefore undermines the power of the press significantly, lowering its prestige, diminishing its usefulness, damaging its credibility—and diffusing its supposedly irresistible effect on public opinion. Spiro Agnew himself never did such damage to the press as dailiness does daily.

Another limitation on the American press is the essential dilettantism of its men and women.

Changes in the nature and scope of news coverage—the postwar interest in science and technology, for one excellent example—have forced reporters into much more specialization than once was the case. Editors now concede their need for science reporters, economic reporters, consumer and legal specialists, urbanologists, and the like; and although many of these are reporters who have merely picked up a specialty, men like Walter Sullivan, the science editor of *The New York Times,* and David Broder, the political editor of *The Washington Post,* would grace any college faculty.

Such genuinely knowledgeable specialists remain the exception in a craft that is dominated by the general reporter on a "beat," a far different thing from a specialist bringing expertise to a specific subject—the Defense Department, for instance, or a city's financial agencies. Of couse, some reporters have been able to master several beats in long careers; my able colleague John Finney has been a science reporter, State Department correspondent, U.S. Senate correspondent, Pentagon correspondent, and distinguished himself at all. He subsequently became the Washington bureau assignment editor for *The New York Times*.

But not many reporters can handle so many challenging assignments. Most tend, as a result, to absorb their knowledge of their beats only from the officials or executives or professionals or spokesmen they are covering. That, all too frequently, produces a reporter who may know a substantial amount about numerous subjects, but who is not really expert in any—and whose knowledge may be warped by the interests and attitudes of those sources who imparted most of it to him or her.

Nor are most beats composed of definable subject matter, which means that greater specialization is not necessarily the antidote for dilettantism. What kind of specialist should cover the Pentagon for a serious newspaper? A former military man? A graduate of a defense think-tank like the Rand Corporation? An international-affairs student and strategist? An aerospace or weapons technologist? A student of budgeting procedures and the political linkages between Congress and the armed services and the bureaucrats? Obviously, it would be nice to have a reporter who could wear all those hats; or to assign a group of reporters representing among them all those specialties; but alas! not even the *Times* or the *Post* disposes of that kind of man-and womanpower.

Similarly, a State Department correspondent ideally would know much about the domestic economy and American politics, which have great impact on foreign policy. And should a government antitrust action properly be covered by an economics specialist or a legal reporter or both? Besides, in Washington and even in most state capitals, only the largest newspapers, the networks, and the wire services can afford more than small staffs; in other bureaus, many of which are one-man or one-woman, reporters *have* to be generalists, with wide but thin knowledge of many subjects. As noted earlier, this increases their dependence on official government sources of news and makes it difficult for any but the best of them to do a tough, challenging, skeptical job, or much outside research and study.

It used to be—sometimes still is—the proudest boast of press traditionalists that "a good reporter can do a good story on any subject." And indeed some of the great general reporters—Peter Kihss of *The New York Times,* Homer Bigart of the New York *Herald Tribune*, later the *Times,* Peter Lisagor and Ed Leahy of the *Chicago Daily News* are four I have known—justified that boast time and again. Bigart's work was as distinguished in uncovering starving children in the backwaters and tenements of America as it was when the South Vietnamese government threw him in jail for reporting too critically on its ineptitude and repression, or when he went to Israel to cover the Eichmann trial.

But what that boast comes down to most of the time is that a "good reporter" can put together six or eight hundred acceptable words on any subject and do it against a deadline. He or she "covers" the story, hits its high spots, manages a quote or two, maybe a line of color, and a paragraph of official-source interpretation, and gets it all done with a slight gilding of expertise and in time for the first edition. That kind of skill is highly admired in most newsrooms, and well it should be; it holds newspapers together and gets them out on time.

It still is not necessarily the same thing as producing a really good story—one that actually explains what happened, and why, that raises the right questions even if the full answers can't be had (and confesses that fact, if necessary), that offers nuance and subtlety and shades of meaning as well as simplifications, and that is literately written as well. Any good reporter usually *cannot* write such a story unless he or she already has a thorough grasp of the subject and personalities involved, as well as the context in which they interacted. Ironically, a training and a reputation as a "good reporter," able to handle any subject on short notice, may have precluded the development of precisely that kind of grasp on any particular subject.

Russell Baker, one of the best of reporters before he became the *Times*'s resident satirist, once devised the ideal journalism school. It would have, Baker decreed, but one course: a student would be required to stand in front of a closed door for six hours, at the end of which the door would open, an official spokesman would look out, and speak two words—"No comment." Whereupon the door would close and the student would be required to go to the typewriter and turn out six hundred words against a deadline.

Every reporter will recognize that problem; and any "good

reporter" could pass the test—far better than in the same time he or she could absorb some complex story, economic, say, or having to do with the urban crisis, and write about it intelligently and lucidly. But it is the latter test, rather than Baker's, that reporters in the real world of the news most often have to pass. That all too few can do it with more than a gentleman's C is one more inherent reason why the American press is neither as persuasive nor as respected as it would have to be if it really were to have "unchecked" power.

When I first went to Washington for the *Times*, it was supposedly to cover "the regulatory agencies." As I quickly found out, all reporters coming to Washington for the *Times* in those days got that assignment; but as in my case few ever actually covered the regulatory agencies, because they didn't really make a coherent beat—but also for the more important reason that their work was so largely dull, routine, and unexciting—albeit important—usually without glamorous personalities or splashy headline stories.

That suggests another limitation on the power of the American press—its definition of news. "Man bites dog" is the most serviceable statement of it, for what the press is constantly in search of is action, movement, new developments, surprises, sudden reversals, "catch-up football," the ups and downs of fate, the cataclysms of nature, the perversities and follies of mankind. Even sober-sided coverage of government and politics is imbued with the search for drama and conflict.

A two-term senator safely being elected to a third term, for example, is hardly news at all, as American journalists define news; but if some unknown suddenly appears to be upsetting the same senator, the political press will flock in and cover the story exhaustively. Yet, depending on the constituency involved, the feat of that senator in making himself politically invulnerable might be a greater value in understanding politics and American society than the relatively commonplace story of one more young upstart knocking off an old head. What most appears as news to the press is often stale stuff in the long history of human events.

Much that transpires in the world—some of it of great importance—is not in the nature of action, motion, upset, man bites dog. And these events, or processes, certainly the absence of action, seldom rate much notice in the press. Nothing is *happening*—although that in itself may amount to action, as when, say, a third-world country does *not* have a birth-control program, or a city is *not* afflicted with high and rising rates of crime.

A classic example is that of American prisons. More than a quarter of a million persons populate these grim fortresses on any given day; most Americans advocate sending more criminals to them for longer terms; and their cost is astronomical—over $12,000 per year per inmate in New York, for domiciling and security alone, before any "rehabilitation" or "corrections" program is paid for. There is much persuasive evidence—widely discussed in professional and intellectual publications—that for that kind of money American society is getting little in the way of protection and almost nothing in the way of lower crime rates.

But in American newspapers, the prison system exists—it is only a slight exaggeration to say—only when there is (a) an escape, particularly of anyone convicted for violent crime; (b) a prison-related sensation—as when, say, an inmate on parole or work-release commits a crime. He or she may be the only work-release subject in a thousand to stumble into trouble; but that one, not the successful nine hundred and ninety-nine, will get the headlines and the work-release program very likely will come under instant editorial and political fire.

But when "nothing's happening" at the prison, it isn't news—although revolt may be generating itself, brutality may be rampant, Malcolm X may be reforming himself into a powerful leader, ambitious "rehabilitation" schemes may be failing or being abandoned, drug traffic, violence, rape may be pervasive, and race warfare may be commonplace. Not to mention the $12,000 per year per inmate of taxpayers' money being mostly wasted. Nothing is *happening*.

This might not matter so much except that, so far as the press is usually concerned, "nothing is happening" in all too many other vital American institutions and processes. Many powerful business organizations, for example, can influence millions of lives through unreported internal developments. When a major corporation runs publicly afoul of the antipollution laws, that makes a big story. But the press seldom if ever makes much of an effort to find out *before* the fact what such a corporation is planning, to defeat with publicity what may be the despoiling of a river or the ruination of a community by some building project or obnoxious manufacturing process.

"Nothing is happening," too, in an unfortunate number of cases, if the information is turned up by the "provincial press," rather than by *The New York Times* or *The Washington Post* or one of the news magazines or networks. These organizations have the power to focus national attention on almost any development they concentrate on; but if *The Des Moines Register* details manipulation and price-fixing in the nation's multi-billion dollar commodity exchanges, as it did in 1975, readers of the *Times,* the *Post,* and the news weeklies may never know about it because these organizations don't necessarily pick up on what's printed out in what they think of as "the boondocks."

In *The Washington Monthly* for March 1977, Nick Kotz, formerly a reporter for the *Register,* then for the *Post,* pointed out that the so-called national press never had paid attention to a Knight Newspapers series, published in September 1976, about the highway-construction politics practiced in Georgia by Governor Jimmy Carter and Bert Lance; or to a *Philadelphia Inquirer* exposé of Internal Revenue Service field-office practices; or to *Newsday*'s reportage on the Nixon administration's improper use of federal funds to support the maritime industry. Unfortunately, all too often, it isn't news if it isn't discovered by the *Post* or the *Times* or Walter Cronkite.

In 1971 Frank Wright of the *Minneapolis Tribune* Washington bureau won the Worth Bingham Award for an outstanding series that cited chapter and verse on how dairymen's groups had made enormous political contributions to Richard Nixon's forthcoming re-election campaign, and on how dairy price supports subsequently had been raised. Except for the award, Wright's stories attracted little attention; but when the metropolitan press began to focus on Watergate a year later, the milk-price controversy became a major element of the story, and of Nixon's downfall.

Hospitals, mental institutions, schools—like prisons—all are usually not covered by the press, except when involved in sensations of some kind; the same applies to numerous obscure city, state, and federal bureaucracies that are no more exciting or "newsy"—usually less—than the federal regulatory agencies.

The women's movement had to institutionalize itself, burn bras, and put forward challenging spokespersons before the daily and broadcast press paid much attention. Consumerism was nowhere in the news columns until Ralph Nader gave it a star spokesman, some underdog glamour, and an institutional structure. From the early fifties onward, the press amply covered the civil-rights movement with its forceful spokespeople, its marches and demonstrations, its victories and defeats, its numerous organizations; but at the same time one of the great migrations of history—of blacks from the fields of the South into the great cities of America—was changing the nature of those cities forever, while going virtually unremarked in the press until the change had been wrought. Effective as it was, the civil-rights movement—so thoroughly covered—may have had less significance than the migration—so nearly uncovered.

Again, therefore, the press's concentration on action, sensation, measurable developments, organized movements, personalities, surprises—natural though that concentration is, and no doubt congenial to most readers—limits the usefulness and the impact of the so-called media. When great developments in American society can take place almost unnoticed by major American newspapers and broadcasters, and when important institutions and processes find the American press mostly indifferent to their functioning, it's hard to make the case for that press as a superpower.

It seems to be recognized more by critics on the political left than by others that newspapers, radio, and television are full-fledged participants in the free-enterprise system. They are businesses, in the fullest sense of the word, and somewhere in the office of every publisher and network president the proverbial "bottom line" works its inevitable influence.

In any discussion of the press as business—particularly when it is being argued, as I shall, that the press as business is another limitation on the press as powerhouse—two clichés have to be dealt with. The first is that the press deliberately does unethical and unprincipled things to "sell papers," and the other is that advertisers dictate content. But, like most clichés, these contain enough truth to sustain them far past any real relevance.

The sensational "Son of Sam" coverage by the *New York Post* and the *Daily News* showed that a rousing crime story, expertly "hyped," can still "sell papers." *Advertising Age* reported on August 15, 1977, that *Post* sales—normally somewhat in excess of 600,000 daily—had risen steadily during the "Sam" hysteria, with about 100,000 extra sales the day the paper ran a police sketch of the hunted man.

When David Berkowitz was arrested and charged with the "Son of Sam" murders, *Post* sales for the day approached the 1,020,000 record the paper had set on June 5, 1968, when the report of the shooting of Robert F. Kennedy was featured. The *News*, on the day of Berkowitz's arrest, printed an extra 350,000 copies. Even the *Times*, with coverage that was sober by comparison, ran off an extra 35,000 copies, according to *Advertising Age*.

In general, however, the idea of "selling papers" with spectacular stories is something of a hangover from an earlier, pre-TV era. Newspapers like most of those run by Rupert Murdoch still operate largely in the old "yellow" tradition, but they are the exception rather than the rule. The *Daily News*, for example, is an excellent newspaper that rarely stoops to the level of its "Sam" coverage and did so in that case only under the goading of Murdoch's *Post*.

Of course, newspapers, television, and radio try to give their audiences what they think is wanted, and at their worst pander shamelessly to what they perceive as the lowest common denominator of audience taste. That is not much different from the sales practices of any business. And it's true that newspapers engage in intense circulation competition, as the broadcasters do in ratings wars, as all businesses do in sales efforts.

But the phrase "selling papers" conjures up particular tricks of pandering or vulgarity to boost sales—a picture of a woman in the electric chair, for example, or of some brutally murdered person, or a headline proclaiming some horror story—"Killer Bees/Move North" in Murdoch's San Antonio paper is a classic of the genre. That sort of thing *did* "sell papers" in the old days of the penny press and "extra" editions; and it did again in the "Son of Sam" frenzy in New York. But those days are mostly gone; today, street and newsstand sales are a small part of most newspapers' circulation, which now fluctuates less according to news developments than to sales and distribution efforts.

It's often charged, for example, that *The New York Times* published the Pentagon Papers in 1971 just to "sell papers." In the first place, the Papers didn't sell papers; circulation records don't disclose any significant rise at the time. In the second place, the costs of such a massive undertaking—editorial preparation over a period of months, clearing space in the paper that could have gone partially to remunerative advertising, legal defense—were heavier than any conceivable circulation returns could have offset. In the third place, all that was well known to *Times* executives before they decided to publish the Pentagon Papers. (Profits from a later book publication may have put the entire operation modestly into the black.)

As for advertisers' influence:

Undoubtedly it exists, and perhaps to a considerable degree on small, more vulnerable news outlets—for instance, those Robbins Mills ads I used to run in the *Sandhill Citizen* more than a quarter of a century ago. But many newspapers and broadcasters have more advertising than they can handle, and have no real need to pander in some shabby way to advertisers' interests. It's true, for example, that when *The New York Times* in recent years decided to seek ads from major grocery stores—which produce sizable revenues—part of the resulting arrangement was that the *Times* would begin to run more articles on food and dining and wine-buying; but it's also true that the *Times*'s new food and "living" sections are literate, informative, and by no means "puff jobs" for any particular advertiser. Over the years, moreover, the *Times* has rarely hesitated to *remove* ads from the paper when a major story demanded more space than normally available.

No doubt the *Times* and every other newspaper have occasionally altered or even omitted a story to avoid real or imagined offense to some major advertiser. Many, like the *Times,* are in the contradictory position of accepting lucrative cigarette advertising while criticizing smoking (as injurious to health) on their editorial pages. It's probably no accident that companies with enormous ad budgets—say, Coca-Cola—don't suffer much muckraking from the press or television.

My point is not that deference to advertisers doesn't exist, particularly on smaller papers heavily dependent on a few major ad customers, but that most newspapers are by no means such slaves to their advertisers as myth would have it. Direct pressures from advertisers, in my opinion, play a relatively small part in editorial decisions and content—and would be bitterly resented by most publishers and editors and reporters. And to the extent that it exists, I believe the sin is more nearly one of omission than of commission.

That newspapers and broadcasters are businesses, however,

is an important and limiting fact of their strictly journalistic lives. Payrolls have to be met, taxes have to be paid, stockholders want fair returns, and costs—notably that of newsprint—keep on rising like everyone else's. As a consequence, most publishers and broadcasters have to put profits ahead of political power; the long-term stability of the enterprise is likely to mean more to most of them as businessmen than any particular effect they might achieve by editorial power—say, the election of a certain candidate or the passage of certain legislation. Not that publishers or network executives are uninterested in such editorial power, but the demands of the *businesses* for which they are responsible make it impossible for them to pursue editorial power at any cost and to whatever lengths.

Perhaps even more important, the press in America is a free-enterprise institution, and that gives it an Establishment character. Its executives are respected, usually affluent figures in any community; its institutions share fundamentally in the economic fortunes, good or ill, of the nation and the locality; its stake *as a free enterprise* in the established economic, political, and social systems is as great as that of any other free enterprise of comparable value (no conceivable revolution, from right or left, would leave the press in America to private ownership and control, or preserve the First Amendment). The growth in recent years of "underground" and "alternative" publications—most of them leftish—is in itself graphic evidence of the Establishment nature of the conventional press. And that's true no matter what the editorial-page policy of some newspapers or the personal politics of editors and reporters.

In one sense, of course, being part of the Establishment may testify to the power of the press. In a stronger sense, I believe, to be part of the Establishment is to accept certain real limitations, conventions, attitudes; to be part of the Establishment is to play fundamentally on the team, not to strike out for more singular glory and power. That Establishment of which the American press is usually a card-carrying member is therefore one of the most effective checks on the theoretical powers of the media.

What *is* the power of the press, anyway? Patently, it isn't the power, say, to send troops to Vietnam or bring them home, to cut or raise taxes, to appoint high officials or manage the national economy.

Is it the power, then, to *cause* such things to be done, or done in a certain manner? Tom Bethell, a Washington editor of *Harper's,* and a thoughtful press critic, wrote in the January 1977 issue of the magazine that in confrontations between "government secrecy and the people's right to know," the media "must always triumph, because they have securely in their grasp the means of forming a public opinion sympathetic to their cause."

The media, Bethell asserted, "very largely control public opinion with the same channels of communication that they use to present the news." He wrote also of "those people who own or control the means of producing public opinion."

Clearly, if the media can "produce" or "form" or "control" public opinion, then the media—perhaps slowly and tediously, but surely—can cause just about anything to happen that the media want to happen. But is that really the case? And even if it were, doesn't it presuppose that the media are monolithically united on what they want?

Taking these questions in reverse, I see no evidence to support the idea that the media will ever be that united on any important question. Even on the press's rights and privileges under the First Amendment—to which Bethell was specifically addressing his article—there's plenty of dispute *within the press*. Both *The New York Times* and *The Washington Post,* for example, were quite cool editorially to Daniel Schorr's publication of the Pike report on the CIA. CBS made no effort to defend Schorr other than legally, or to retain his services. Numerous journalists questioned his action—as some had questioned publication of the Pentagon Papers.

And as one who has confronted many an audience of nonjournalists on the question of First Amendment interpretation, I can testify flatly that even on a matter of such fundamental importance to the media, those same media have abysmally failed—if they've tried—to "produce" or "form" a public opinion favorable to them. Quite the opposite, I'd say.

Even if the media could be monolithically united—and on what controversial subject has that ever happened, or is it likely to happen?—it's not clear that public opinion could then be easily formed or controlled. Highly organized opinion-forming campaigns to make people stop smoking or start using seat belts in their autos or practice birth control haven't come close to succeeding—granted that these campaigns are not all-pervasive. Even in authoritarian societies like Nazi Germany or the Soviet Union, with absolutely controlled media, unanimous by decree in their opinion-forming efforts, a police-state apparatus, from concentration camps to the midnight knock, has proved necessary to control, even more to "produce" opinion.

Literally hundreds of newspapers have editorialized against cigarette smoking; their headlines warn of its dangers; some of them no longer accept cigarette ads; television carries numerous "public service" ads against smoking, and every pack carries its own health warning. But the cigarette companies keep advertising on television, in magazines, in many newspapers, on billboards—the cigarette sales keep going up, particularly among the young.

It may be argued that it isn't necessary for a monolithic media to produce monolithic opinion, in order for the press to have too much power to affect public attitudes. But "affecting" opinion, even greatly, is by no means producing or controlling it. To take only one example, television news coverage no doubt affected public opinion during the 1976 election—but so did the paid advertising of all candidates, the three debates between the two major party candidates, and such directly broadcast events as Ford's White House news conferences and ceremonies. With so many conflicting forces at work on public opinion—not to mention those in the printed press—how can any single force be said to "produce" or "control" opinion?

In fact, the impact of "the media"—far from being that of deliberately forming public opinion—is diffused even within its own organs, as among news, editorial statements, and advertising. It is Balkanized among literally thousands of news organizations—daily and weekly newspapers, television and radio stations. The consequence, in my judgment, is that Woodrow Wilson had it about right when he wrote—before television and radio—that "the news is the atmosphere of events."

I have already called the media "the arena of politics" today. Both atmosphere and arena are environmental terms and perhaps this is the more useful metaphor—the media provide an environment within which things happen and are perceived.

And the way things are perceived—public opinion—undoubtedly produces or at least affects further events.

But the media environment is not everywhere and always the same, any more than the earth's physical environment. Just as cold fronts and high-pressure areas move across the country, rain follows sunshine, and snow falls in Vermont while the weather clears in Connecticut, the media environment changes and conflicts and confounds itself. And that environment does not finally control human behavior and attitude—granted that it has great effect on them, as does the weather—any more than other environmental forces. The experiences and attitudes, even the heredity, of that infinite variety of individuals who perceive what happens within the media environment can't be that easily blotted out or overcome. I doubt seriously if any single media influence was as important in the 1976 election as the basic intention of most Americans either to vote for the conservative, familiar Ford, or to vote for change.

One other point may be relevant here. Reporters, editors, and columnists—all of whom have more to do with the content of newspapers and news broadcasts than publishers and network executives do—are a peculiar breed of cat. Irreverent, skeptical (if not always skeptical enough), broadly albeit dilettantishly informed, competitive, operating in a world somewhat set apart from the ordinary—what is a reporter if not first and foremost a privileged spectator?—the reporter's Mecca is always the story, *not* the more conventional forms of power.

I have never known a reporter who actively sought real political power for himself. Those who may have wanted great economic power surely left the press as soon as they could. Aside from a few television newsmen—former Governor Tom McCall of Oregon, Representative Lionel Van Deerlin of California, and Senator Jesse Helms of North Carolina come to mind—most reporters I've known have made poor politicians when they ventured across the line.

Reporters want *journalistic* power and eminence, all right. Power struggles for important newspaper posts or executive positions within the network news operations are savage and frequent. Beyond that, reporters want to be first with the story, distinguished among their colleagues, well paid, influences or checks upon the mighty, giant-killers perhaps, iconoclasts always. But, basically, they want to catch the scoundrel with his hand in the till—rarely to replace him. Reporters love to be heeded by powerful personages, but most wouldn't know what to do with *actual* power (outside their own news organizations) if they had it; and they hold almost as an article of faith, anyway, that power is dangerous unless closely monitored. By whom? By reporters, of course. The monitoring of power, to a reporter, is more important and exciting by far—and a lot more gratifying—than the exercise of power.

What examples does history offer of a journalist who seized dictatorial power and threw generals and politicians in jail? The breed begins and ends—fortunately and significantly—with Mussolini.

No discussion of the limitations that restrict—however subtly—the power of the American press would be complete if the point were not made that the federal government's "national security" powers profoundly inhibit the national press. This may surprise a nation shocked by publication of the Pentagon Papers and Dan Schorr's release of the Pike report, but these really are exceptions to, rather than examples of, the rule.

Take the case of Daniel Ellsberg and those Pentagon cables with which this chapter begins:

The salient fact is that we didn't print or even write Ellsberg's story, even though I was persuaded of its truth, even though it fitted what was then our emerging knowledge of the government's duplicity concerning Vietnam, and even though Ellsberg actually turned over to us one piece of corroborating evidence. We didn't write or print it because we believed we couldn't.

First, the cables were classified Top Secret. This meant that heavy security protected them physically and psychologically, so that ultimately it was impossible to secure basic documentation. And to have been caught trying, it was then believed, might make a reporter or his source liable to legal action.

Second, without such documentation—the cables themselves—this kind of story has little impact anyway. Perhaps Ellsberg might have produced one or two witnesses to support his story. Ordinarily that would be enough—three persons' testimony—to justify a news story. In this case, had we had such witnesses, they would have had to be anonymous, their charges would have been sensational, the government's credibility would have been at stake. Obviously the reader still would demand, and rightly so, the documentary evidence the *Times* could not supply.

Third, the government had a position of assumed probity and knowledge—more so then than now—from which to declare its version of events, as Westmoreland and Bunker had been doing. It did not have the need for documentation that the press had. The government could claim: "What we say is true; but the documents that prove it are Top Secret; and you'll have to take our word for it." No newspaper or broadcaster can take such a position.

Fourth, there's a mystique about government secrets, not much less powerful now than in 1967 and 1968. The government can and does classify old newspaper clippings, and nobody yet has shown, for example, that publication of the Pentagon Papers "blew" a single secret of any value. Nevertheless, if the government—particularly the President!—labels something secret, Top Secret, or even just "national security" the mystique sets in immediately. The label makes all but sacrosanct whatever it covers. To publish a "secret" or a "national security" matter is at once to invite charges of lack of patriotism, culpable irresponsibility, endangering the nation, and in extreme cases even treason or espionage.

Nixon almost whitewashed Watergate with "national security" claims. Time and again it has been shown that government officials from presidents down will cover anything embarrassing or inconvenient or duplicitous or scandalous with the "national security" label. Yet, the myth persists that the government's secrets are vital, and the national security depends on their being kept.

No newspaper or broadcaster, therefore, lightly violates classification rules or "national security"—not least because editors, publishers, network executives, and most reporters share the mystique of government secrets and a horror of disclosing them. National security—aside from the difficulty of penetrating its far-flung screen—thus becomes a major inhibition on the national press and its supposedly unchecked power.

10

National Delusion

Just as no reporter turns down an interview with the president, no group of editors and reporters turns down a group meeting with a president. And as anyone in the White House soon discovers, such a meeting is one of the best ways to get his views across and create a favorable reception for them among people who are highly likely then to interpret a president to their readers or viewers in the same favorable fashion.

No one on the *New York Times* editorial masthead was surprised, therefore, when in January of 1975 we all received notes from Ron Nessen, President Ford's press secretary, inviting us to lunch. With a certain *Times*-style solemnity, our group gathered in the office of Clifton Daniel, then the Washington bureau chief, and proceeded to the White House in two rented limousines. Like innumerable other visitors before us, we entered by the Southwest Gate, well out of sight of the White House press room in the West Wing, and were driven to the entrance under the South Portico.

It was January 16. Just a few days before, Gerald Ford—then less than half a year in office after having succeeded Richard Nixon in August 1974—had reluctantly called for tax reduction to stimulate a lagging economy. This was embarrassing, since in the fall he'd asked Congress for a tax *increase* to combat inflation.

Only three weeks earlier, moreover, the *Times* had printed as its lead story, under a multicolumn headline, a sensational article by Seymour M. Hersh. It disclosed with copious supporting detail that the Central Intelligence Agency had been conducting for years "a massive, illegal domestic intelligence operation" against at least ten thousand American citizens— some political dissidents, some caught up innocently in matters of interest to the CIA. At first, agency officials had denied the story, although J. J. Angleton, mentioned most prominently by Hersh, had abruptly resigned; and Ford had appointed a commission headed by Vice-President Nelson Rockefeller to investigate Hersh's charges. But just the day before the *Times* luncheon at the White House, CIA Director William E. Colby, in testimony to the Senate Appropriations Committee, had confirmed everything Hersh had written—except that he denied that the offenses thus detailed constituted a "massive" operation.

Ford, however, obviously wanted most to talk to the *Times* group about the economy; in addition to Nessen, the President had bought along Alan Greenspan, the articulate chairman of the Council of Economic Advisers. Robert A. Goldwin, a resident academic and intellectual at the White House, also was present. Luncheon was in the so-called Family Dining Room, where eleven years earlier I'd listened to Lyndon Johnson ebulliently congratulating himself on having just knocked Robert Kennedy out of the running for the vice-presidency in 1964.

Over lamb chops, the seven-man *Times* contingent, the President, and Greenspan kept the conversation centered mostly on the economy and other relatively routine matters. Inevitably, however, the subject of the CIA and the Rockefeller "blue ribbon" Commission arose. I knew Ford better than most of our group, having dealt with him often when he was House minority leader and in 1968 and 1972 when he'd been chairman of the Republican national conventions that nominated Nixon to be their presidential candidate. Ford was genial and forthright as I knew him to be, but even I was surprised at the candor with which he talked about the CIA.

Managing Editor Abe Rosenthal raised the subject. The Rockefeller Commission seemed somewhat loaded in favor of the CIA, Rosenthal said, and he could see only two possible reasons. One was to get a soft report that would not damage the CIA (a prospect that particularly worried Abe, since it might seem to discredit Hersh's story in the *Times*). The other was that the case against the CIA was so damaging that only an apparently sympathetic commission could give it credibility.

Ford replied that he had very carefully provided the Rockefeller Commission with a charter quite specifically limiting its scope to the investigation of illegal domestic activities by the agency. Then he had just as purposefully chosen each member for his "responsibility"; he had selected a commission that he could be sure would not exceed the limits of its charter (which, ironically, was just what the CIA had done in slipping into domestic intelligence operations).

Ford went on to say that this kind of caution was necessary to make sure the commission did not delve into the CIA's activities abroad. He didn't want it to do so, he said, because as president he had learned enough about the CIA to know that there were things on its record that would "blacken the name of every president back to Harry Truman"—the phrase rings as clearly in my ear now as it did then. The American people would be shocked, Ford said, if such information came out.

At some point in this monologue, Ford had used the word "assassinations," and this clearly seemed to be the dark secret he had in mind. (He had been told by Colby on January 3, as it later developed, of the long and sordid record of the CIA in attempting to murder foreign leaders.) I was not much surprised by the substance of what Ford had said. Allegations of involvement in assassination plans had been swirling about the CIA for some time. As early as eleven years before, on the weekend of January 4-5, 1964, at the LBJ Ranch, Lyndon Johnson had described to me and two other reporters his own shock at first learning of some of the "black" activities of the CIA—including, Johnson said flatly, complicity in the murders of Rafael Trujillo in the Dominican Republic and Ngo Dinh Diem, just two months earlier in South Vietnam.

Ford's discussion of this subject with the *New York Times* staff *did* surprise me. As he talked, I tried to remember if Nessen had put the session "off the record"; I couldn't remember that he had, and certainly Ford's discussion of the economy had been intended for "background"—that is, we could use it but without attribution to him. On one or two points, Ford *had* specified as he talked that he was speaking off the record—which tended to confirm my notion that everything else, including the CIA material, had *not* been put specifically off the record. It occurred to me then that despite what Ford was saying about shocking the American public, maybe he *wanted* us to print what he was saying about the CIA—or at least to investigate it, as Hersh had investigated the agency's domestic abuses.

That was not so farfetched as it may seem. Ford, in office so briefly, had no responsibility for the secret acts he was talking about. He might have wanted them brought into the open to prevent any possibility of a cover-up—at that time a bad political word—being charged to him, as well as to make sure that the CIA would not embarass his own administration with more such misdeeds. He might even had had political motives, if the record would tend to discredit Presidents Kennedy and Johnson—thus to some extend balancing off Nixon's and the Republicans' Watergate disgrace. Or Ford could just have been deeply shocked at the CIA's actions.

If he had had any or all those motives for tipping the *Times* to the story, Ford still would not necessarily have wished it to be the Rockefeller Commission that brought the record into the open. He had to work with the CIA, which would not thank him for appointing a commission to expose its deepest secrets. The agency had considerable capacity to embarrass or harass or damage him; and he might even have noted in Hersh's December 22 story that when former CIA director James R. Schlesinger first began an internal investigation of the agency's excesses, he prudently had had his personal bodyguard expanded.

Besides, how would the people *really* react, in view of the national-security mystique? As a veteran of government well acquainted with that mystique, Ford might have been reluctant to scourge the CIA directly and through his own commission; while as a neophyte president he might not have been sure enough of the reaction to proceed openly against the CIA. Leaking the story to the *Times,* moreover, would almost surely result in investigation by the Democratic Congress rather than the Republican White House.

Aside from motive, why would a politician as experienced in the ways of politics and publicity as Gerald Ford discuss such a matter at all with seven newspapermen, if he really wanted the CIA's secrets to remain secret? I could only speculate, but one thing thirteen years in Washington had taught me: that Ford had said these sensational things in such a setting meant that one way or another the substance of what he had said was going to become public. Even if he did not actually want the *Times* to follow up on his monumental leak, the likelihood was that if he would say such things to one group he would say them to someone else; and whether that someone else was in or out of the White House or the administration made little difference to the near-certainty that sooner or later these remarks would find their way into public circulation.

I was reasonably sure, for example, that neither Goldwin nor Greenspan had high security clearances, not ordinarily needing them for their work. Either might confide what they had heard to someone else; no matter how trusted, that person—even a wife—might tell a third party, after which the fat could be in the fire. If of seven *Times* representatives not one confided such remarkable statements to another soul, my entire experience of human nature—particularly of newspaper people, whose stock in trade is information and the reputation for having it—would have been confounded.

It's not for nothing that any well-kept secret is kept by the minimum number of people who necessarily must know it; such things as Gerald Ford had told us cannot be said in the presence of eleven persons, none of whom other than Ford and possibly Nessen had any "need to know," with the reasonable expectation that they will go no further.

For the rest of the leisurely luncheon, I was distracted by mental speculation as to how such a windfall of information ought to be handled—which in itself suggests the extent to which I and the press in which I had spent my life were different from what both had been on that long-ago weekend when LBJ had confided his shock at "black" CIA activities. Then, it had not occurred to me that we should print such things; when my colleagues Doug Kiker of the *Herald Tribune* and Phil Potter of *The Baltimore Sun* and I later made notes—which I still have—of Johnson's conversation, we carefully entered only a cryptic note ("Trujillo and Diem") for that part of it, lest the notes fall into irresponsible hands.

But that had been before Vietnam and Cambodia and the Pentagon Papers and Watergate, in a different world of government and journalism. I am not sure, in retrospect, that I was even particularly outraged by Johnson's disclosures, since like most Americans then, I was persuaded that "anything goes" in the righteous cause of defeating communism and defending freedom. Nor did I then have any particular reason for mistrusting either the wisdom or the probity of the government; if such things were done, I believed, it was only because they *had* to be done.

By 1975 I thought it intolerable that American government should sponsor such criminal and indefensible acts as political assassinations, and I saw no reason why *The New York Times* should protect Ford against his own disclosures of such acts. If the people had a right to know anything, surely they had a right to know murder was being done in their name.

Ford did catch my further attention that day with a spirited defense of appropriating another $200 million for military aid to South Vietnam. Some note in his remarks even suggested to me the insane possibility of the return of American troops to Southeast Asia. On the way out after coffee, I pulled Ron Nessen aside; some years earlier, as an NBC correspondent, Nessen had been badly wounded while covering the war in Vietnam.

"You've got better reason than most of us to know that Vietnam chews up everybody who touches it," I said. "Don't let this guy get chewed up too."

Nessen knew what I was talking about. Some of the White House staff, he suggested, were working on Ford with just that in mind. He made no mention of the CIA remarks, or that anything was off the record except what Ford had specified.

After the luncheon, Max Frankel, then the *Times* Sunday editor, went directly to the airport and returned to New York. The rest of us went to Clifton Daniel's office and I immediately raised the question of how the CIA leak should be handled. Not quite to my astonishment, I found that only Abe Rosenthal, the managing editor, seemed to agree that the story should be published in some fashion. But in this case, he said, he was not sure of the ground rules for the luncheon and for Washington generally. Had the luncheon been off the record or not?

Not specifically, Daniel said, but it had to be assumed that such luncheons were off the record. James Reston and John Oakes both believed there was no question but that such explosive remarks had to be off the record; obviously, they said, the President had been talking in confidence. Arthur Sulzberger was properly willing to let his editors decide the issue, but said he had assumed the luncheon was off the record.

Even if it was, I argued, Ford had given us a lead on a story that was going to come out. It couldn't hold. And we didn't need to pin the story on Ford, or rush into print the next day with what he'd told us. Why not give the information to Hersh—even he wouldn't have to be told where the lead came from, just that it was from an unusually good source—and let him take it from there? We couldn't really rule out the possibility that Ford *wanted* us to print the story. And hadn't we learned the hard way during the long Vietnam years that our job was to print what we knew, at the least to decide for ourselves whether or not to print what we knew?

I deeply respect all the colleagues with whom I was discussing the matter, and I understood their different views. If Ford really had thought he was speaking in confidence and off the record, to print his remarks, perhaps even to set Hersh to work on the basis of those remarks, might be construed as an extreme violation of traditional journalistic ethics; certainly it would go against the ingrained instinct of every journalist who ever agreed to an off-the-record conversation. If publication led, moreover, to the actual blackening of the names of every president back to Truman, that would be a serious responsibility to undertake—particularly for men who only a few years before had been taken by the government all the way to the Supreme Court on the issue of the Pentagon Papers.

Besides, it was not *my* decision to make or my responsibility to bear; I was a columnist with no authority over the news department or anything but my own small corner of the paper. It was easy for me to urge Abe Rosenthal and "Punch" Sulzberger to be bold. They were the ones who'd have to take the rap.

Nevertheless, I thought then and still believe that the national-security mystique was principally at work in Daniel's office. Neither Ford's confidences nor the reputations of his predecessors were really the issues, and the question of journalistic ethics seemed to me subordinate to a larger ethical problem: if the activities of the CIA had been as shameful as Ford had suggested, did we have the right to keep that secret to ourselves? Was there not in fact an *obligation* on our part to use our constitutionally privileged position to inform the public of such deeds rather than tacitly to help the government cover them up?

But the national-security mystique arises from another idea, which can hardly be disputed. It is—as Carl Rowan described it when he was a State Department official—that "the people have a right *not* to know" certain things that, if generally known, would endanger the same people's safety and well-being. The most obvious examples might be wartime military codes or troop-movement information. Some details of weaponry no doubt fall into this category, as do some delicate diplomatic missions and some military-preparedness matters—for example, nuclear-missile targets in the Soviet Union.

Two demurrers necessarily have to be filed, however, as to the people's right *not* to know. Particularly in peacetime, it is a limited right—there just aren't all that many secrets that, if disclosed, would actually endanger the national security. Other secrets, if cracked, would make government more difficult perhaps; many would embarrass or discredit numerous officials; some might produce awkward diplomatic situations. But disclosures in these categories of secrets, at worst, cause difficulty for those involved, which is not the same thing as threatening national security; and such lesser disclosures—say, as to cost overruns on a new weapons system—more often than not concern matters about which the people of a democracy *do* have a right, and a clear right, to know.

Second, the officials who decide what the people have a right *not* to know are unchecked, save by congressional investigations and the press, in what they may choose to place under the cloak of national security. Nixon thought having Dan Ellsberg's psychiatrist's office burglarized could properly be so categorized. Nor is there any reasonable limitation on *who* can make such decisions; literally thousands of officials are empowered—not by law but by executive order—to wield the Top Secret stamp. Some of these officals have nothing to hide but their own inefficiencies and corruption; most have nothing whatever to do with genuine national security.

But those two words are magic, an incantation, vibrating with the ideas of power, knowledge, authority, responsibility. National security!—the phrase rings with masculinity, patriotism, heroism. Used in tones of proper solemnity by someone from the White House or the Pentagon, those words can mesmerize most Americans; and a generation of Washington reporters stood mostly in awe of them—not least, I believe, because a reporter who knows something that can't be printed for national-security reasons is elevated himself into that prized masculine circle of power, knowledge, authority, responsibility. He becomes the ultimate insider; and the reporter's deadliest enemy—the desire to be an accepted part of the world of power all around him—has won its final victory.

The national-security mystique, particularly as it grips reporters, is a powerful product of the same Cold War mentality that had caused me, a decade before, not even to consider writing about what Johnson had said about Diem and Trujillo. In 1964 before the Marines went ashore at Danang and the bombers began going north after Pleiku, to a reporter of my generation, national security seemed to have literal meaning. What was done under its arc was not something to be interfered with or too deeply questioned. When John Kennedy had proclaimed in 1961 the nation's determination "to assure the survival and success of liberty" at any cost, he perfectly exemplified the Cold War mentality then prevailing.

The hard, disillusioning years since Kennedy's death had not released everyone from the grip of the national-security mystique he had done so much to further. The outcome of the debate in Daniel's office was that, despite Rosenthal's and my misgivings, Daniel called Ron Nessen and asked him whether Ford's remarks about the CIA were off the record. I could have told him what the answer would be before he picked up the phone.

Nessen was aghast. If it hadn't been a president speaking, he told Daniel only half in jest, everybody at the table could have been arrested just for hearing what was said. *Of course* it was off the record. This didn't kill my hunch that Ford had deliberately let a very dark cat out of the bag; he wouldn't necessarily have told Nessen what he was doing if he had wanted us to print the story, because he wouldn't have wanted Nessen to know that. Ford would have wanted Nessen to be able honestly to have denounced the *Times* for breaching the President's confidence. Ford, speaking through Nessen, thus would have "deniability," but the CIA story would be out as he desired.

The call to Nessen settled the issue; and Rosenthal insists that it was not national security but the "off-the-record" problem that caused the decision not to publish. Had the story been obtained in any way other than at the President's luncheon table, in his view, it would have been published.

Let those who will say that anyone who felt as I did—about journalism and this particular story—should have done something dramatic, perhaps resign, or at least write a column about Ford's sensational remarks. But I wanted neither to affront esteemed colleagues, as sincere in their judgments as I was in mine, nor to sever myself from an institution I cherish. Besides, I had put up a reasonably good fight for my point of view; and I was certain the story was going to come out, whether or not in the *Times.*

It did. I got up early Saturday morning, March 1, to write the next day's column. Opening the *Times,* I was infuriated to find a wire story reporting that the evening before Dan Schorr—not yet in trouble over the Pike report—had made a startling broadcast. President Ford, Schorr said, had warned "associates" that investigation of the CIA might disclose its involvement in assassinations. Our story—on CBS! Every competitive bone in my body—a lot of bones—cried out in anguish. That I had expected it was poor consolation for being scooped, and less for the *Times* having let slip—I thought—its own standard, set by publication of the Pentagon Papers.

A footnote: on May 4, Schorr wrote a piece for the *Times* Op-Ed page, of all places, disclosing that Ford had first mentioned the assassination problem at a White House luncheon with *New York Times* executives. He didn't say who *his* source was, but I'd bet my framed photograph of J. Edgar Hoover that his story originated, one way or another, from that luncheon conversation.

After Schorr's broadcast, the assassination story could not be contained. Numerous news articles appeared, and Ford ultimately either requested or permitted the Rockefeller Commission to look into the matter after all. He then turned its report on assassinations over to a special Senate committee, rather than making it public. The Senate committee's report specified CIA attempts in varying numbers on the lives of *eight* foreign leaders, either directly or as the possible result of agency-assisted coups d'état.

What is pertinent here is that neither because of Schorr's

broadcast nor any of the newspaper stories can it be demonstrated that the national security was in any way endangered. When the Senate committee's report appeared, these news stories were vindicated as to fact, and far more details were made public. Still, no wars were declared, no diplomatic relations were broken, no threatening military confrontations occurred. Once again, "national security" was shown to be a label that more often protects the convenience and reputations of high officials than the actual security of the American people.

The convenience of officials in making government work admittedly is of considerable value; so, at least to them, are their reputations. But these hardly warrant the kind of secrecy tolerated so often by the press and encouraged by the national-security mystique. And murdering foreign leaders, even obstreperous ones, or trying to, is considerably more than a convenience, anyway; it's an international crime.

It might be argued that exposing the CIA's murder plots generally blackened the agency's name, hence that of the United States, and in that way created problems for the government and perhaps set back American purposes in the world. If so, the root cause was CIA crimes, not their exposure. Besides, the argument has the weakness that, had these excesses remained secret, either by successful secret-keeping or by press cooperation, the agency could have gone right on committing more such crimes. And a hoary old technique of any bureaucracy under fire—the national-security bureaucracy in particular—is to try to shift the point of controversy to the propriety of *exposing* misdeeds or blunders, and away from the fact of their having been committed.

Another example of this diversionary technique had been seen in Colby's skillful defensive focus on Seymour Hersh's description of the CIA's domestic abuses as "massive." Of course the CIA had made a few errors, Colby conceded suavely (actually confirming all Hersh's factual allegations), but it really was just going too far to call these errors a "massive" illegal operation. This concentration of attention away from Hersh's facts to his characterization of them actually caused some early congressional and press comment that Hersh had overstated his case. He hadn't, as later investigation confirmed, but he concedes today that the use of the word "massive," even accurately, gave Colby an opportunity to hold down the public impact of the admitted facts.

But the Senate was preparing to investigate the CIA anyway. So it might be asked if Schorr's broadcasts and other news stories concerning the assassination attempts were necessary. Wouldn't the story have come out anyway, and in the proper form of a Senate report?

In the first place, the Senate investigation might not have been scheduled except for press disclosures, including Hersh's of December 22, 1974. Beyond that, the official events that followed Ford's disclosures to the *Times* on January 16—his direction to the Rockefeller Commission to get into the assassination matter (or his acquiescence in its decision to do so), his turning over the commission's assassination report to the Sentate committee—were the clear result of Schorr's broadcast and other disclosures in the press. Had it not been for that exposure, the Senate report *could* have been quite different.

At the least, Schorr's and other stories made it inevitable that the Senate committee could not ignore the assassination matter, or succumb—as so many other "oversight" groups had—to the agency's blandishments that it was all a question of national security, not for the public to know about.

Congressional "oversight" and the supposed diligence of administrations of both parties in "controlling" the CIA had not, after all, prevented the agency from making eight attempts to murder Fidel Castro in the name of national-security—or even from a comic-opera effort to make his beard fall out with a depilatory powder. Senators and congressmen, too, share the national-security mystique; officials directly responsible for the actions of the CIA can hardly be relied on to report to the people on the agency's mistakes, excesses, and crimes. Press scrutiny and exposure are therefore a vital part of a system of checks and balances that in the case of the security agencies is weak at best.

Press exposure is, of course, not the only check or even perhaps the most important. It *is* one without which—as the record plainly shows—the government's own "oversight," whether by the executive or legislative branch, is likely to be limited and ineffective.

The national-security mystique goes so little challenged, in or out of government, for several reasons. One is embodied in the phrase "if you only knew what I know." In practice, of course, it may not be put so bluntly; but anyone raising questions about "national security" can in any number of ways be given to understand by an official that the official knows something that journalists, members of Congress, the general public do not and may not know; and that this knowledge—if it could only be shared—would justify what might seem to the unknowing to be unjustifiable. No check, of course, can easily be made on such a claim to superior knowledge, which if made by so exalted a personage as a president makes him appear to have received something like divine revelation.

From the "if you only knew" tactic naturally flows the assumption that the government, particularly the president, "knows best." With its sources of information and its expertise, the government seems obviously to know more than ordinary citizens—hence, in a leap of faith all too easy to make, to "know best."

Equally important is the natural fear of anyone in a position to breach what is claimed to be the national security that to do so really would cause a war or a diplomatic setback or some other consequence far outweighing the public's right to know. Why would something be classified—one is naturally inclined to ask—why would the government want to keep it secret, if it were not really important national-security material?

Sometimes, perhaps often, no one would dispute, the government *does* know more, *does* know best, *does* have sound reasons for secrecy. To assume that it *always* does, however, presupposes information of never-failing accuracy; interpretation and analysis of impeccable insight; and officials both reporting and interpreting who are free of such human failings as fear and ambition, and who can come to unanimously agreed conclusions. The record of Vietnam alone ought sufficiently to discredit the notion of government infallibility and the assumption of selfless government virtue. But it hasn't. The mystique persists.

Never mind that after the Bay of Pigs President Kennedy sternly and publicly warned broadcasters and newspapers to "re-examine their own responsibilities" and ask of every story they proposed to print: "Is it in the interest of national security?"—but two weeks later, in the privacy of the White House, told Managing Editor Turner Catledge of *The New York Times:* "Maybe if you had printed more about the operation you would have saved us from a colossal mistake."

The national-security mystique persists, moreover, despite

other examples of publications that either have saved the government from its own folly or, at least, made it far less likely that the government would commit some "colossal mistake." A classic of the kind was the publication by the *Times* on March 10, 1968, of the story that General William Westmoreland, following the Tet offensive, had asked for 206,000 more American troops. Written by Hedrick Smith and Neil Sheehan, with research aid from Max Frankel and Edwin Dale, the story also disclosed the deep internal divisions within the Johnson administration over the request and about how and whether to proceed with the war.

The Smith-Sheehan story was denied and denounced as exaggerated and a disservice to national security, by the administration and even by some journalists. Ken Crawford wrote in a signed article in *Newsweek* that the *Times* had become "a pipeline for anonymous dissent from the inside," attributing political motives to the newspaper (and hence to the reporters presumably doing the *Times*'s bidding) and implying that the story had exaggerated an unimportant possibility into a high policy question. But the troop request *had* been made and the debate *was* going on—ultimately to be settled against further escalation, and to result in Johnson's decision to withdraw from the 1968 election.

No story I remember had more important public impact. If that many more troops had been sent, the money cost of the war would have risen by at least $5 billion a year, as then estimated; the death and destruction would have increased immeasurably. The publication, coming hard after the disillusionment of Tet, just two days before the 1968 New Hampshire primary, and less than a month before Johnson quit the presidential race, probably did not alone turn around public opinion and the course of the war. Nevertheless, the story so fired domestic opposition—whatever the value of the war, few even of its proponents thought it was worth half again as many troops as already had been invested—and so bolstered Johnson's political opponents that it played a major part in preventing the possibility of further escalation and forcing his withdrawal. Eight years later not many would suggest that that story should *not* have been published for reasons of "national security."

The national-security mystique persists, too, despite evidence of how often the phrase is used merely for purposes of covering up what an administration does not *want* to be known, as Nixon tried to use it to contain the Watergate investigation. Domestic politics appear also to have been the prime reason for Nixon's fury at one of the major "leaks" to appear during his administration. It came early, on May 8, 1969, when William Beecher reported in *The New York Times* that American planes had secretly been bombing Cambodia, where Viet Cong and North Vietnamese forces had "sanctuaries."

These forces knew their "sanctuaries" were being bombed; they got the news from overhead. The Cambodian peasantry, informed in the same direct way, was in on the secret. The Soviet Union and the Communist Chinese could have known, and probably did, from the North Vietnamese and V.C. forces who were suffering the bombing. Henry Kissinger later said secrecy had been necessary so that Prince Norodom Sihanouk, then the Cambodian chief of state, would not be forced to protest, at least *pro forma,* border incursions by American ground forces into Cambodia; the United States had kept right on making the ground raids, despite the protests.

The only people kept from knowledge of the bombing of Cambodia were the American people, who happened *not* to be at war with Cambodia. Not only would publicity about the war having been spread to another country, even after peace talks had opened in Paris, possibly confront Nixon and Kissinger with a sharp upturn in domestic political opposition to their war policy; but to bomb a country with which the United States officially was at peace, and to deny doing it, as Nixon publicly did, may well have exceeded even a president's vast constitutional powers. Five years later the House Judiciary Committee considered—but rejected—an impeachment plank against Nixon, based on the secret bombing of Cambodia.

Oddly, neither in the press nor the general public did Beecher's story cause any excitement in 1969 (it was not prominently displayed in the *Times*) and the matter dropped out of sight with little follow-up—a victim no doubt of "dailiness." It caused Kissinger and Nixon, however, to initiate a wiretap program on newsmen and government servants, in an effort to find the leaker. Disclosure of these wiretaps also came to be part of the general "Watergate" charges against the Nixon administration.

The national-security mystique has even survived disclosure of deliberate lying by the President and the sensational news that the Pentagon was stealing the White House's "national security" secrets. In December 1971 the columnist Jack Anderson was able to publish materials from the minutes of the Washington Special Action Group, a "crisis management" unit under Kissinger, which was then dealing with the India-Pakistan war. Nixon had insisted publicly that the United States was strictly neutral in that conflict.

But on December 14 Anderson in his column quoted Kissinger from the Action Group minutes of December 3, as saying: "I'm getting hell every half-hour from the President that we're not being tough enough on India. . . . He doesn't believe we're carrying out his wishes. He wants to tilt in favor of Pakistan."

Typically, the White House steered public attention to Anderson's "breach of national security," trying to deflect criticism from what he actually had done: expose Nixon's duplicity and his one-sided policy. When the usual White House hunt for the leaker followed, he or she was never certainly found; but it was disclosed—in the press, of course—that a Navy enlisted man working in Kissinger's office had been passing numerous classified documents to the Pentagon, even though the White House had decided that the Department of Defense was not entitled to see them.

If this opera bouffe did not demolish the national-security mystique, even in the press, probably nothing can. Its persistence, of course, is to some degree owing to the facts that there *is* a national security and there *are* some secrets vital to it. But this truism is consistently blown out of all proportion to what are probably relatively few secrets truly vital to national security.

In February 1977, when Bob Woodward of *The Washington Post* told the story of secret CIA payments to King Hussein of Jordan—over twenty years and running to millions of dollars—loud charges were heard that the national security had been endangered because (a) Hussein's cover was blown, and (b) the story appeared just as Secretary of State Cyrus Vance was about to land in Amman for conferences with Hussein.

In fact, the Hussein payments had been labeled an "impropriety" by the Intelligence Oversight Board in the Ford administration; neither the House nor Senate committees that had investigated the CIA had been told of the payments; and President Carter had not been informed of them until told by Woodward. In those circumstances, the story raised such legitimate questions as whether the CIA determined the necessity for the payments and deceived or persuaded one administration after another to go along with the subversion of a foreign head of state; or whether five succeeding administrations decided as a matter of policy to make the payments and used the CIA only as a secret bank. And how many more such explosive secrets might the CIA or the other security agencies have been keeping from Congress and the new president?

Unfortunately, Mr. Carter defended the Hussein arrangement as "legitimate and proper," although he stopped the payments. By April he was urging the Senate Intelligence Committee not to release a report critical of the CIA for improper "microphone surveillance" of Micronesian negotiators in talks with the United States over the future status of Micronesia. That quickly, Carter began to share the national-security mystique, although he frequently had promised less secrecy in government.

In his Pentagon Papers decision, Supreme Court Justice Potter Stewart wrote that the executive had an "awesome responsibility" to pursue the necessary internal security, and added:

> I should suppose that moral, political and practical considerations would dictate that a very first principle . . . would be an insistence upon avoiding secrecy for its own sake. *For when everything is classified, then nothing is classified,* and the system becomes one to be disregarded by the cynical or the careless, and to be manipulated by those intent on self-protection or self-promotion. I should suppose, in short, that the hallmark of a truly effective internal security system would be the maximum possible disclosure, recognizing that secrecy can best be preserved only when credibility is truly maintained. [Italics mine.]

But in the shadowy Washington world of national security, things unfortunately don't work that way—as was seldom better illustrated than in the case about which Stewart was writing.

The most celebrated "national security" violation of modern times was the publication of the Pentagon Papers, a documentary history of the war in Vietnam through 1968, officially compiled within the Department of Defense and classified Top Secret.

No detailed retelling is needed here of how *The New York Times* obtained and began publishing massive excerpts from these documents in 1971, whereupon *The Washington Post, The Boston Globe,* and others soon obtained and began publication of the Papers, too. The Nixon administration quickly went into federal court for an injunction against the *Times* and the *Post;* the newspapers ceased publication under the first real "prior restraint" the government had ever imposed on the American press; but ultimately, upon the newspapers' appeals, the Supreme Court by a vote of 6-3 held that the government had not shown sufficient reason for preventing publication, which was resumed immediately—but only after fifteen days of restraint by government decree.

This history is well known but not necessarily well understood. Beyond the notion of a "great victory" for the press—in itself a dubious proposition—the Pentagon Papers story tells much about the national-security mystique, and the government's exploitation of it.

Why, for example, did the Nixon administration go to such lengths to suppress publication of the Pentagon Papers? In the month before publication, I thought of several ways in which the administration might counter; the most threatening to the *Times* and to the press, I thought, would be a bitter televised attack by Nixon himself, accusing the *Times* of having endangered the "security" of every American but disclaiming any thought of trifling with the First Amendment. It never occurred to me that the government actually would try to stop publication, something that never before had been attempted, even in wartime.

The Papers, after all, were an account primarily of the mishandling of the Vietnam war in two *Democratic* administrations—as Nixon himself acknowledged to Republican congressional leaders two days after the first publication. Some experienced Washingtonians even assumed at first that the administration had itself leaked the papers to embarrass the Democrats. The Papers also were historical in nature; they had little if anything to do with current operations or the Nixon administration's own plans and policies. The government's experts must quickly have established that publication did not "blow" codes or other secrets of that technical and highly sensitive nature.

As far as is known, Kissinger sparked the Nixon administration's vigorous reaction. He was at the time deeply involved in secret negotiations through Pakistan with Communist China, with the ultimate aim of rapprochement, and also in secret talks with North Vietnamese officials in Paris, in an effort to settle the Southeast Asian war. The Pentagon Papers had no direct bearing on either set of delicate contacts—except that Kissinger, almost conspiratorially secretive himself, feared the publication might scare off both Peking and Hanoi, on grounds that the American government could not keep secrets or proceed confidentially.

As soon as Dan Ellsberg was believed within the administration to have been the source of the Papers, a new fear spread rapidly—Ellsberg, formerly of the Rand Corporation and the Defense Department, might have all sorts of secrets to leak, including the targets of American nuclear missiles. White House paranoids, including Nixon himself, also thought Ellsberg might be the first surfaced agent of a vast conspiracy, possibly including other knowledgeable mid-echelon government servants. And even if there were no conspiracy as such, these paranoids feared, Ellsberg's example might inspire others to turn over sensitive documents to the press, in an effort to stop the war.

Creative political operators also saw certain opportunities arising from the publication and the prevalence of the national-security mystique. "We can discredit the peace movement and we have the Democrats on a marvelous hook because thus far most of them have defended the release of the documents," Charles Colson wrote H. R. Haldeman in a memo two days before the Supreme Court invalidated the government's injunction.

All this leaves little doubt that the major reason the administration reacted as it did, beginning with Kissinger's concerns about Peking and Hanoi, was to preserve the importance of government secrecy—the *principle* of secrecy—and to uphold the national-security mystique. According to Colson, Nixon told his inner circle that June:

"I don't give a damn how it is done, do whatever has to be done to stop these leaks and prevent further unauthorized disclosures; I don't want to be told why it can't be done. This government cannot survive, it cannot function if anyone can run out and leak whatever documents he wants to.... I want to know who is behind this and I want the most complete investigation that can be conducted.... I don't want excuses. I want results. I want it done, whatever the cost."

Remarkably, none of this has anything to do with *the content and substance of the Pentagon Papers*. Whatever the validity of other reasons it may have had for seeking prior restraint, there is no evidence that the Nixon administration believed the documents themselves seriously threatened the national security. The system of secrecy, not any particular secret or group of secrets, was perceived to be endangered; and it was the national-security mystique, not any specific material in the Papers, that the administration went to court to protect.

This conclusion is supported by a further study of what did happen after publication of the Pentagon Papers. Very little happened, except further public controversy as to whether the press or the government was telling the truth. The American people did not rise in anger to demand the end of the war, as Ellsberg in his most optimistic moments might have hoped. Nor did drastic damage to "national-security" result.

In fact, the government made no real effort during the various court proceedings to claim that specific damage would result from publication. William B. Macomber, then the deputy under-secretary of state for administration, testified for example in an *in camera* hearing before Federal Judge Murray Gurfein in New York that publication of the Pentagon Papers in the *Times* had given the Soviet Union valuable insight into the kind of information that Llewellyn Thompson, in the sixties an American ambassador to Moscow, had sent back to Washington. Even if that were so, it scarcely seems earthshaking, since Thompson had been a leading Soviet expert for the American government since the twenties! Whatever the Russians learned about him and his views from the Pentagon Papers in 1971 can hardly have come as much of a surprise.

Yet, *in open court,* Macomber and other government witnesses took the position that they could only testify *in camera* as to the damage done by the Papers, lest press reports of their testimony compound the damage. Here was another example of the old device—shift public attention from the facts to the supposed damage exposure had done to national security. Inevitably the public impression was created that matters of grave import, badly breaching security, had been irresponsibly made public; and the damage was so great—it was suggested—that it could only be discussed in the secrecy of a judge's chambers. Note that there is an element here, too, of the "if you only knew what I know" tactic.

The same *in camera* technique was followed in Washington when the *Post* case came to trial in a different federal court. Five years later the sad truth came out. The Justice Department, responding to demands submitted under the Freedom of Information Act, made public in 1976 the record of the *in camera* hearing before Federal Judge Gerhard Gesell—a hearing once again featuring Macomber, as well as Dennis J. Doolin, who in 1971 was an assistant secretary of defense dealing with the problems of American prisoners of war in Vietnam. Here is the *Times*'s account of their testimony as to the grave damage done to national security by publication of the Pentagon Papers.

> Mr. Doolin said, addressing the judge:
> "I can say, sir, that I have lost the one contact that I personally had in Hanoi. It dried up last week." Mr. Doolin did not identify the contact, even by nationality, but said that "I had a private relationship with him, and he does not feel with certain items that have been in the press that he can talk to me any longer. . . ."
> [Macomber] testified in an affidavit that Canadian officials had called in the American Ambassador. The officials, he said, "expressed concern over impressions created in Canada" that the Ottawa government was "either a rogue or a fool" for helping the United States to search for peace in Vietnam.
> Mr. Macomber also testified personally that the 1971 Prime Minister of Australia, William MacMahon—whom Mr. Macomber did not name—had let the United States know privately that he found the disclosures "appalling."
> Mr. Macomber's affidavit, however, quoted a telegram from the American Embassy in Canberra that said that Australian officials "have not said so, but we expect for some time to come they will be more than normally cautious in discussions with U.S. officials."
> The State Department had sent a telegram to all

embassies asking for reactions from host governments and the independent assessment of American ambassadors. In his affidavit, Mr. Macomber quoted from several, contending that continued publication of the papers could jeopardize national security.

But in later testimony before the judge Mr. Macomber acknowledged that other telegrams, not mentioned in his affidavit, had said that "it was too early to tell."

"Occasionally," he went on, "some would say 'We will get along all right.' There was a spectrum of them."

Measured against the immense store of historical information in the Pentagon Papers, as well as the appalling picture they presented to the American people of the ineptitude, self-delusion, and duplicity of successive administrations, these seem small setbacks indeed to the national security. Yet, Solicitor General Erwin N. Griswold—no doubt himself barred by "national security" from any real knowledge of the impact of the Papers—insisted in his Supreme Court brief that publication "could have the effect of causing immediate and irreparable harm to the security of the United States."

Since available legal precedents held that "any system of prior restraints of expression comes to [the Supreme] Court bearing a heavy presumption against its Constitutional validity" and that the government "thus carries a heavy burden of showing justification for the enforcement of such a restraint," it was no wonder that the Court majority agreed that "the government had not met that burden" in the Pentagon Papers case, and allowed publication to resume.

This necessity distressed Justice Harry A. Blackmun, who delivered a wholly gratuitous lecture to the press in his dissenting opinion:

I strongly urge, and sincerely hope, that these two newspapers will be fully aware of their ultimate responsibilities to the United States of America.... I hope that damage already has not been done. If, however, damage has been done, and if, with the Court's action today, these newspapers proceed to publish the critical documents and there results therefrom "the death of soldiers, the destruction of alliances, the greatly increased difficulty of negotiation with our enemies, the inability of our diplomats to negotiate," to which list I might add the factors or prolongation of the war and of further delay in the freeing of United States prisoners, then the Nation's people will know where the responsibility for these sad consequences rests.

His fears were as ill-founded as those of Kissinger and Nixon, and as informed with disdain for the press. But even in terms of the Nixon administration's *real* fears, not just its court testimony, little justification developed following publication. Kissinger's negotiations led on to a successful "opening to China" and finally even to a tenuous peace settlement with Hanoi (if not with Saigon). No great new spout of leaks opened; government employees with secrets to spill did not flock to press offices in Ellsberg's footsteps with the goods on the war or anything else. Dan Ellsberg himself became a political voice of some importance, to the administration's extreme anguish, but not a fount of more secret information. And while Charles Colson may have tried, he did not discredit the peace movement or the Democrats owing to their support of publishing the Pentagon Papers.

It might be argued that most of these things did not happen *because* the government went to court and enjoined publication for fifteen days; thus, the leakers were frightened off and both the Chinese and the North Vietnamese were reassured. But this argument would be hard to sustain in view of the Supreme Court's ultimate rebuff to the government. Logic suggests that if Nixon's and Kissinger's various fears had been well grounded *before* the Court acted, they would have been even more justified *after* its ruling that publication could proceed.

But one goal the Nixon administration might have had, and which it might have at least partially or temporarily achieved, was the intimidation or the inhibition of the press in America. Evidence that the government was prepared to go as far as the administration did might well have suggested to numerous publishers and broadcasters who lacked the resources and legal staffs and prestige of the *Times* and the *Post* that discretion was the better part of valor—even while they piously toasted victory for "the press" in the Supreme Court.

Even the literal "victors," poring over the Court's various opinions, felt a certain chill that might later have restrained their bolder editorial impulses. They had won the immediate battle, but further study inevitably suggests that if the war should resume, the Pentagon Papers opinions by no means guarantee a final victory.

During oral argument in the Supreme Court, Justice William O. Douglas roused himself from what appeared to be a nap to address himself to Alexander Bickel, the Yale law scholar acting as special counsel for *The New York Times*.

The First Amendment, Douglas reminded Bickel, says that Congress shall make "no law" abridging the freedom of the press. Did Bickel, Douglas asked, interpret that to mean that Congress could make "some law" abridging the freedom of the press?

"Yes, sir, I do," Bickel replied, to the consternation of most of his *Times* clients, but in pursuit of his basic strategy, as most of them later realized. Douglas and Justice Hugo L. Black were First Amendment absolutists; they held that "no law" meant "no law" so that freedom of the press was absolute, and—in the Pentagon Papers case—the orginal injunctions had been improper. In their view there should have been no prior restraint because there could be no *constitutional* prior restraint, whatever the circumstances. That was probably the instinctive position of most of the journalists who were hearing the case argued.

But that was not a majority view on the Supreme Court in 1971, although Justice William J. Brennan, Jr., agreed that the injunctions should never have been issued. He argued that only in time of war and after proof of specific consequences—he gave as an example "imperilling the safety of a transport already at sea"—might a prior restraint on publication be proper. In Brennan's opinion, only *after* the government had offered conclusive proof of such a consequence—not the mere assumption that it *might* occur—could an injunction against publication have constitutional validity. An injunction could not be issued even to give the government time to prepare such proof, he wrote; only the proof itself would warrant an injunction against publication.

Justice Thurgood Marshall joined the majority on still other grounds—that the administration, in effect, wanted the Supreme Court to make a law that a publication could be restrained to protect national security. The Supreme Court had no such power to make law, Marshall wrote, particularly when Congress had refused to make the law it was proposed that the Court should make.

These four votes against prior restraint were more or less predictable but the keys to the case, Bickel and the other *Times* attorneys believed, were Justices Potter Stewart and Byron R. White. Bickel's reply to Douglas really was addressed to them, and embodied as well his own central conviction that there are no absolutes in the Constitution.

The apparent absolute of the First Amendment, for example, inevitably must collide with some other apparent absolute in the Constitution—say, the right to fair trial. At that point, Bickel believed, some accommodation between these apparent absolutes had to be made; something had to give. In the Pentagon Papers case, Bickel's view of the Constitution comported well with a plausible strategy to win the support of Stewart or White or both.

That is, a plea that the *Times* could never, under any circumstances, be restrained from publication—the absolutist view—was not likely to appeal to these moderate justices. But they might concur in an argument that while *some* circumstances might warrant prior restraint, no such circumstances were present in the Pentagon Papers case. Interestingly enough, Bickel's refusal to claim an absolute right of publication was echoed by Solicitor General Griswold, who argued for the government *in support* of prior restraint:

"Now, Mr. Justice [Black], your construction of . . . [the First Amendment] is well known, and I certainly respect it. You say that no law means no law, and that should be obvious. I can only say, Mr. Justice, that to me it is equally obvious that 'no law' does not mean 'no law,' and I would seek to persuade the Court that that is true. . . . [T]here are other parts of the Constitution that grant power and responsibilities to the Executive and . . . the First Amendment was not intended to make it impossible for the Executive to function or to protect the security of the United States."

Prosecution and defense, in other words, were making the same interpretation of the Constitution. But Bickel's strategy prevailed. Stewart, in an opinion joined by White, wrote that the executive had a "constitutional duty" to protect the "confidentiality necessary to carry out its responsibilities." He added further that Congress could pass and the administration could use "criminal laws . . . to preserve government secrets"; Congress might also pass a law authorizing "civil proceedings in this field." The courts might properly pass on the constitutionality of any such laws, or of any regulations the executive might, in pursuit of such laws, promulgate to protect its confidentiality.

But, Stewart concluded, the government was not asking the Court to construe regulations or to apply laws of Congress, since none existed, but to make a judgment on the confidential nature, if any, of the contents of the Pentagon Papers—to prevent publication of material that the executive insisted should not, for reasons of national security, be printed. Stewart thought that claim might even be true of some of the documents involved "but I cannot say that disclosure of any of them might surely result in direct, immediate, and irreparable damage to our nation or its people."

White's own opinion, joined by Stewart, concurred almost grudgingly with the majority, but added pointedly: "I do not say that in no circumstances would the First Amendment permit an injunction against publishing information about government plans or operations." And he noted ominously that dismissal of the injunctions would not mean that if the newspapers resumed publication they would be 'immune from criminal action.' He thought the government had "mistakenly chose[n] to proceed by injunction" but declared that "failure by the government to justify *prior restraints* does not measure its constitutional entitlement to a conviction for *criminal publication*." (Italics mine.)

Justice John Marshall Harlan—like Black, participating in one of his last major cases—wrote the primary dissent, Chief Justice Warren E. Burger and Blackmun concurring. After strongly protesting the pressures of time the Court had had to work under, and at that on "great issues as important as any that have arisen during my time on the Court," Harlan expressed the view that the judicial branch had only "very narrowly restricted" functions in passing upon the essentially *political* activities of the executive in the conduct of foreign affairs. He thought the judiciary could determine no more than that the "subject matter of [a] dispute" lay within the President's "foreign-relations power" and that the executive's decisions on such a matter had been properly made at the appropriate level of responsibility.

Echoing Stewart to the opposite point, Harlan wrote that, beyond these basic determinations, "the judiciary may not properly...redetermine for itself the probable impact of disclosure on the national security." Thus, he thought an executive decision in the field of foreign relations, made at the proper level, such as classifying the Pentagon Papers Top Secret, was not reviewable by the judicial branch· but in the Pentagon Papers cases, Harlan saw no evidence "that the conclusions of the executive were given [by the newspapers] even the deference owing to an administrative agency, much less that owing to a co-equal branch of the government operating within the field of its constitutional prerogative."

The respected constitutionalist, Justice Harlan, therefore seemed to believe that if the executive determined at a certain official level that material pertaining to foreign affairs could not be published, the courts could not even review that determination and newspapers would ignore it at their legal peril.

The sum of the justices' views, while they permitted publication to resume in the case of the Pentagon Papers, can hardly be interpreted other than to say that prior restraint might well be justified in other cases; that Congress might pass laws permitting prior restraint in certain circumstances; that Congress might also provide stronger sanctions for what White grimly termed "criminal publication"; and that if the government had proceeded under criminal law rather than by injunction, convictions might well have resulted even under unspecified existing law for those responsible for publishing the Pentagon Papers.

With Black and Douglas no longer serving on the Supreme Court, the Pentagon Papers case itself might be lost if it had to be heard today. And if the Nixon-Ford appointees have converted the minority that concurred in Harlan's opinion into a majority, the next prior restraint case the government might bring in the interests of "national security" could well result in a vast accretion of power for government officials to act in secrecy—which approaches the power to do what they want, without hindrance from public opinion or political opponents.

They could classify anything remotely covered by the foreign-affairs powers of the executive, and the judiciary could not "redetermine for itself" whether the matter was really a vital secret or not. The secret classification would be enough in itself either to prevent publication or to subject anyone who did publish to criminal sanction—thus writing by judicial interpretation an Official Secrets Act into a Constitution that *seems* to say that "no law" may be made abridging the freedom of the press.

That would be an ironic—to say the least—result of the Pentagon Papers, the Pike report, and other breaches of "national security." For there really have not been all that many such breaches, and *none of grave, demonstrated consequence.* And, unfortunately, the American press has been more often hesitant than aggressive in pursuit of its constitutional obligation to act as a check on the power of government. All too often, the press has been a collaborator in the national-security mystique, rather than a challenger of it.

11

Let 'em Eat Handouts

Sometime in 1973, while talking to an official of the Central Intelligence Agency, Seymour Hersh first heard of "Project Jennifer." Something to do with a Soviet submarine, the official said, rather vaguely; he didn't know much about it but thought that if Hersh dug around a little it might make a fascinating story.

Dangling that kind of lead in front of Seymour Hersh was about like turning a mule loose in a brier patch. Hersh began to follow up and learned enough to suggest to him that the CIA was putting heavy money into deep-diving equipment, perhaps—he thought—to pick up Soviet intercontinental ballistic missiles test-fired into the Pacific Ocean from Siberia.

The story did not much excite Hersh and anyway, the *Times* Washington bureau had diverted him into its Watergate coverage in an effort to catch up to the *Washington Post*'s numerous disclosures. Hersh plunged heavily and successfully into Watergate and thought little more of Project Jennifer—until sometime in February 1974. William Colby, the director of the CIA, called to say he'd heard Hersh was sniffing around Jennifer. Could Colby drop by to discuss this with Hersh?

Hersh and the *Times*'s Washington news editor, Robert H. Phelps (now managing editor of *The Boston Globe*), jumped at the offer. CIA directors don't drop in every day. But when Colby arrived at the *Times* bureau at 20th and L streets, N.W., Hersh and Phelps still were more interested in Watergate, and Colby proved cooperative and informative. When the matter of Jennifer did come up, Phelps and Hersh readily acceded to Colby's request that Hersh talk to him before going back to work on whatever story Jennifer might offer.

The final stages of Watergate and Nixon's resignation followed. Hersh also went intensively to work in 1974 on what became his smashing story, on December 22 of that year, about "massive" illegal CIA domestic operations. Jennifer was far down the scale of his priorities, and by early 1975 he was more preoccupied with the consequences of his December 22 story. Much of the press was hesitating to follow his lead, he had little if any editorial support, and Colby was scoring points with his denials of Hersh's characterization of CIA misdeeds as a "massive" operation.

On May 13, 1973, however, the *Philadelphia Inquirer* had commented on the near-completion at the Sun Shipbuilding and Drydock Company in Chester, Pennsylvania, of a strange-looking ship, 618 feet long, more than 115 feet wide, 36,000 tons displacement, and mounting a 209-foot derrick capable of lifting 800 tons, as well as three other lifts almost as powerful.

The *Glomar Explorer*—the first word came from Global Marine, Inc., the company that had contracted to operate the ship—was being built for the Howard Hughes industrial and financial empire, the *Inquirer* reported. "If all sails smoothly," its story said, "the mystery ship may be at work next year scooping such metals as titanium, manganese, uranium, copper and nickel up out of the depths to add to the fortune of the world's wealthiest recluse."

Other newspaper stories had appeared about a giant, 106-foot-wide barge being constructed by the National Steel and Shipbuilding Company at its San Diego yards. In October 1973 the London *Observer* reported that the *Glomar Explorer* was beginning to mine the ocean floor near Nicaragua. By then, the *Explorer* had completed its first test run, from Chester to Long Beach, California. And the previous August *The Washington Post* had reported that Hughes had sunk $250 million into the ship, with the expectation that it could suck five thousand tons of minerals daily from the ocean floor.

In July 1974 Hughes officials told the *Inquirer* that the *Glomar Explorer* was "systems testing" in the Pacific. The *Honolulu Advertiser* reported on August 17, 1974, that the ship had visited Hawaii. Adopting the *Inquirer*'s terminology, the *Advertiser* called it a "mystery ship" and later reported that it lay at anchor near Maui for two weeks, disappeared for a week, reappeared for four days, and sailed away in September 1974.

In Los Angeles, another story had appeared that summer of 1974. On June 5 a four-man burglary team had entered and robbed Hughes headquarters at 7020 Romaine Street. A police burglary bulletin said $68,000 in cash, some antiques, and two butterfly collections were missing.

As later learned by James Phelan, a free-lance investigative reporter extremely knowledgeable about the tangled affairs of Hughes's business and private life, the real burglary was quite different from the one described in the police bulletin. The robbers had burned open an office safe and a vault with a two-tank acetylene torch and had got away with two footlockers full of documents. Ten days later one "Chester Brooks" phoned the Romaine Street offices and said someone should pick up an envelope from a trashcan in a nearby park. If the envelope's contents interested Hughes officials, they should place an ad in the *Los Angeles Times*, with the text "Apex OK" and a telephone contact number written backwards.

The envelope contained a handwritten Howard Hughes memo. The ad was placed and a series of telephone talks began, in which "Brooks" demanded $1 million for return of the documents stolen on June 5. But the talks broke down and "Brooks" was not heard from again. Some time later, about the time other Hughes officials were reporting that the *Glomar Explorer* was "systems testing" in the Pacific, Kay Glenn discovered that a certain memorandum was not in a briefcase where he had left it. Glenn was an assistant to a member of the executive committee that ran the Summa Corporation, the Hughes holding company, and it was Kay Glenn's office safe that had been burned open on June 5.

The missing memo—as Phelan reported later—was no ordinary document. It outlined for Howard Hughes himself the details of how the Central Intelligence Agency had financed construction of the *Glomar Explorer*. The "mystery ship" was not intended for ocean-floor mining; that was only the cover story the CIA had devised for the Hughes officials. The ship's real purpose was to recover Soviet hydrogen-warhead missiles and code books from a Russian submarine that had exploded and sunk in three miles of water in the mid-Pacific northwest of Hawaii. The *Explorer* was on that mission—accompanied by the mammoth barge from San Diego, designed to transport the recovered submarine hull—when Glenn discovered the memorandum was missing.

Hughes officials informed Bill Colby of the loss; Colby relayed the problem to Clarence Kelley, the director of the FBI, with the request that contact with the burglars be reopened in secret. Kelley passed the matter urgently to the Los Angeles police, who redoubled their efforts; at one point a trap for the supposed burglars was baited with a million dollars in federal—presumably CIA—cash. But the trap failed.

Except, however, for the *Honolulu Advertiser*'s reports on the "mystery ship" and the *Glomar Explorer*'s mostly unremarked return to Long Beach in the fall of 1974, all these matters dropped out of sight for a while. The *Explorer*'s real mission in the Pacific remained secret and unsuspected.

Then, on February 1, 1975, Jim Phelan got the tip that the June 5 burglary had resulted in the loss of more than two butterfly collections and some cash. He confirmed this information and prepared for *The New York Times* a story that the burglars had carried off Hughes documents so valuable they'd tried to sell them back to the Summa Corporation for a million dollars. But Phelan's story contained no mention of the *Glomar Explorer* or the actual contents of the missing documents.

On February 6 a *Los Angeles Times* reporter heard that Phelan was writing a story on the burglary. He went to work with the Los Angeles police to match or top Phelan and got the story of the missing documents—plus, more importantly, a garbled account of the Hughes-*Glomar Explorer* contract. Incorrectly assuming the submarine story also was part of the Phelan story for *The New York Times*, the *Los Angeles Times* published its version on February 7, before anything had appeared in New York.

The published story, hastened into print under competitive pressure, was incomplete and inaccurate—it had the submarine being recovered in the Atlantic—but it rang bells all the way across the continent. At Langley, Virginia, Colby reacted as if a burning cigarette had been pressed into his palm. Two West Coast CIA representatives immediately called on William F. Thomas, the editor of *The Los Angeles Times,* pleading grave danger to national security. As it so often does with the American press, the plea had its effect; in succeeding editions Thomas cut the length of the story and moved it off page one far inside the paper. Even so, a Hughes official quickly denied what had been printed.

But from the CIA's point of view, the damage had been done. Re-enter Seymour Hersh.

Well over a year after he had first heard of Project Jennifer, Hersh was reading inside pages of the New York *Daily News* when he noticed the *Los Angeles Times* story about the *Glomar Explorer*; the *News* had picked it up from the *Times*'s news service. The deep-sea salvage mission immediately connected itself in Hersh's mind to his own almost-forgotten information about Project Jennifer, which he had supposed had to do with salvaging Russian ICBMs from the Pacific test range.

Hersh immediately called Colby. Now he saw the significance of Jennifer, he said; he hadn't realized its importance before; and as agreed he was notifying Colby that he was going back to work on the story.

According to a transcript of the conversation later released by the CIA as a result of a lawsuit brought under the Freedom of Information Act, Colby told Hersh: "You have been first-class about this thing for a long time . . . you have been damn good."

"I am a citizen, too," Hersh replied.

But then he took a plane to the West Coast; exactly what he did and whom he saw remains in his own files, but at his usual headlong pace within a week he was able to find the major outlines of the story of the *Glomar Explorer*—a story he estimated would take six columns in *The New York Times.*

But Colby had not been idle. Again, he had reached for the phone—this time to call Arthur Sulzberger, publisher of the *Times.* Hersh was digging into a serious national-security matter, Colby told Sulzberger. The *Los Angeles Times* had patriotically soft-pedaled that same story; there could be grave international repercussions if *The New York Times* printed it. Sulzberger conferred with Abe Rosenthal, his managing editor.

When they queried Hersh, he said he was not quite ready to write his story anyway.

Rosenthal says he never spoke to Colby directly. He asked Clifton Daniel, the Washington bureau chief in 1975, to confer with Colby and pass along the CIA director's arguments. Colby's basic request was for sufficient delay—Rosenthal understood this could mean several months or more—in publication so that the *Explorer* could try again to recover nuclear warheads from the Soviet sub. That had weight with Rosenthal; in his long reporting career he had many times covered disarmament conferences, and he believed the recovery of Soviet warheads could be of considerable help to the United States in strategic arms limitation talks.

Meanwhile, as a result of the Los Angeles publication, Colby was getting queries from other news organizations—*Time* magazine, for example. He put it to them all that the *Los Angeles Times* had played down the story at his request, and claimed that *The New York Times* was holding off publication. Either to *Time* or to other inquirers, he also made the point that even ferocious Seymour Hersh had backed off the story, at the CIA's request, for more than a year—so grave could be the consequences of publishing. He did *not* say Hersh was furiously back at work on Project Jennifer; perhaps he thought the *Times* had in fact called Hersh off the story.

When Hersh did turn in his article, late in February or early in March, Abe Rosenthal pondered the matter for several days. Ordinarily, Rosenthal is fiercely committed to the post-Vietnam ethic of disclosure; he has also been a staunch defender of Hersh's most controversial stories. But this time he told Hersh he had a "feeling in my stomach" that it would be wrong to publish the story. It concerned an "on-going intelligence operation"—Colby had said the *Glomar Explorer* might return to the salvage site—in international waters, and further disclosure could have grave consequences.

Stunned, the volatile Hersh—whose articles on CIA domestic spying had yet to be fully vindicated—asked in an outraged memo to Rosenthal how the case was any different from Rosenthal's and Sulzberger's epochal decision to publish the Pentagon Papers, four years earlier, in the midst of an "on-going war"?

But Rosenthal, in consultation with Sulzberger, maintained his position through further exhanges of memos. The story would not be published in the *Times* until the CIA either completed a second attempt to salvage the submarine or abandoned the project altogether—or until someone else published the story.

Hersh was given to understand that his story was being "held up" pending further research rather than being killed outright. Daniel relayed Rosenthal's decision to Colby, who was at that point triumphant. According to the documents released in the lawsuit, he even had a letter from the *Times* (the signature was deleted before the letter was released) agreeing to hold the story. Colby could and did tell other news organizations that the *Times* and Hersh were holding off publication, using that to bolster his argument that the *Glomar Explorer* story should not be published in the interest of national security.

Colby is known to have talked at least the following out of publishing or broadcasting, in addition to the two *Times*es and *Time* magazine: *The Washington Post*, NBC, ABC, *Newsweek*, *Parade*, and *The Washington Star*. All had been zealous pursuers of the Watergate story; the *Times* and the *Post* had been the Pentagon Papers defendants; and, taken together, their acceptance of Colby's arguments seems astonishing.

Yet the question has to be asked: were the editors of these news organizations all so sensitive to their long conflict with succeeding administrations—on the Bay of Pigs, Vietnam, Agnew's charges, leaks, sources, the Pentagon Papers, Watergate, CIA and FBI abuses—that they were unconsciously willing to be persuaded not to precipitate another "national security" fight? My instinct is that they were, whatever may have been their conscious reasoning. And *tactically*, in March 1975, so soon after Nixon's resignation, there may have been something to be said for a "low profile" by the most controversial organs of the press. The *Times*, in particular, was already embroiled with the CIA over Hersh's December allegations.

Rosenthal vigorously disputes this notion. "The *Glomar* [incident] was the first time that I ever felt that the arguments against immediate publication outweighed the arguments in favor," he told me later. "I do not believe in delaying publication of stories. . . . In this case, I felt that the goals were so important that a reasonable case had been made for delay." His experience in disarmament coverage was a "definite factor" in his decision, he said; so were Hersh's own delays in getting the story ready to print.

Colby succeeded in tying up the *Times* on another front.

Inviting Hersh, Daniel, and Bill Kovach, the Washington bureau news editor, to Langley for a briefing, he offered to fill them in more completely, and generously said he'd be happy to tell them when the national security would permit publication. To the dismay of Hersh and Kovach, Daniel accepted this proposition; but Hersh did get in return some information he hadn't had—for example, a more precise location of the salvage site in the Pacific.

But—for the same reason that Ford's luncheon leak to the *Times* could not possibly be kept secret—Colby's deft scotching of the *Glomar Explorer* story could not long be sustained. There was just too much known, by too many people. Soon, Daniel was calling Colby to complain that the story was "all over town." Boldly, Colby said he was holding Daniel to his agreement not to publish until the CIA gave permission. Bill Kovach, meanwhile, was working strenuously to persuade *Times* editors to go ahead with the story.

Then, on March 18, Hersh had a call from Les Whitten, a tough and perceptive reporter for columnist Jack Anderson. Did Hersh know anything about the submarine story? Was it valid? Anderson was thinking of using it on his radio program that night. (Anderson had picked up the story from Charles Morgan, Jr., in 1975 the director of the Washington office of the American Civil Liberties Union, a lawyer who would have made a great reporter. Morgan then believed the *Explorer* was an American effort to steal a march on the world in the area of ocean-mining rights, and since a United Nations conference on the law of the sea had convened the day before at Geneva, he was making strenuous efforts on March 18 to get the story into print.)

Hersh gave Whitten some suggestions on further sources; Whitten followed up and called back at about 5:30 P.M. to say that Jack Anderson would broadcast the story that night, on a program that began at 7:55 P.M., before the first edition of the *Times* would appear in New York. Hersh informed Daniel, who called Anderson, who confirmed his intention to broadcast the story. With that assurance, and urged on by Kovach, the *Times* decided that it would publish Hersh's "delayed" article in the editions of March 19—first letting Jack Anderson break the story and the national-security mystique.

But the dogged Colby was not done. Getting wind of Anderson's intention, he tried to stop the columnist from broadcasting the *Glomar Explorer* story. Anderson refused to heed Colby's plea. He later said he thought that since Watergate "a lot of reporters are wearing a hairshirt—sackcloth and ashes . . . and they're overdoing it a little bit, trying to prove too hard how patriotic and responsible we are."

Seymour Hersh could not resist calling a *Times* editor that night to inquire why, if his story should not have been published for national-security reasons in February, it could be published in March, national security or no national security?

In the *Glomar Explorer* case, it turned out not to matter. Colby had done yeoman work—but not to protect national security. As Hersh's nine-column story made clear when it finally appeared, Colby had been covering up an important CIA *failure,* in which at least $350 million, perhaps as much as $750 million, had been spent on the recovery of one-third of an old submarine hull and the bodies of seventy Soviet seamen—but no hydrogen warheads, no code books, and little else of substance.

When Hersh, Daniel, and Kovach met with Colby at CIA headquarters, Hersh had noticed a slight loss of composure by Colby when it became clear that Hersh knew that only a third of the submarine hull had been recovered. That crucial fact had not appeared in the *Los Angeles Times* story, the only published reference to the salvage effort. Colby's behavior tended to confirm Hersh's view that Project Jennifer had been a costly failure.

He was even surer after his story appeared and government officials corrected one of his assertions—the sunken sub, they said, had not been nuclear but diesel-powered. Colby had not bothered to make *that* point in his generous briefing at Langley. Hersh deduced that he had wanted to make the project seem as important as possible, and recovering a nuclear sub would have been far more useful than salvaging an older diesel model.

That may have been one point Senator Frank Church—who quickly announced plans to add Jennifer to his Intelligence Committee's agenda—had in mind when he said caustically: "If we are prepared to pay Howard Hughes $350 million for an obsolete Russian submarine, it's no wonder we're broke."

Senator W. Stuart Symington, usually a staunch CIA backer, was miffed that his friends in the agency had not informed him of the project, despite his membership on the

Intelligence Subcommittee of the Armed Forces Committee. "What would be on a submarine built in 1968 that we didn't know about in 1974 or 1975?" he asked, reasonably enough. But Representative George Mahon of Texas, chairman of the House Appropriations Committee, had been briefed in advance and he shrugged off Jennifer as a "gamble that lost." This is an odd phrase to apply to a "grave national-security matter," to say the least.

Still, Mahon might have been right had it been a question only of whether the *Glomar Explorer* recovered all or only a third of the Soviet sub. Any mechanical equipment can fail, as the *Explorer*'s lifting apparatus had when the sub had been raised about halfway to the surface, approximately eight thousand feet above the ocean floor; two-thirds of the hull broke off and fell back into the depths. But the real question was not one of mechanical failure, or even a third of a loaf, but whether the operation ever had been worth its risks. Was it a gamble worth taking?

A Ford administration official put the matter in this perspective for Hersh: "If the project was sold on the basis of what we're going to get, okay—we didn't get it."

Project Jennifer of course offered certain possibilities. Even old code books might have shed some light on pre-1968 Soviet communications traffic, for whatever that could have been worth. Recovery of a missile might have helped weapons experts check against their more theoretical evaluation of Soviet arms. Metallurgical analysis of the submarine's hull would no doubt have been useful. Knowledge of design changes since the submarine's construction might have given American negotiators some leverage in arms limitation talks. Any additional knowledge of Soviet submarines would almost certainly be of some advantage. Whatever advances, if any, the *Explorer* herself represented in ocean-mining techniques still are not known. They could have been significant.

These possibilities have to be weighed against more than the probable half-billion dollars or more that Project Jennifer cost. Numerous authorities argued before the project was authorized and after the story appeared that outmoded code books and missiles—at least six years old—could have yielded little useful information. It was not possible, moreover, to give the *Explorer* a naval escort *and* maintain secrecy, so that the real possibility of a Soviet attack on her existed—particularly if the Soviets knew of some vital secret that might be found aboard.

Even if Moscow could be counted on sensibly to refrain from going that far in the event of exposure of the project, such exposure was an ever-present danger to Soviet-American relations, then in the development stages of détente. The operation was an affront to the Russians in two ways—that the United States had located the sub when the Soviet Navy could not, and that the United States was trying to salvage Soviet military property in secrecy. And Global Marine had joint undersea research ventures going forward with the Soviets; the company's participation in the salvage job could also jeopardize those joint projects, and by that much diminish Soviet-American détente.

After the failure of the first salvage job, in 1974, Colby might have had at least two legitimate reasons for trying to maintain secrecy. He wanted, no doubt, to protect the exotic details of the *Explorer*'s constructions and operations—but, as it developed, these were not exposed by stories on Project Jennifer and still are not generally known. Colby also was trying, as he had told Abe Rosenthal and Arthur Sulzberger, to protect the possibility of another effort in 1975 at raising the rest of the submarine hull. Exposure of the 1974 effort could cause the Soviets or Congress or American public opinion to act against its repetition—but a repetition would be sensible only if Project Jennifer itself had been sensible, on a cost-and-risk vs. benefit basis.

That is highly doubtful, not just because only a third of the hull and no useful Soviet secrets were recovered, but because there never was much probability that the operation would bear fruit anywhere near commensurate with its costs and risks. Henry Kissinger, for one, told Hersh he had had little use for the project and had never expected much from it.

Why, then, did Kissinger—who could have stopped the project—let it go forward? "Frankly," a Kissinger aide said, "I don't think we cared that much about it." But Hersh's private theory—one that squares with bureaucratic practice since time immemorial—is that Kissinger, knowing his cloak-and-dagger colleagues, approved their pet project of derring-do, and thereafter had a certain leverage—or "stroke"—on the CIA for things *he* wanted from the agency.

That reading of the episode is bolstered, and a good deal is told about the CIA mentality, by the comment on Jennifer of an agency wizard queried by Hersh. Even if the project *was* only partially successful, he said, "it was a fantastic operation." He meant the CIA's success in carrying out Jennifer under a complicated cover story had been "fantastic." It didn't much weigh with him that nothing had been gained but seventy Soviet corpses.

What is most pertinent here is that had *The New York Times* printed what it knew a month sooner that it did, had the *Los Angeles Times* known and printed the full story on February 8, had any of the other news organizations who tinkered with the story overriden Colby's protestations and published or broadcast what they knew, *nothing adverse to the national security would have happened.* It is, of course, arguable that had anyone learned of the story while the *Glomar Explorer* was actually engaged in salvage, publication should have been withheld until the operation was completed, in deference to the safety of the men aboard the ship.

Once the *Explorer* was safely in harbor, there was little justification for withholding publication—certainly not on grounds of national security. As so often happens, the press had yielded to the national-security mystique, only to learn later that it had actually been protecting nothing but the CIA's dubious project, and its desire to try again what it perhaps never should have attempted in the first place.

A lesson learned? Not exactly. Just a year later the press again showed its vulnerability to the national-security mystique, though not so blatantly as the House of Representatives did. Once again, the CIA was at the center of the controversy.

A House committee investigation of the agency had gone forward somewhat parallel with the Senate probe headed by Frank Church; but since the Senate inquiry had focused heavily on the assassination issue, the House committee, chaired by Representative Otis G. Pike of New York, had taken a different tack. It went beyond the question of CIA illegalities to that of its efficacy. Was the agency any good? Was it doing its job?

This approach might have been taken, also, because the House committee was less "manageable" than Church's group, with a membership less inclined to awe of the agency and of "national security," and less linked to CIA interests by long association. But this was in one sense a disadvantage; it enabled the CIA to denounce the Pike committee for leaks, faulty security, and hostility toward the intelligence community—in effect to mount a counterattack, using the old bureaucratic ploy of shifting the focus from the thing being investigated to the alleged faults of the investigators.

Nevertheless, by January 1976, the Pike committee had completed its inquiry and drafted a powerful report, amply documented, mostly from the agency's own files. It detailed, for example, a particularly shocking American double cross—there is no other term—of the CIA-armed Kurdish rebels in Iraq, a betrayal which permitted Iraqi troops to wipe out the rebellion Washington had encouraged. And the report contended that for all its expenditures, secrecy, lawbreaking, far-flung operations, and proud boasts of mighty contributions to the national security, the CIA had *failed* to give political and military leaders sufficient advance warning of:

- The Tet offensive in Vietnam in 1968.
- The October 1973 war in the Middle East.
- The Portuguese revolution of 1974.
- India's explosion of a nuclear device in 1974.
- The coup on Cyprus, also in 1974, which led to the Turkish invasion of Cyprus.

Here was *news*. Not vital secrets but well-supported allegations from a public body that the CIA as an intelligence agency was rather like Richard Nixon as a guardian of law and order—not quite so good as claimed. Even before the report could be published, the CIA reacted to drafts as if to a rattlesnake and in the finest bureaucratic tradition—with outrage and charges that the report was biased, distorted, inaccurate, and seriously threatened—you guessed it—the national security. Since the Pike committee *was* rather leaky, *The New York Times* was able to publish several stories detailing the major points of the as-yet-unpublished report; and the persistent Dan Schorr, who had broken the assassination story nine months earlier, was broadcasting stories on CBS which could only have been derived from ample access to the committee's draft report.

These disclosures prompted one of the most startling acts that history records of locking the barn door after the theft of a somewhat spavined horse. Late in 1975, responding no doubt to accounts of CIA excesses, several publications, mostly in Europe, had begun listing the names of CIA agents and their stations. One so named was Richard S. Welch, an agent in Athens. On December 23, 1975, Welch was shot and killed by persons unknown, possibly because of his public identification—although any determined assassin could have learned his identity, since the various Athens station chiefs for the agency had always succeeded each other not only in office but in the same comfortable house!

From that day forward, the CIA had been able to orchestrate an effective campaign against breaches of national security—which, as we have seen, is easy enough to do. Welch's murder dramatized the issue; the Pike committee's leaks exacerbated it. The *Times* publications and Schorr's broadcasts brought matters to a head. The national security—particularly the lives of CIA men abroad—seemed to many to be threatened by an irresponsible press.

On January 30, 1976, the House of Representatives voted 246 to 124—virtually two to one—*not* to publish the Pike committee report, ostensibly on grounds of national security. Probably the House was within its rights in so doing, although the report had been compiled by public servants, paid for by public funds (about a half-million dollars), analyzed the activities of a tax-supported agency, and had been developed partially in public hearings.

Reporters familiar with the House knew that this ludicrous step—the House, after all, had established the Pike committee for no other reason than to report on the CIA—was a direct result of the countercampaign against leaks that had risen to a crescendo since Welch's murder. But 1976 was an election year and every member had to face his or her constituency; few wanted to do so while vulnerable to charges of indifference to national security.

The vote appeared futile at first, since the *Times* and Schorr had already disclosed so much of the report. Most of the content that might actually have been construed to have something to do with national security had been made public; there was no evidence of substantial inaccuracy, other than self-serving CIA charges. Only if the House was acting out of political caution did its vote make any sense. Members of the House clearly feared the voting public's devotion to the idea that secrecy means security and vice versa.

On February 16 and 23, however, *The Village Voice,* a New York weekly, published long excerpts from the text of the Pike committee report. They took disclosure little further than Schorr and the *Times* already had, but they added textual authority. And they directly challenged the House's decision not to publish the report officially. If the House chose to make an issue of the *Voice* publication, someone could be in trouble for contempt of Congress.

The day after the *Voice* published the Pike report, *The Washington Post*, in a story by Lawrence Stern, identified Daniel Schorr as the person who had made the Pike report available to the Manhattan weekly. Schorr quickly confessed, although he at first denied to Stern that he had given the report to the *Voice*.

Schorr's identification raised the definite possibility of contempt action. If the House pursued the matter, and officially demanded to know from whom Schorr had got the report, he might be voted in contempt of Congress if he refused to answer. Almost immediately, the House *did* vote instructions to its moribund Committee on Standards of Official Conduct— which had *never* investigated any member of Congress—to investigate Dan Schorr and the leaking of the Pike report.

CBS almost as promptly suspended Schorr from active practice as a correspondent,* although the network agreed to pay the legal costs of defending him in the congressional investigation and any litigation that might follow. Once again, "national security" had produced a direct clash between the government—this time its legislative branch—and the press.

As conceded, the House may have been within its rights when it voted not to publish the report. But its legal right to have proceeded *further* is disputable. Surely the House had no right to decree that *no one* could publish an existing document, especially the official report of an official committee. The Supreme Court had held in the Pentagon Papers case of 1971 that the executive branch had no power except in the most narrowly defined circumstances to impose prior restraint on publication. Neither the espionage statutes nor those concerning disclosure of classified communications intelligence information appeared, in the opinion of authorities, to apply to what Schorr had done.

---

*Schorr has since disclosed that he was asked to, and did, sign a letter of resignation; it was not then disclosed, so that his legal defense would not be jeopardized.

But no one—least of all anyone in the press—should have been under any illusion about the chilling effect of the Schorr case. Even if Schorr himself suffered no further penalty from the House and was reinstated by CBS News, that he was being investigated by the House committee and had been suspended by the network were facts likely to cause some reporters to tread more carefully when in the neighborhood of so-called national-security information.

If the House acted against Schorr, or if it didn't and CBS News did not reinstate him, the chilling effect would become freezing. If both penalized him, many reporters and more publishers would think long and hard before they dared challenge the power of the government—whether the executive or the legislative branch—to suppress information, and to cloak its activities in the secrecy to which claims of national security inevitably lead. Moreover, Schorr himself would have suffered a grave injustice.

Schorr first thought of publishing the report as a paper-bound book, to which he would contribute an introduction. He gave CBS News a Xerox copy of the document and asked if any publishing subsidiary of the network wanted to handle the job. Receiving no answer, he sought the help of the Reporters' Committee for the Freedom of the Press, an organization whose title describes it. The committee put him in touch with its lawyer, Peter Tufo, who was a member of the board of the New York Magazine Company, publisher of *The Village Voice*.

Tufo could make no book-publishing arrangement and quickly turned to Clay Felker, the operating chief of the New York Magazine Company. Felker agreed to publish the report, and to make a money contribution to the Reporters' Committee. None of the contribution was to go to Schorr; the committee ultimately decided not to accept it; and Felker never in fact made the contribution. Still, this part of the transaction led to the idea that Schorr was "selling secrets" and *The New York Times*—publisher of the Pentagon Papers!—even rebuked him with an editorial under that headline. This editorial undoubtedly stiffened the House's determination to go after Schorr.

The *Voice*, despite its anti-Establishment history, struck many critics as an inappropriate place for the report to appear; particularly when it had been provided by a CBS reporter. Schorr may have made some preliminary efforts, after first denying to Stern that he had been the *Voice*'s source, to hint that another CBS reporter might have been responsible; but in less than a day he was taking full responsibility. Schorr was an abrasive reporter anyway, and a hard competitor with his CBS colleagues and with other reporters. As all these elements of the story became known, many who should have supported release of the report held back, instead, from defending the man who had released it.

But I. F. Stone, never one to be put off the main point and reliable as ever in defense of knowledge, wrote that Schorr and the *Voice* had "performed a public service. They acted to print the text only after the House vote to suppress, when there was clearly a duty to make the text available." But the *Times* editorial, the *Washington Post*'s eager identification of Shorr, his suspension by CBS, Schorr's own panicky early attempts to evade responsibility, the adverse reaction of many of his colleagues, however motivated—all tended to make Schorr appear to have carried disclosure to lengths that the press itself would not support.

The ethics committee was voted $150,000 for its probe of the leak and employed twelve ex-FBI agents to track down the culprit who had given the report to Schorr. All that was clearly permissible; the House had every right and a clear duty to try to enforce its own security procedures. But the leak was never discovered, and as had been almost inevitable, Schorr was finally called as a witness and directed on September 15, 1976, to tell the committee who had given him the report.

He refused numerous times to do so; each was a possible act of contempt, if the committee and the House so voted. But Schorr eloquently proclaimed a reporter's right to protect the identity of his source, at least before a congressional committee. He made a strong case in his own behalf, undistracted by the peripheral charges of "selling secrets" and blaming colleagues that had at first weakened his position. The political panic over "national security" had waned since January, and good head-counts in the House suggested that members had no real stomach for a constitutional confrontation with the press on First Amendment grounds. Six months after publication of the Pike report, members reasoned, better to forget the whole thing.

So the committee recommended no contempt charges but offered a lecture to the press as gratuitous as, if somewhat less offensive than, that by Justice Blackmun in the Pentagon Papers case:

"Newsmen, just like anyone else, are not infallible in their judgments of what is right or wrong, good or bad for our nation. The mere assertion by a newsman that he revealed government secrets 'for the good of the country' does not insure the country actually will benefit...."

To which it is appropriate to respond: of course not, but neither does the mere assertion by some official that he is keeping information secret "for the good of the country." There is far more evidence to show unnecessary, self-serving, damaging, and deceitful classification of information by the government than to demonstrate unnecessary, self-serving, damaging, and deceitful publication by the press.

"The fact is [the ethics committee continued] the news media frequently do not possess sufficient information on which to make a prudent decision on whether the revelation of a secret will help or harm. We suggest caution and discretion should be the watchwords."

Of course they should be and of course newspapermen and broadcasters may be in some cases insufficiently informed to predict all the repercussions that might result from publication. The committee did not here acknowledge, however, the other side of that issue—that news organizations are not as limited by self-interest, official policy, and bureaucratic procedure as would be any government department or official in making such evaluations of information. Who is the better judge—one who is personally and politically disinterested, or one whose career may be at stake or whose policy is at issue or whose interests are otherwise served by the secrecy he or she has the power to impose?

Or, in the case of Daniel Schorr, was an uninvolved reporter as good or better a judge of the national interest as the 246 members of Congress—all of them facing an election—who voted to suppress the Pike report over the votes of 124 colleagues and the strenuous objection of Otis Pike and his committee majority? I'd argue that Dan Schorr *was* a better judge in that instance—but as soon as the House committee retreated, CBS News announced Schorr's resignation.

No doubt network executives had reasons beyond Schorr's literal responsibility for handing the Pike report to *The Village Voice*. But those reasons were never made clear and the net public effect was and is that after Schorr caused the report to be made public he was out of a network job. In the years to come,

no one will be able to show how many stories did *not* make the
nightly news or the headlines because those who might have
reported them took due note of the departure of Daniel Schorr,
and chose the better part of valor. I fear they will be many.

The echoes of the Schorr affair had scarcely faded with his
departure to the faculty of the University of California when the
national-security mystique claimed another victim—or at least
was made the instrument by which he was eliminated. He was
another "leaker," or so his critics charged—Theodore C.
Sorensen, the brilliant former counsel and speech-writer for
John Kennedy, later a successful attorney and unsuccessful
Senate candidate in New York.

When President-elect Carter in late 1976 appointed Sorensen
to be the director of the CIA, no real opposition was anticipated.
Sorensen had had little experience, on paper, in intelligence
work, but he had been at Kennedy's side in the Bay of Pigs and
Cuban missile crises, an important White House adviser in every
national-security crunch of the period. He had been a World
War II conscientious objector, but that had been known during
his White House days and had not troubled anyone he had then
worked with. He had little administrative experience, but the
real problem was not just to administer the CIA but to control it,
make it bend to the President's will, serve his foreign-policy
needs, and honor the Constitution, the law, and its own charter.

Aloof and chilly in personal relations—or appearing
so—Sorensen was not popular, but he was respected for his
intelligence and for what had been highly prized in the Kennedy
era, a "hard nose." Many thought he would control the agency
strongly—that a hard-nosed conscientious objector who
remembered the Bay of Pigs was just what the doctor ordered.

Apparently the intelligence community also believed Sorensen would tighten control over the agency, owing to his tough
statements against covert operations and the like. Suddenly, like
wildfire, opposition to his appointment flashed through
Congress, especially the Senate Intelligence Committee. Ignit-
ing it was testimony Sorensen had given years earlier, including
an affidavit he had written when *The New York Times* published
the Pentagon Papers.

After publication was enjoined and the case went to court,
the *Times* and its attorneys had sought in various ways to show

that the government and many government officials did not necessarily regard classified documents as sacred. Sorensen, as a former White House official with a top security clearance, wrote that he was thoroughly familiar with classified documents, many of which he had written for President Kennedy. Having read the documents the *Times* had published, he said in his affidavit, he did not believe they would embarrass foreign governments, nor did any of the "information and opinions revealed appear to have any current facets requiring continued secrecy."

Then, in 1973, Sorensen stuck his neck out further. For the Ellsberg defense in the second Pentagon Papers case, he filed an affidavit in which he described how he had taken boxes of documents, some classified, from the White House when he left it in 1964 to write a book on Kennedy's administration. His point was not that he had been a grievous leaker of secrets, but that classification was usually so routine and meaningless that his mere use of these documents in writing his book had not been a security breach at all. Many other government officials, including presidents, can be shown to have done the same thing upon returning to private life.

Almost any reporter, in fact, has had the experience of receiving a classified document from a government official, sometimes a president. Secretary of State John Foster Dulles personally handed the Top Secret Yalta papers to James Reston, intending them to be published. Morton Halperin has pointed out, for more recent examples, that Secretary of Defense Robert S. McNamara, annoyed at being accused of "de-nuclearizing" Europe, told a European news conference that there were more than seven thousand American nuclear weapons in Europe; and that President Nixon, while insisting that an American reconnaissance plane shot down off the North Korean coast had not strayed over that country's waters, told the press that the United States had tracked Soviet radar tracking the American plane. These were major leaks of properly classified information, but the skies didn't fall, nor any major crises result; and such disregard of classification by the government itself points up the frequent meaninglessness of the classification stamp.

Nevertheless, the sudden circulation of Sorensen's affidavit in the Ellsberg case made him appear an irresponsible handler of secret materials. Some Republicans on the Senate Intelligence

Committee suddenly saw a chance to rebuff the new Democratic President; other members of that committee were anxious to assert its independence. Some senators were more genuinely disturbed over the affidavit itself—Adlai E. Stevenson III of Illinois, for example, thought it reflected on Sorensen's judgment that he had not discussed its existence with Carter; Charles McC. Mathias, Jr., of Maryland thought the affidavit suggested an "everybody does it" rationale too much like Richard Nixon's Watergate defense. Besides, the abrasive Sorensen had no real depth of support to fall back on. As his chances slipped, all the other possible charges against him—lack of experience, conscientious objection—were quickly brought out.

Primarily, however, it was his candid testimony on classified documents that did in Sorensen. There was not much doubt that its circulation had been sped along, if not by the CIA itself, at least by those in, near to, or once a part of the intelligence community who did not want a director from outside the community's old-boy network, one who was not deluded by the national-security mystique, and who stated flatly his intentions to curb the agency's activities to the limits of the law and administration policy. One intelligence community hawk told *New York Times* reporters reconstructing the episode that Sorensen would be "about as welcome at Langley as Sherman was in Atlanta."

As always, it was not hard for these anti-Sorensen forces to find allies in the Senate and even in the press—from which Sorensen got so little editorial support as to suggest again how susceptible the press is to the national-security mystique. Even *The New York Times,* which he had supported with his affidavit in 1971, expressed only lukewarm regret at his forced withdrawal in 1977.

There seems to be a public impression that the press leaps at any chance to rush into print with government secrets, scarcely pausing to think about, or happily ignoring, the consequences. If so, few impressions are more erroneous. Neither does the press leap at such chances nor does it brush off the possible consequences.

It's true, as I've suggested, that in the post-Vietnam, post-Watergate era, the press is becoming more aggressive, even as to "national security." But that may be no more than a temporary trend; the longer history is of a press not anxious to challenge or antagonize either the government or other powerful institutions.

In 1965, to cite one example in which I was involved, a story broke from Singapore that Prime Minister Lee Kuan Yew had been offered a $3.3 million bribe by the CIA to cover up an agency operation that had misfired in 1960. Secretary of State Dean Rusk, it developed, had been obliged to send Lee a note of apology. This piqued the interest of Turner Catledge, the executive editor of the *Times,* and he set in motion an assignment that resulted in a five-part "takeout" on the CIA, about twenty-three thousand words in all, to which dozens of *Times* correspondents around the world contributed. As Washington bureau chief, I was in charge of the project, with principal assistance from Max Frankel, E. W. Kenworthy, and John Finney of the bureau.

A project of that magnitude can't be carried out in secrecy—as the government itself would do well to learn. We sought, therefore, as much cooperation as the Johnson administration would give us, Frankel and I interviewing, for example, McGeorge Bundy, then the White House national-security adviser, and I talking separately to Richard Helms, the agency's deputy director, and Clark Clifford, a member of the President's Foreign Intelligence Advisory Board. We received enough cooperation to suggest that someone in the administration, perhaps Bundy, had concluded it was better to have an administration "input" to our articles than to let us work only with what we could turn up on our own.

Our activities nevertheless produced trepidation in Langley and a phone call from Rusk to Catledge and Arthur Sulzberger. As Catledge recalls in his memoirs,* Rusk, a fellow Southern Presbyterian, asked him to give "prayerful consideration" to whether or not the *Times* ought to publish a series that—as Rusk saw it—might upset intelligence operations, endanger agents, offend allies, encourage adversaries, and otherwise damage— the magic phrase!—national security. The series survived this and some other high-level expressions of concern; but those inquiries did cause Catledge and Managing Editor Clifton Daniel to have the series read before publication by John

---

*My Life and The Times (New York: Harper & Row, 1971).

McCone, formerly the director of the CIA during the Kennedy years.

Catledge's account of his reasoning is significant:

"Our purpose in working with McCone was not to protect the government but to protect the *Times*. Any newspaperman is liable to error, and when fifty or a hundred newspapermen file stories from around the world on an espionage agency the possibilities of error are very high indeed. It is better to correct errors before you make them than to apologize for them afterward. In this case, there was the risk that the CIA would use one error to attack the entire series."

There certainly was that risk; and Catledge's view can be seen as little different from that of whoever in the government decided to cooperate with the *Times* in order to influence the series as much as possible.

More than ten years later, it's not clear to me whether I was a party to the decision to bring in an "expert" to monitor the series. I *was*, I recall, one of those who recommended McCone, if anyone was to do the job. I did not, I'm sure, make much protest, if any at all. As had been the case when LBJ told me, in December 1963, about the possibility of CIA assassination attempts, I was myself something of a victim of the national-security mystique. The last thing I would have wanted—then or now—would be to endanger agents' lives or to "blow" some sensitive operation in an important part of the world. Now, however, I would be much less likely to believe that publication would have such dire results.

To this day, I regard Catledge's reasoning, quoted above, as sound, if—two very large ifs—the appointed monitor can be counted on to do a fair, honest, disinterested job, and the editors he works with maintain a rigid distinction between demonstrable errors and security threats, on one hand, and government value judgments or unsupported assertions that there *might* be adverse reaction, on the other. It goes without saying that no cover-up of mere embarrassments should be permitted by editors, who must reserve all final judgments for themselves. If all these conditions can be met—which is admittedly not easy—it seems to me that the public's right to know is better served than by a quixotic display of press independence which, by error and inadvertence, might well bring the press into deserved opprobrium.

With due respect to John McCone, however, I now would

insist on some less committed monitor than he, and I would have much more skepticism about any government-connected person doing "a fair, honest, disinterested job" in such circumstances. I might also be less willing to rely on the stout insistence of editors that they would exercise the right of final judgment. Catledge's report, in a memo to Arthur Sulzberger on the results of McCone's work, is a little dismaying:

"Every point raised [by McCone for the CIA] has been carefully considered and in almost every case the piece has been revised or modified in line with [McCone's] suggestions. Here and there when he raised points in which nothing but pure value judgments were involved we have preserved our own language. . . . I don't know of any other series in my time which has been prepared with greater care and with such remarkable attention to the views of the agency involved as this one."

That memo, it should be said, was written in the pre-Vietnam, pre-Watergate period, and was an internal document intended to make the case for publication and to assure Sulzberger that every precaution had been taken. It proved persuasive, the CIA series was published, and the episode might well have steeled Punch Sulzberger for the greater ordeal of the Pentagon Papers five years later. And whatever concessions were made to McCone, I don't remember feeling that the series had been much or seriously altered.

But although we congratulated ourselves at the time on the most extensive newspaper reporting that had then been done on the CIA, I'm afraid in retrospect that McCone didn't have to argue to suppress a lot of material; there just wasn't that much in the series, I can see now, to cause the CIA undue alarm—much less to threaten national security.

Two footnotes to this tale of another era:

At a social occasion on perhaps the third or fourth night after publication of the CIA series began, a ranking CIA official accosted me drunkenly, loudly, and abusively. I should be proud of myself, he said, with scorn; my name was being mentioned on Moscow Radio. Later he sent me a handsome note of apology.

After several weeks in which numerous book publishers approached the *Times* about fashioning the series into a book, I was having a splendid lunch with my old friend Wallace Turner, the *Times*'s West Coast bureau chief, at Bardelli's in San Francisco. I was paged to the phone. Catledge came on the line to tell me a decision had been made—there would be no CIA book. There would be no explanation, either.

The CIA series was only another instance of the *Times*'s concern for national security—and, indeed, until the Pentagon Papers, the *Times* was more often criticized by dissidents for playing "on the team" than by security buffs for disclosing secrets.

In 1960, for example, the *Times* had had knowledge of U-2 overflights of the Soviet Union *before* a U-2 was shot down over Russia that year—and after President Eisenhower issued an untrue "cover story" that the craft was off course, letting the cover story stand until the Soviets shattered it. Even now, withholding publication of the overflight story in those presatellite days seems responsible, since publication either would have put an end to the profitable flights or resulted in a U-2 being shot down. Whether or not the *Times* or any newspaper should have acquiesced in Eisenhower's lie is another matter entirely, particularly since the lie couldn't hold anyway.

In 1962, after a personal appeal from President Kennedy, the *Times* withheld publication of the fact that operational Soviet missile bases had been discovered in Cuba, within range of American cities. On that occasion, Kennedy first called James Reston, the Washington bureau chief, who advised the President to call Publisher Orvil Dryfoos. In 1966, in a speech to the World Press Institute, Clifton Daniel quoted Reston as telling Kennedy that "if my advice were asked I would recommend that we not publish." After Kennedy called Dryfoos, he did put the issue to Reston and others and the decision was made not to publish.

This led Kennedy, in May 1963, after Orvil Dryfoos's untimely death, to write Mrs. Dryfoos in praise of her husband's decision "to refrain from printing on October 21st, the news, which only the man for The Times possessed, on the presence of Russian missiles in Cuba, upon my informing him that we needed twenty-four hours more to complete our preparations."

More than a decade later, it's hard to assess this episode. The missile story was withheld when American forces already were in motion toward the blockade of Cuba that Kennedy soon announced. Would publication have forced him to change that plan, or lessened the possibility of confrontation, or given the

Soviets and Cubans an important advantage comparable to that actually attained by Kennedy through surprise? By giving Kennedy the opportunity to shock the nation with his television announcement of the presence of the missiles and his blockade plans, did the *Times* let him color public opinion irrevocably to the not necessarily accurate view that the United States was intolerably menaced by the Soviet missiles? Would publication, in short, have heightened or eased the risks of war, at the most precarious point in post-World War II history?

Whatever the answer, my point here is that both the U-2 episode and the missile crisis importantly support the idea that the American press usually has been reluctant—not eager—to publish stories supposedly dealing with national security. The Bay of Pigs fiasco of 1963 provides a better example and clearer consequences.

The story has been told too often to need detailed repetition. The essential facts are that on April 6, 1961, the *Times* had in hand a story more than two columns long by Tad Szulc, in which Szulc documented the training of a Cuban exile army in the United States and Central America, declared that its invasion of Castro's Cuba was "imminent," and specified that the operation was CIA-sponsored and planned. News editors understandably enough "dummied in" this story to run under a four-column headline as the page-one lead for April 7.

Catledge, then the managing editor, sought Reston's advice from Washington. Reston, who had been working hard to pin down the same story, said that his information was that an invasion was *not* "imminent." With Dryfoos's consent, Catledge took three steps (according to his account):

• He ordered the reference to an "imminent" invasion deleted, on grounds that it was an undocumented prediction, however logically deduced.

• He excised references to the CIA and substituted such descriptions as "U.S. experts," explaining that there were numerous intelligence agencies and the *Times* might not be able to support Szulc's specific references to CIA sponsorship.

• Having demoted an imminent, CIA-sponsored invasion to a more vaguely sponsored operation that had "reached the stage of adequate preparation" (a Szulc phrase in the story's fourth paragraph), Catledge killed the four-column headline and moved the story to column four, top of page one, under a one-column head: "Anti-Castro Units/Trained to Fight/At Florida Bases."

Catledge had to fight these decisions through, over the protests of Assistant Managing Editor Theodore Bernstein and News Editor Lew Jordan. In his World Press Institute speech five years later, Daniel recounted that they primarily protested the headline change, on the ground that "never before had the front-page play of *The New York Times* been changed for reasons of policy." Daniel quoted Jordan as believing that the change in play was important because "a multicolumn head in this paper means so much." But Catledge dismisses concern over the size of the headline as "putting the cart before the horse, to say the least."

The two protesters succeeded only in getting Dryfoos to give them a personal explanation of his and Catledge's decisions—at least until Daniel publicized their actions in his WPI speech years later. At the time, Catledge's orders were upheld. The story appeared as he wanted it on April 7, and the invasion began on April 17 as scheduled; Szulc had thought it would be April 18, although he had not used that date in his original story. Was his use of the word "imminent" therefore justified? Is an invasion twelve days away "imminent"? Can any question more pointedly suggest how subjective such news decisions are?

Ironically, the *Times* itself all but negated Catledge's decision to excise the "imminent" reference. Directly following the Szulc story was a so-called "shirttail" (a separate but connected piece from another source). It quoted Stuart Novins of CBS Radio as having said that preparations for the operation were in their "final stages," with members of invasion units ordered to their assigned bases, and contingents in Florida already having put to sea. This, of course, is a tried-and-true evasive technique for editors; the *Times* merely reported that CBS had said what the *Times* had not been willing to say on its own responsibility.

As has been pointed out, Kennedy told Catledge in the White House a few weeks later: "Maybe if you had printed more about the operation you would have saved us from a colossal mistake." Still later, on September 13, 1962, as is not so well known, Kennedy told Orvil Dryfoos: "I wish you had run everything on Cuba . . . I'm just sorry you didn't tell it at the time." Coming scarcely a month before the missile crisis and his calls at that time to Reston and Dryfoos, the last remark is ironic in the extreme.

In a view I find impossible to dispute, Daniel told the WPI that the Bay of Pigs invasion might have been canceled and the country saved "enormous embarrassment" if the *Times* and "other newspapers"—unspecified—"had been more diligent in the performance of their duty." The possibility of *preventing* an obviously risky and debatable act of war is something quite different, I believe, from breaching security in the middle of an invasion or tipping off the location and course of a troopship or supply convoy. And Lew Jordan seems to me to have been exactly right—that four-column headline, leading the front page of the sober-sided *Times*, would have rung through the country, particularly Washington, like an alarm bell. But Catledge eased the story down almost to routine news.

My view is influenced by an interview with Allen Dulles, who was in 1961 the director of the CIA. In 1965 or 1966 I talked with him at the Georgetown house where he was in retirement. Specifically putting the information off the record for purposes of our series on the CIA, Dulles told me the Bay of Pigs disaster was *his* fault, because he had known Kennedy instinctively did not want to go through with it and might therefore pull back from its requirements at the crucial moment. Yet, Dulles said, he had talked Kennedy into proceeding with the invasion by asking him if he was "going to be any less anti-Communist than Eisenhower."

If Kennedy was that uncertain, newspaper exposure might very well have caused him to back off the invasion. Again, however, Catledge's memoir is revealing. Asking himself the question whether the *Times* would have been responsible if publishing Szulc's story as originally written and dummied had caused the deaths of hundreds or thousands of Cuban exiles, Catledge responds with an echo of his reasoning later about McCone and the CIA series:

"I suspected that Castro already knew about the pending invasion, and the real question was not whether we would be responsible for deaths during the invasion, but whether, *however unfairly, we might be blamed for them.*" (Italics mine.)

However else it might be stated, and in whatever circumstances, that is a fundamental—perhaps the major—reason for the restraint of the American press in its repeated encounters with the national-security mystique. Endangering the "national security," or appearing to, will almost inevitably threaten the standing and reputation of the newspaper or broadcaster that does it. It's hard to be sure, moreover, when the national security really might be endangered, or at least will be made to *seem* endangered or damaged.

In these circumstances, not many editors and broadcasters are eager to take chances in the service of the abstract principle known as the people's right to know. That attitude may be changing, since Vietnam and Watergate, but it is still prevalent. When the national-security mystique is involved, it's safer to let 'em eat handouts.

Further details of the press's reluctant-dragon attitude—even in its more challenging recent history—toward national-security claims are not hard to produce. One good example is provided by Vietnam itself—the years that had to pass before most of the press began to express editorial reservations, much less criticism, about the war, despite the press's own discouraging reports from the field. The claims of the government were consistently given greater weight, so that it sometimes seemed that two wars were being covered—the shooting war in Southeast Asia, the handout war in Washington.

Or another example from Vietnam: the so-called My Lai massacre took place on March 16, 1968, and that night the American spokesman at the "Five O'Clock Follies" in Saigon routinely announced a body count of 128 "enemy dead." But National Liberation Front publications and broadcasters in Vietnam and Paris within the next few days described a massacre as having taken place; little credence, of course, was given to this "Communist propaganda."

Six months later a former soldier named Ronald Ridenhour realized that his report of the massacre was being ignored by or had never reached the Johnson administration's highest officials, including the secretaries of state and defense; so he turned to the mass circulation press. *Life, Look, Newsweek,* and *Harper's* rejected the story. *Ramparts's* interest in it was rejected by Ridenhour, who apparently didn't want the story discounted for having been run in a "radical" magazine. He then offered his material to newspapers in Boston and New York and the two wire services; there were no takers, although Ridenhour was not seeking money.

By September 1969, a year and a half after the event, David Leonard of the *Columbus Enquirer* had enough interesting information to publish a story about the massacre and Lieutenant William L. Calley, Jr. The national press and the wire services displayed not the slightest interest. A month later,

Seymour Hersh, then a free-lance writer, began investigating My Lai. When he had a story ready, *Life* and *Look* turned him down, too. On November 1, 1969, the minuscule Dispatch News Service offered Hersh's story to forty-five clients. Only thirteen took it, but they projected the story into the open and, herdlike, most of the press at last moved to cover it.

So far as is known, the government was not actively trying to discourage use of the story; the press either failed to see its significance, which is doubtful, or was reluctant to muckrake American military men and the actions of American troops in a controversial war. Why be the messenger bringing such unpopular tidings—at least until someone else brings them first and takes the heat from the public and the inevitable official complainers about national security?

Supposedly liberal editorial pages that hung back from support or encouragement of Hersh's later *Times* pieces on massive CIA domestic spying; journalists and news organizations that seized a variety of excuses not to back Dan Schorr's release of the Pike report; the reluctance or failure of most of the press to join *The Washington Post* in its early exposures of Watergate abuses; Pulitzer judges who refused a prize to Harrison Salisbury of *The New York Times* for his extraordinary journalistic feat of visiting Hanoi and reporting from there in 1966, while the Vietnam war was raging (and journalistic colleagues who denounced him for articles using "Communist" statistics)—these and many other examples raise the question not so much *whether* the press has lacked aggressiveness in challenging the national-security mystique, but *why?*

Catledge supplied one powerful answer (quoted above); the risks—not to the national security but to the news organization involved—are usually too great. Since metropolitan press organs are virtually all card-carrying members of the Establishment, among the largest of these risks is Establishment disapproval—not just government denunciation but a general attitude among "responsible" people and groups, even other journalists, that to "go too far" or "get too involved" is bad for the country, not team play, not good form, not *responsible*. This may seem at first a frivolous point, but in publishing as in any other endeavor the approval of one's peers is a powerful force; and since Establishment disapproval conceivably could have business repercussions, it has a cutting edge as well as great weight—particularly with publishers themselves, all too many of whom are fundamentally businessmen unaccustomed to making national-security decisions, and not eager to do so.

The Pentagon Papers demonstrated the legal problems that can be encountered—and the legal costs. Not every paper or broadcaster can afford, or is willing, to underwrite the cost of extensive investigations, or big staffs in Washington, Vietnam, and other places where the national-security mystique is likely to flourish. Many rely on wire-service reporting—so many, in fact, representing so many parts of the country and so many attitudes, that most wire-service reporting tends to be bland, homogenized, unchallenging to the official point of view.

Broadcasters have a more specific problem—the requirement that they be licensed by the Federal Communications Commission, with the license subject to periodic renewal. However unconsciously, the next license renewal may well be on the mind of any broadcaster contemplating some breach of government "national-security" claims. This is particularly so since the Nixon administration actually raised the question of challenging the license renewal of television stations owned by *The Washington Post.*

The television and radio networks need not be licensed; but each is permitted to own five broadcasting stations that do need licenses. These network-owned stations tend to be among the networks' biggest sources of revenue, so that network news executives also cannot be totally free from the specter of real government retaliation.

Both the "fairness doctrine" and the "equal time" rule also act to limit the freedom of broadcasters in a manner not applicable to publishers of print journals. Both doctrine and rule are derived from the idea embodied in the Communications Act of 1934—which still governs broadcasting—that the airwaves belong to the public and their responsible use has to be guaranteed by law. Court cases and congressional revision of the 1934 act, together with technological developments that could substitute cables and satellites for "over-the-air" broadcasting, may perhaps produce extensive changes in—if not the elimination of—such rules within a few years.

In both broadcasting and publishing, reporters themselves play roles of some significance in the national-security deference of the press. Aggressive challenges to the official version of things can result in lost access, complaints to editors and publishers, social penalties, leaks to competitors, a variety of responses no one wants. Perhaps as important, too many reporters get "tied up" on what they ought to be publishing—through friendship, or unwary acquiescence in off-record sessions (like my agreement not to publish Allen Dulles's remarks on the Bay of Pigs), or by swapping silence on one story for a leak on another, or fear of losing a source, or even appeals to their "responsibility" and patriotism and anti-communism. Dulles knew how to bring John Kennedy around; should reporters be less susceptible to such methods than presidents?

Even after Vietnam, the American press, not unnaturally, is heavily tinged with nationalism and Cold War loyalties and hostilities. Reporters, editors, publishers are Americans, too, not uninterested in their nation's success and security, their own freedom and prosperity. They are vulnerable (and who would not be?) to the arguments of presidents, cabinet officers, generals that they should be responsible, put the nation's best interest first, not endanger its security.

That kind of vulnerability was never better described than by Egil Krogh, not a reporter but the Nixon White House aide who was jailed for his part in supervising the 1971 break-in at the office of Dr. Lewis Fielding, Daniel Ellsberg's psychiatrist. After being sentenced to six months' imprisonment, Krogh published a statement in which he said that the "key" to his guilt was "the effect that the term 'national security' had on my judgment. The very words served to block critical analysis.... The invocation of national security stopped me from asking the question, 'Is this the right thing to do?'"

Too often, reporters have been deluded by that same invocation into protecting disastrous government policies or culpable officials or embarrassing blunders or the attitudes of men like Maxwell Taylor, the supposedly "intellectual" general, who could say when the Pentagon Papers were published:

"I don't believe in [the people's right to know] as a general principle. You have to talk about cases. What is a citizen going to do after reading these documents that he wouldn't have done otherwise? *A citizen should know the things he needs to know to be a good citizen and discharge his functions,* but not to get into secrets that damage his government and indirectly damage himself." (Italics mine.)

There was no question in Taylor's "intellectual" mind, obviously, as to who should decide what a citizen "needs to know to be a good citizen"—which suggests that the power to operate in secrecy is not only the power to do what officials want to do but that it breeds contempt for that very public in whose name and interest officials claim to act, and which they claim to be protecting.

Finally, I think the canons of "objective" journalism have acted to restrict disclosure. Official spokesmen obviously don't leak secrets publicly; highly classified documents usually are hard to come by and have impressive and forbidding stamps on them; and objective journalism almost demands that controversial charges or allegations be made, not by even the most knowledgeable reporters, but by official spokesmen or by quotations from official documents. If these are not available and a story is published quoting unidentified sources or merely reaching logical conclusions from other facts, with serious charges unsupported either by official spokesmen or documents, the story can be persuasively denied by officials. Its publisher or broadcaster is likely to be denounced for "irresponsibility." Nor, in most cases colored by national-security allegations, can any non-official spokesman of sufficient weight be found to carry the burden.

The result is that objective journalism works strongly against disclosure. The good side of that is that it imposes caution and restraint, which is certainly appropriate in possible national-security matters. My own experience and the record of the postwar decades nevertheless convince me that the greater effect has been an important factor in the press's reluctance to challenge the government.

Owing to all these factors, including warranted fear of the government's power and its willingness to retaliate, that reluctance has been, I think, mostly self-imposed; not the government but the press itself has been most responsible for its timid record of disclosure. And if the recent tendency of the press to be more challenging, particularly in national-security matters, proves to be temporary, I believe the press itself will largely be at fault.

12

Robust and Uninhibited?

SAN FRANCISCO (AP)—Former San Francisco Mayor Joseph Alioto has begun his fourth libel trial against Look magazine.

He claimed here yesterday an article linking him with the Mafia used false information....

The previous three trials ended in hung juries. Parts of the article were found false and defamatory, but jurors were unable to reach any decision on the question of malice.

—*New York Post*, March 22, 1977

SAN FRANCISCO, May 3—After almost eight years and four federal trials, former Mayor Joseph L. Alioto today was awarded a libel judgment of $350,000, plus costs, against Look Magazine, which had said that he was "linked" to the Mafia....

"These allegations have heretofore been found to be false and defamatory," the judge said. "The court now finds that they were made with actual malice, i.e., with reckless disregard for the truth."

—*New York Times*, May 4, 1977

It may seem strange that Mayor Alioto—one of the most skillful American trial lawyers—had been able to prove that *Look* in its last years printed "false and defamatory" information about him, yet in eight years and three trials could not win a judgment against the magazine. The problem was that until the fourth trial, Alioto could *not* prove that *Look* "maliciously" printed the defamatory allegations, hence he could not prove libel or collect damages.

Worse, for a man who at one time had hoped to run for governor of California and in 1968 even had harbored vice-presidential dreams, the three "hung juries" in the first three libel trials conveyed the impression to many that Alioto had "lost" the cases, and that *Look* must therefore have been right in its charges. If not, why couldn't the mayor collect?

In that sense, Joe Alioto is a victim of the American libel law; there's not much doubt that being unable at first to collect damages from *Look* hurt his political career—although the public inference was wrong, and although Alioto's prospects suffered other damaging blows, too. But was Alioto constitutionally entitled to more protection from *Look* and from false publication than he received?

The United States Supreme Court has unequivocally declared that he was not so entitled—although for the first 188 years of the republic, if a libel defendant could not prove the *truth* of what he had published, he was generally held responsible for damages to the person libeled. But in 1954, in the complex case of *New York Times* v. *Sullivan,* the Supreme Court articulated a new concept; public officials—like those of Birmingham, Alabama, who were suing the *Times* for alleged libel—could not thereafter recover damages even for falsehoods published about them unless they could prove the false material had been published deliberately and with knowledge that it was false, in "reckless disregard of the truth"—in effect, with malice toward the official or officials concerned.

As a consequence, since 1954, public officials in America have almost no chance to prove a libel or collect damages for it, for the simple reason that malice is a state of mind and exceptionally difficult to prove. Put another way, the American press is virtually immune from libel suits brought by public officials; after his fourth trial, Joe Alioto became a rare exception.

This immunity is one of the most important factors in a

growing American concern that the free press is a threat to the fundamental rights of privacy of every American citizen. Privacy, in fact, may soon become the most clangorous battleground between a press dedicated to what the Supreme Court in the Sullivan case called "uninhibited, robust, and wide-open debate" and those many Americans who believe they have not only a free but an irresponsible press that needs at least limited forms of restraint—stronger libel laws, as an example.

Actually, press immunity to libel actions has been extended even further than it was in the Sullivan case. In a later suit brought by the former University of Georgia football coach, Wally Butts, against the Curtis Publishing Company and the *Saturday Evening Post,* the Supreme Court let stand a lower court decision that the ruling in the Sullivan case should apply not only to "public officials," but to "public figures" as well. The problem with that, of course, is to define who is a "public figure"—obviously Frank Sinatra or Joe Namath or Eugene McCarthy or Betty Friedan, all of whom deliberately hold themselves out in one way or another for the attention, approval, or support of the public. But what about, say, the pilot of a hijacked aircraft, or the wife or husband of someone involved in a sensational crime or accident, or anyone thrust by mere circumstances suddenly into the public eye? Or someone who actively sought fame and public position but failed to achieve it, or won it only temporarily—as, say, the leader of an urban rent strike? (Butts, as a famous coach, was obviously a public figure; but he won $460,000 damages when the court ruled that a *Post* article about him showed reckless disregard for the truth.)

In more recent cases, the courts have appeared to be pulling back from the broadest implications of the "public figures" ruling. In one case, it was held that a Chicago lawyer who had written books and appeared in numerous television and radio broadcasts was not a "public figure." In another, Mrs. Mary Alice Firestone, though possessing a famous name and place in Palm Beach society and involved in a sensational divorce case, also was held not to be a "public figure."

An interesting example of the ambiguity involved in defining the term followed an assassination attempt against President Ford in 1975. A woman outside a San Francisco hotel produced a pistol as Ford emerged and walked toward his car; a bystander grappled with the woman and her shot missed Ford. The incident naturally received wide press coverage, including the identity of the man who probably had saved Ford's life.

Obscure as he was until that identification, did he become a "public figure" because of his timely act? The question became relevant when members of the homosexual community in San Francisco told the columnist Herb Caen that Ford's rescuer was "gay." This statement was then extensively published and broadcast, and the man brought numerous suits in state and federal courts against those who had circulated the report. He maintained that the most intensely private fact of his life had been published without his consent and to his great disadvantage and embarrassment, although he was not truly a "public figure." In 1977, his suits were still pending.

Nevertheless, a broad immunity from libel suits by public officials and real public figures—absent evidence of reckless disregard for the truth—gives the American press a freedom probably unmatched anywhere to discuss individuals, even the most powerful, their actions, their motives, their characters. The Supreme Court's theory in the Sullivan case is clear and—at least to journalists and their lawyers—consistent with the First Amendment. "A robust and uninhibited press" is not to be deterred even by the threat of libel suits from holding public officials and public figures, and through them the institutions and processes they represent or control, responsible to the public.

Without such broad immunity, *The Washington Post* might well not have printed the charges it did in 1972 and 1973 about the public officials of the Nixon administration. Even if the charges could have been proven true in a court of law—a difficult matter, since Deep Throat and other unidentified sources would hardly have been willing to take the stand, even had the *Post* been willing to identify them—the likelihood of a libel suit and its attendant costs, troubles, and time consumption might well have inhibited publication or significantly lessened the sweep of the Woodward-Bernstein stories.

Similarly, the news that numerous American corporation chiefs had authorized illicit payments—bribes—to facilitate foreign sales might well have had to be significantly diluted if these public figures (few of whom actually were prosecuted) had been able to make newspapers prove the charges to the satisfaction of a jury in a libel case.

On the other hand, the same "robust and uninhibited" press,

effectively immune as it is from legal retaliation by public officials and public figures, conceivably could destroy the reputation and career of a public official or public figure with false information that could not be proved to have been published or broadcast maliciously. This could happen because a newspaper or broadcaster purveyed false information on purpose but covered its tracks well enough to prevent a finding of malice; or, more likely, because of honest error—the publication or broadcast of a story, damaging to a public official or public figure, for which the news organization responsible had a reasonable source or sources, which had been honestly checked and which the editors had no reason to believe was erroneous, but which nevertheless proved untrue.

The latter is the eventuality that American libel law—as interpreted by the Supreme Court—is designed to protect. And such protection is vital; for as Gabriel Perle, a counsel for *Time* magazine and president of the Copyright Society of the United States, once put it:

"No one believes that the press has a right deliberately and knowingly to publish 'lies.' But it must be able from time to time to make honest errors if it is to fulfill its duty to inform the public in a timely and professional manner."

Error, that is, can sometimes be a vital or unavoidable consequence of the search for truth, and error must therefore be tolerated, or at least not punished by law, lest there be no search for truth.

This proposition can scarcely be doubted by anyone who looks at the sharply different situation of the press in Britain, where press laws are far more restrictive. A spokesman for Prime Minister Harold Wilson, for example, brought suit against a London newspaper for a facetious reference in an editorial to "spokesmen for No. 10 Downing Street and other liars." Imagine a White House press secretary being able to bring such legal action; if he could, of course, so could his boss.

Numerous British reporters and editors have stated that had something like Watergate occurred in their country, the combination of strict libel laws and the Official Secrets Act would have made it impossible for the press even to report most of the story, much less pursue its own investigation and print the results. For more than a decade, as another example, restrictive laws prevented *The* (London) *Times* from printing further stories about how English children were born malformed and crippled because Thalidomide had been placed on the market by drug companies and prescribed for their mothers. While negotiations for a settlement of suits brought in the case dragged on through the courts, *The Times* would have been in contempt to have published additional details long in its possession.

Even in the United States, the libel laws are not necessarily settled. Some attorneys, jurists, and journalists believe the "public figures" ruling too broad, yielding the press too much immunity and too much power to publish and broadcast irresponsibly. And in one case, a federal judge called for specific answers to a sweeping set of questions about all the elements of a network news decision to broadcast a news story in a particular form—an unprecedented judicial inquiry into an editorial decision that a higher court later overruled.

"Sixty Minutes," the CBS "magazine" news program broadcast a story on Colonel Anthony Herbert, a Vietnam war hero who said his army career had been ruined by his efforts to report war crimes. Army colleagues interviewed on the show said he had never made such efforts. Colonel Herbert brought suit against the network in federal court; and his lawyers put a long list of questions to producer Barry Lando in twenty-five days of oral pretrial testimony. Included were such questions as:

Did Lando ever consider including the information in his script that Pentagon officials were speaking about Herbert at Army bases? Did he consider including the fact that a comment by one soldier had been contradicted by another? Why had one soldier been interviewed three times and some others not at all? Why had some statements about Herbert been broadcast but not others?

These and many other questions asked by Herbert's lawyers, if put to a newspaper or a network by a congressional committee, would not be answered, because they would be held highly offensive to editorial freedom. But Federal District Judge Charles J. Haight allowed these and many more such questions to be put to Lando and CBS because, the judge said, such a heavy burden rested on a public figure like Colonel Herbert in a libel case that he deserved a "liberal" interpretation of the rules of "discovery"—in the Herbert case, a detailed explanation from the network of the elements of its decision to broadcast the "Sixty Minutes" story as it had.

The judge's reasoning, plausible on its face, was that if libel can be proved only if the plaintiff also proves malice—"reckless disregard for the truth"—which is a state of mind, the judge and the plaintiff are entitled to know all the elements that went into an editorial decision, so that a reasonable determination can be made as to whether such malice was present in the editor's—or the producer's—mind when the decision was made.

If that novel approach had prevailed, then the present effective immunity of the press from libel suits by public officials and public figures would have disappeared under a wave of judicial second-guessing of crucial editorial decisions. The inhibition or "chilling effect" that surely would have resulted would have negated the hard-won freedom of action the American press has had since 1954—and that the "Warren Court" of that era intended to give it.

In a 2-to-1 decision, the Second Circuit Court of Appeals rejected this doctrine. Chief Judge Irving R. Kaufman, terming the questions put to Lando an "inquisition," wrote that "we cannot permit inquiry into Lando's thoughts, opinions and conclusions to consume the very values which the Sullivan landmark decision sought to safeguard.... We must permit only those procedures in libel actions which least conflict with the principle that debate on public issues should be robust and uninhibited."

Judge Thomas J. Meskill, dissenting, conceded the chilling effect of such an inquiry into reporters' and editors' motives. But that chilling or "deterrent effect," he wrote, would discourage the publication of lies. The two opinions thus expressed opposite preferences for the values involved—robust and uninhibited debate, on one hand, and protection of individuals from possibly untrue charges, on the other.

If the case ever reaches the Supreme Court—now the Burger Court—how it might choose between those values is anybody's guess.

Libel is not the only element in the gathering fears of many Americans that a free press threatens their rights and privacy. Laws purportedly assuring individual privacy exist in virtually every state and in the federal code; the concept of privacy is firmly rooted in the common law; and the Supreme Court has indicated that the right of privacy, though not specified in the Constitution, nevertheless in some circumstances "rises to constitutional dimensions."

Most newspapermen and broadcasters—and not a few lawyers—believe the threat of state intrusion, not only on privacy but on legal rights, far outweighs any such threat from the press. As late as 1977, for example, bills were only just being introduced to prevent government examination—without a proper court order—of an individual's bank and telephone records, and to make government surveillance or harassment of political dissidents unlawful. And some measures aimed at protecting privacy from being trampled by the press succeed more often in shielding police and governmental agencies from press scrutiny. Nevertheless, millions of Americans, unconvinced even by Vietnam or Watergate, the CIA and the FBI, that the government can be duplicitous or repressive, see a greater threat to their privacy and security from the press than from the government's massive police agencies.

Some of the developing body of privacy cases raise serious First Amendment questions. On Staten Island, New York, in 1976 a local television news organization was admitted to St. Michael's Hospital for neglected and dependent adolescents by a child-care counselor—a classic whistle-blower—who was disturbed by allegedly callous treatment of children in the hospital. Some of the children were questioned and filmed, and a broadcast critical of the institution and its treatment of its patients was developed.

Less than an hour before the story was to be aired, the hospital authorities, having learned of the planned broadcast, got an injunction banning the television station from "causing, permitting or allowing any broadcast or dissemination to be made or rendered in any manner" about St. Michael's. The ground for this broadside order, astonishing in its sweep, ostensibly was that the film crew and reporters had committed a trespass and that the broadcast would violate the privacy of the children interviewed—although the only evidence for either proposition was an affidavit by the attorney for the hospital.

Appeals were heard, of course, but it was *forty days* before the appellate division finally permitted the report to be aired; and still more time would have been consumed in further appeals had not the television station altered its film so as not to identify the children interviewed.

Few cases have more clearly shown the extent to which the laudable concept of privacy can be used to conceal legitimate public information and cover up scandalous situations. The appellate division *did* rule that the film could not be enjoined even though the purpose of the news organization was not solely or primarily to change conditions at the hospital—a salutary decision for the First Amendment right to publish and broadcast *aside from* the consequences, for good or ill, of doing so.

On the other hand, the original injunction barring any discussion of conditions at St. Michael's shows how willing some courts are to muffle the press at any cost to the First Amendment; and the consequence, as in the Pentagon Papers case, was a very real prior restraint on publication (broadcasting in this instance), resulting in a substantial delay during which the hospital's conditions conceivably could have caused much harm to its young patients.

That may have been only one state court expressing an attitude; a federal court case growing out of a California suit against *Sports Illustrated* magazine has actually provided as a precedent for other courts a "standard of newsworthiness" to apply to material that might be claimed to be protected from publication by the right to personal privacy. This case raises the grim specter not of prior restraint but of juries ruling on editorial decisions—deciding whether published information was or was not "newsworthy" and thus "privileged," or legally publishable under the First Amendment.

Sports Illustrated had published an article on one Mike Virgil, a West Coast surfer, in which it informed readers that at one time or another Virgil had engaged in such conduct as "putting out cigarettes in his mouth and diving off stairs to impress women, hurting himself in order to collect unemployment [insurance] so as to have time for body surfing . . . fighting in gang fights as a youngster and eating insects." Not contesting the truth of these allegations, which he had himself confirmed to the magazine's reporters, Virgil contended that he had not intended for them to be published and brought suit in the California courts for unlawful invasion of his privacy.

Time Inc., publisher of *Sports Illustrated*, had the case removed to federal court but District Judge Thompson denied Time's motion for summary dismissal of the suit. Time Inc. then took an interlocutory appeal to the Ninth Circuit Court of Appeals, which ordered Judge Thompson to reconsider the matter under the following "standard of newsworthiness" established by the appeals court:

"In determining what is a matter of legitimate public interest, account must be taken of the customs and conventions of the community; and in the last analysis what is proper becomes a matter of the community mores. The line is to be drawn when the publicity ceases to be the giving of information to which the public is entitled, and becomes a morbid and sensational prying into private lives for its own sake, with which a reasonable member of the public, with decent standards, would say that he had no concern."

The appeals court contended that in ordering such a strict standard it had "avoid[ed] unduly limiting the breathing space needed by the press for the exercise of effective editorial judgment." And Judge Thompson then granted Time Inc.'s motion for summary dismissal of the suit, holding that the statements *Sport Illustrated* had made about Virgil were "generally unflattering and perhaps embarrassing but they are simply not offensive to the degree of morbidity or sensationalism." Besides, the judge held, even if the facts disclosed had had "a degree of offensiveness equivalent to 'morbid and sensational,'" Virgil could not have won his suit under the Ninth Circuit's standard. For it also required him to show that the revelation of those facts had been "for its own sake"; but the article clearly had included the statements about Virgil in a bona fide effort to "explain Virgil's extremely daring and dangerous style of body surfing."

So Time Inc. won its battle but the press may have lost a war. The Ninth Circuit's "standard of newsworthiness" is now in the law, since the Supreme Court declined to review the Virgil case (although other cases in which it may be used as a precedent undoubtedly will reach the high Court). That means, as Judge Thompson pointed out, that newsworthiness in privacy cases has become not just a matter of an editor's or a producer's judgment but "an issue dependent on the present state of community mores and, therefore, particularly suitable for jury determination." Consequently, persons bringing invasion of privacy suits may now subject editorial decisions to review by juries, not as to the truth of factual statements, but as to whether they offend community mores by "morbidity" and "sensationalism"—terms subject to interpretations as widely varying as "community mores."

And in an ominous footnote, Judge Thompson also noted

that he had concluded that in the *Sports Illustrated* article on Mike Virgil there was "a rational and at least arguably close relationship between the facts revealed and the activity to be explained." But this did not endorse, he said, "no-holds-barred rummaging by the media through the private lives of persons engaged in activities of public interest under the pretense of elucidating the activity or the person's participation in it."

Thus, the Ninth Circuit's "standard of newsworthiness" means that numerous editorial decisions involving the privacy issue may also have to be defended before juries on a second issue—again, not as to the truth of published facts but on the question of their relevance to the story being presented. But what may seem a "pretense" of relevance to a jury may seem to be a sound editorial judgment to a journalist; and what may to a journalist seem a pertinent link between a news subject's personality or character and his or her public activities may nevertheless appeal to a jury as mere "rummaging" through the private lives of people in the public eye.

The entry into the editorial field of juries authorized to judge the fitness of stories by the jury's interpretation of "community mores" and its view of the relevance of facts is not likely to improve the quality of editorial decisions; only to make them more cautious and restraining (which is not necessarily better). But to a journalist the most chilling effect of the Ninth Circuit's "standard" is that it seems to signal that the judicial branch may be moving to assert a power to intervene in the editorial freedom of the American press that the same judiciary has never permitted to the legislative or executive branch of government.

But government is government, and the courts are a part of it; and if Congress "shall make no law" abridging the freedom of the press, shall the courts nevertheless interpret the law and the Constitution to abridge that freedom? Sadly, that has seemed to be the recent trend of a judiciary determined to enforce the "responsibility" of a press the Warren Court once urged to be "robust and uninhibited."

The First Amendment does not say anything about "responsibility." This observation, which I have offered to hundreds of disbelieving and usually disapproving audiences, invariably brings some challenger to his or her feet with something like the following inquiry (usually varied more in its degree of choler than in wording): "Do you mean to say that the press has a right to be irresponsible?"

I mean to say nothing of the sort—although it's true, just to be argumentative, that irresponsibility does not appear to the layman's eye to be a *constitutional* violation. But it's just as well for journalists, particularly, to recall the skeptical judgment in *The Federalist* of Alexander Hamilton—who opposed as unnecessary a Bill of Rights for the Constitution:

"What is the liberty of the press? Who can give it any definition which would not leave the utmost latitude for evasion? I hold it to be impracticable; and from this I infer that its security, whatever fine declarations may be inserted in any constitution respecting it, must altogether depend on public opinion, and on the general spirit of the people and of the government."

Just so. And with that in mind, no journalist should advocate to the public the idea that the press has "a right to be irresponsible"; no one could agree to that. Nor should any journalist wish the press or broadcast news to *be* irresponsible. Aside from their pride in the craft and its institutions, their desire to do their personal work well, and their concern that the public should be informed, all journalists know that popular contempt for and fear of press "irresponsibility" is as grave a threat—and more justified—to a free press as government attempts at silencing it. And, as Hamilton foresaw, that part of the First Amendment might not long survive a hostile, determined public opinion.

Granting all that, a certain case for tolerance of irresponsibility still has to be made—basically the same case made earlier for the tolerance of honest error as necessary to the search for truth. That is, if the American press is to remain "free"—even in the somewhat limited sense that necessarily results from the conflict of this "freedom" with other equally guaranteed "freedoms" in the Constitution and the Bill of Rights—it cannot have "responsibility" imposed on it by legislation, judicial interpretation, or any other process. And as Supreme Court Judge Harry Blackmun observed—rather unhappily—from the bench during oral arguments in *Miami Herald* v. *Tornillo:* "For better or for worse we have opted in this country for a free press, not fair debate."

Freedom necessarily contains within itself the *possibility* of irresponsibility. No man is truly free who is not *permitted* occasionally to be irresponsible; nor is any institution. Responsibility, it goes without saying, is profoundly important; and the highest freedom of all may well be the freedom to conduct one's life and affairs responsibly—but by one's own standards of responsibility. It's a mean freedom in which a mere failure of responsibility necessarily brings a jail term or a fine or some other societally imposed penalty—and no freedom at all if standards of responsibility are uniform, designed to *prevent* rather than punish failures, and set by higher authority.

Yet, in the name of preventing "irresponsibility" in the press, some of the most sweeping restrictions on the freedom of the press have been proposed. What is lost sight of is that if responsibility can be *imposed,* freedom must be lost; and of those who advocate various means of insuring the "responsibility" of a supposedly free press, two questions should be asked:

Who defines responsibility? In numerous instances in this book, the difficulty editors and reporters face in determining a responsible course in disputed circumstances has, I believe, been demonstrated—notably in the case of the *New York Times*'s treatment of the Bay of Pigs story. In literally thousands of less important instances—and not a few at the same level of seriousness—editors have no hard-and-fast rules to follow, save those of experience, ethics, and common sense—all of which vary from person to person. Nor *can* there be more certain guides. Reasonable persons may, and often do, differ on what is "responsible"—even as *Times* editors differed among themselves on handling the Bay of Pigs story. There simply is no certainty, in most instances, as to what constitutes a "responsible" course in an enormous number of cases that editors and reporters have to face.

Most journalists believe that the multiplicity of editorial decisions likely to result in any given case is a major safeguard again "irresponsibility" and misinformation. All editors won't make the same decision on the same set of facts—the same story played on page one by the *Times* may be printed inside *The Washington Post;* a quotation in the one story may not appear in the other; different lines of interpretation may well be taken by the two papers, and any number of others; with the result that the same "story" appears in many versions and within a broad range of prominence. This rich diversity not only works against the possibility that any story can be "covered up" or manufactured; it also offers a reasonable guarantee that differing viewpoints on the same events will reach the public.

Not only, therefore, would the imposition of standards of "responsibility" on the press move it toward uniformity of presentation and away from diversity but it would require an instrument big enough and comprehensive enough to define responsibility in an immense number of instances, for a huge number of publications and broadcasters. No such instrument exists, save the government.

Who enforces responsibility? This is a simpler problem; once responsibility is defined, obviously, nothing of sufficient power and scope exists to force the defined responsibility on the entire press—again save the government.

Thus, if we are to be *sure* of a responsible press, the only way is through a government that both defines and enforces responsibility. Not just Richard Nixon would have leaped at *that* opportunity. It need scarcely even be pointed out that in such circumstances the condition of the American press would be a far cry from freedom.

Would that matter?

Obviously, a totally government-controlled press would make much difference to liberty in America; but that is not what most of those who demand greater press "responsibility" have in mind. They more often set forth a supposedly middle course—yielding a little "freedom" in a beneficial trade-off to gain some "responsibility." Many undoubtedly would endorse the Ninth Circuit's "standard of newsworthiness."

The middle-course argument is respectable. It cannot be maintained by the most ardent First Amendment advocate that *democracy* is not reasonably healthy in Britain, where *the press* is under much greater restraint than it is in the United States. Libel laws that sharply restrict publication and broadcasting; a heavy bias toward other societal interests rather than that of publication in laws governing press reports on criminal justice and other actions of the courts; an Official Secrets Act that governments of both parties frequently invoke, apparently not always for matters of indisputable national security; and a quasi-governmental National Press Council to monitor and criticize press activities—have these stifled the larger British democracy?

From my side of the Atlantic, I cannot say that they have. But British society is not really analogous to American. The question period in the House of Commons, ineffectual though it often is, nevertheless provides a degree of government accountability not afforded by the American system. Confidence votes in the House and the occasional political necessity for the government to call an unscheduled election make British government more responsive than an American administration with its fixed term in office. A more stratified British class system and—until recently—a minimum of racial conflict causes life in Britain to be less violent, turbulent, and crime-ridden than it is in America.

Despite the Magna Carta, a society that derives from monarchy, aristocracy, primogeniture, and class privilege does not have the tradition of bumptious personal liberty that marks a people descended from those who came to a frontier land to escape kings, lords, and caste. And an embattled island long ago came to accept certain government and military exigencies that have been regarded as excessive in a continental and mostly unthreatened land.

For whatever reasons, the history of British politics is by no means as marked by venality and corruption as that of the United States, and governing ethics and traditions there appear so settled that serious violations—for example, power grabs such as that represented by the Watergate complex of offenses—are far less likely. Secrecy by the British government has been widely accepted for centuries. Profound policy miscalculations—the Suez War—bring quick political retribution, Official Secrets Act or no; while even more egregious American blunders in Vietnam and Cambodia for years produced in the United States mostly a "rally-round-the-President" effect, until the press, primarily television, finally turned the public against the war (by printing and broadcasting *news,* not editorials).

Therefore, press restraints perhaps amenable to British democracy—although not many British journalists really consider them so—would not necessarily be fitting in the United States. Should a Watergate occur in the United Kingdom, colleagues in the British press say, a British governing party plausibly accused of conniving at a burglary of opposition party headquarters, then obstructing justice to conceal the crime, would soon be turned out of office, despite restrictions on reporting such a story. But it was only a challenging American press that kept Watergate in the public eye and ultimately forced the various actions that led to Richard Nixon's resignation—at that, two years after the offense.

But the existance of restrictions on the British press, together with the evident survival of the essential British democracy, leads many serious and reasonable persons to suggest not government control of the American press but similar instruments of "responsibility" in this country's journalistic practice.

When the Senate established in 1977 an oversight committee for the so-called intelligence community, for example, one of the committee's first studies was of the need, if any, for a limited form of Official Secrets Act in the United States—an effort to protect the CIA from the public rather than the public from the CIA that stood the committee's supposed responsibility on its head.

The discussed act's reach ostensibly would have been limited to barring disclosures of "sources and methods" in gathering intelligence—ostensibly because although "sources and methods" is a term of an arcane art and therefore is asserted to be capable of strict definition and narrow application, both the FBI and the CIA in the past have shown themselves capable of slipping large abuses through tiny loopholes. It was, for example, supposedly to protect "sources and methods" that some of the CIA's mail-opening and surveillance operations were illegally pursued.

Whatever the situation in Britain, in this country—as I hope I have demonstrated—secrecy has too often been used to shield blunders, crimes, and ineptitude; alert citizens should not accept without sharp questioning a secrecy law supported by a secret agency designed to give that agency even greater powers of covering up its operations than it already has. And unless Congress were to show an uncharacteristic willingness to include a "shield" provision for reporters—which it never has done in other legislation of less importance and which would be of dubious constitutionality—a likely consequence would be about as follows:

A "leak" of a secret protected by the act would appear as a news story in a newspaper or on a broadcast. An inquiry would be launched, but as usual the identity of the leaker (who could be prosecuted under the new law) could not be learned. The reporter-recipient of the leak would be subpoenaed before a grand jury and asked the identity of his source, with a view to prosecuting the leaker. It would be made clear that no other means existed of obtaining this information vital to enforcement of the Official Secrets Act and the orderly administration of government.

The reporter, by his professional code of ethics and his view of the First Amendment, would have to refuse to answer. He would then be held in contempt and ordered to jail—although there might be no evidence of any damage to national security as a consequence of his or her story. A lot of reporters would have a lot of second thoughts—chilling indeed—about accepting leaks of so-called security secrets under such a threat.

Would that serve the cause of "responsibility"? Once again, the answer depends upon who defines responsibility in any given case; but those who place a high value upon a "robust and uninhibited press" and who have learned to be skeptical of the government's assertions of "national security" are not likely to think so.

But even if no such drastic step as an Official Secrets Act was taken, why not more restrictive libel and privacy laws? Would they limit press freedom so severely as to threaten the public's right and need to know? And what about a nongovernmental Press Council at least to criticize—constructively, as well as punitively—press performance, even if the council had no real power to punish or penalize?

The question of more severe libel and privacy laws requires, essentially, a value judgment. There isn't much doubt that greater protection from press charges than now is provided for public officials would limit the ability of the press to act as a check on the power of government; but some reasonable persons believe the press now has *too much* latitude to criticize government, expose its workings, penetrate needed confidentiality, and hinder its effectiveness. Similarly, no one should be in doubt that stricter protection of individual privacy from searching press inquiry would frequently prevent needed public exposure and discussion of personalities, institutions, and processes; but few in the press would care to deny that the power of the press has sometimes been the instrument of unwarranted personal humiliations, embarrassments, misfortunes, and losses of reputation and livelihood.

As for a National Press Council, such an organization has

been financed and supported by the Twentieth Century Fund, which is neither conservative nor antipress. Neither have been the first workings of the council, which has been supported by many in the press and broadcasting and which has no connection with the government. Its purpose is to conduct quiet private investigations of controversial press or broadcasting decisions and to report publicly on whether or not those decisions had been taken responsibly and on reasonable grounds. The council has no power, other than the force of its disapproval, to penalize news organizations.

Some concerned journalists have argued that the press and broadcasting ought to cooperate wholeheartedly with the National Press Council. Most news organizations, they say, would have nothing to fear; and better for those who might be culpable to be censured by a private group with press interests at heart than by unsympathetic courts or legislatures. Besides, they argue, by certifying in most disputed cases that editorial decisions had been responsibly and reasonably taken, the council would more often reassure the public than threaten the press.

In short, these journalists view the National Press Council as a good instrument of public relations for the press. Not only would news organizations appear to be trying to police their own work and that of colleagues; but most periodically would be given a good bill of health by a respected panel of citizens, while "irresponsible" publications and broadcasts could be sternly reprimanded by a council backed by the press itself.

But there is another underlying reason why there has been considerable press support for a National Press Council. Seldom stated outside newsrooms, journalism classes, or press club bars, it is that the Press Council idea offers a safe way to "clean up the press before the government comes in and does it for us." That suggests that even many who are deeply involved in American journalism themselves believe that there are so many "excesses" and malpractices that need to be "cleaned up" that the press really does face possible government control. And that points straight to the fundamental reason why I am personally opposed to the Press Council, to more restrictive privacy and libel laws, and to all other schemes of enforcing the "responsibility" of a supposedly free press—reasonable as some of those schemes undoubtedly appear in their proposals for only limited sacrifices of freedom.

• • •

The overwhelming conclusion I have drawn from my life in journalism—nearly thirty years so far, from the *Sandhill Citizen* to *The New York Times*—is that the American press, powerful as it unquestionably is and protected though it may be by the Constitution and the laws, is not often "robust and uninhibited" but is usually timid and anxious—for respectability at least as much as for profitability. Those whose idea of the press is bounded by the exploits of Woodward and Bernstein on one hand and by the Pentagon Papers on the other, whether or not they view such remarkable efforts as needed or excessive, do not usually understand that they were limited exceptions to long-established practice.

Undoubtedly, in more than a decade since Dwight Eisenhower roused the Goldwaterites with his attack on "sensation-seeking columnists," the press has become more activist and challenging, particularly in covering politics and government—though *not* business and financial institutions. On the evidence of press performance in that decade—the disclosure of duplicity and ineptitude in Vietnam, the exposure of political corruption in the Nixon administration, the demonstration of grave threats to American liberty by the "Imperial Presidency," the FBI, the CIA, and other security agencies—I assert the necessity to *encourage* the developing tendency of the press to shake off the encumbrance of a falsely objective journalism and to take an adversary position toward the most powerful institutions of American life.

By 'adversary," I don't mean a necessarily hostile position; I use the word in the lawyer's sense of cross-examining, testing, challenging, in the course of a trial on the merits of a case. Such an adversary is "opposed" only in the sense that he or she demands that a case be made—the law stated, the facts proven, the assumptions and conclusions justified, the procedure squared with common sense and good practice. An adversary press would hold truth—unattainable and frequently plural as it is—as its highest value, and knowledge as its first responsibility.

Such a press should be encouraged in its independence, not investigated—even by its friends—when it asserts that independence. A relatively toothless Press Council that nevertheless could summon editors and reporters, notes and documents, film and outtakes, in order to determine publicly whether editorial decisions had been properly made *by the Press Council's standards* would be bound to have an ultimately inhibiting effect on editors, publishers and broadcasters—not all of whom would therefore be dismayed. Most, it's safe to say, would rather be praised for someone else's idea of "responsibility" than risk being questioned or criticized for their own independence.

Somewhat similarly, tighter libel and privacy laws surely would narrow the area open to editorial judgment—and some editors and publishers might welcome such laws just for that reason. Some might even yearn privately for an Official Secrets Act, because its proscriptions would relieve them of having to decide such difficult questions as whether to publish so-called "national security" stories, and of the loud accusations of irresponsibility that inevitably follow such decisions, no matter how they are made.

My belief is that the gravest threat to freedom of the press is not necessarily from public animosity or mistrust, legislative action or court decision. Certainly, even though absolute press freedom may sometimes have to accommodate itself to other high constitutional values, the repeal or modification of the First Amendment seems unlikely. At least as great a threat, I believe, comes from the press itself—in its longing for a respectable place in the established political and economic order, in its fear of the reaction that boldness and independence will always evoke. Self-censorship silences as effectively as a government decree, and we have seen it far more often.

In the harsh sunlight of a robust freedom, after all, nothing stands more starkly exposed than the necessity to decide and to accept the responsibility for decision. If the true freedom of the press is to decide for itself what to publish and when to publish it, the true responsibility of the press must be to assert and defend that freedom.

But my life in journalism has persuaded me that the press too often tries to guard its freedom by shirking its responsibility, and that this leads to default on both. What the press in America needs is less inhibition, not more restraint.

Index